NATIVE PERENNIALS FOR THE SOUTHEAST

PETER LOEWER

Published by Cool Springs Press, a Division of Thomas Nelson, Inc., P.O. Box 141000, Nashville, Tennessee 37214.

Library of Congress Cataloging-in-Publication Data is available.
ISBN 1-59186-121-7

First Printing 2005
Printed in the United States of America
10 9 8 7 6 5 4 3 2 1

Managing Editor: Ramona Wilkes
Horticulture Editor: Jenny Andrews
Production Design: S. E. Anderson
Design Contributors: Starletta Polster and Lisa Sarmento

Cover Photo: *Iris cristata* by Brenda Tharp

Cool Springs Press books may be purchased in bulk for educational, business, fundraising, or sales promotional use. For information, please email SpecialMarkets@ThomasNelson.com.

Visit the Thomas Nelson website at **www.ThomasNelson.com** and the Cool Springs Press website at **www.coolspringspress.net**.

NATIVE PERENNIALS FOR THE SOUTHEAST

PETER LOEWER

Illustrations by Peter Loewer

COOL SPRINGS PRESS
A Division of Thomas Nelson Publishers
Since 1798

Thanks are due to my wife, Jean, who helps in so many ways;

to Jenny Andrews and Ramona Wilkes, my cool-headed editors at Cool Springs Press;

Peter Gentling for advice and counsel (not to mention Jasmin for those great lunches);

Barry Glick of Sunshine Farm and Gardens;

all the gardeners who kindly answered my queries and wrote about

their own efforts in the Southeast;

and finally, the often threatening, but in the end,

challenging weather of the Great Southeast.

TABLE OF CONTENTS

Introduction   7

The World of Perennials   11

Ferns   123

Grasses and Sedges   133

Water and Bog Plants   145

Advice from Other Gardeners   161

Bibliography   185

Index   186

Meet the Author   192

All botanical illustrations by Peter Loewer.

William Adams: 7

Liz Ball: 26, 36b, 47a, 61, 65, 90, 91, 106, 111, 129, 148, 153, 160

Cathy Wilkinson Barash: 21, 50

Thomas G. Barnes, USDA-NRCS Plants Database: 88

Laura Coit: 57, 117

Mike Dirr: 68

Tom Eltzroth: 10, 36a, 37, 40b, 41, 44b, 51b, 53, 55, 59, 62b, 66, 74, 79, 84, 86, 89, 92, 98, 104, 108, 112, 121, 125, 155, 165, 169, 172

Peter Gentling: 133, 170

Erica Glasener 18a

Barry Glick: 25, 31a, 32, 43, 44a, 101, 147a

Pam Harper: 22, 93, 134a, 173

Pegi Ballister-Howells: 31b

Dency Kane: 116

Kirsten Llamas: 122

Peter Loewer: 11, 14b, 15, 16, 17, 33, 38, 39, 45, 51a, 62a, 69, 71, 76, 97, 102, 110, 114, 127, 135, 136, 137, 138, 140b, 147b, 151, 152, 161, 171, 174, 175, 176, 179, 180, 183

Charles Mann: 8, 60, 64, 75, 78, 100, 140a, 141

Jerry Pavia: 12a, 14a, 18b, 20, 23, 27, 28, 29, 30, 34, 40a, 47b, 48, 49, 52, 54, 67, 72, 73, 83, 85a, 95, 109, 115, 119, 126, 128, 130, 131, 132, 134b, 142, 162, 163, 167, 168, 182, 184

Carol Reese: 24

Felder Rushing: 9, 12b, 85b, 96, 107, 113, 123, 145, 158, 159, 166, 177

Greg Speichert: 154, 156

Mark Turner: 164

Andre Viette: 82, 103

Photos in order from top to bottom of page, left column first, right column second
A=first photo, B=second

For a long time, nurseries refused to deal with most American wildflowers, believing that the average gardener found them too unassuming, too demure, and too boring (except those in the specialized realms of horticulture). Salespeople would frown and scratch their heads at the mention of plants referred to as native. So folks continued to introduce exotics like delphiniums, hybrid tea roses, and other plants that did well when water was plentiful and the air was cool and calm.

But the droughts came, summers heated up, and water was in short supply. Utility bills climbed to the heavens, the delphiniums needed staking or they collapsed, and the garden required hours of work and a double palm-full of money in order to remain strikingly beautiful. Suddenly, the worm has turned. Native plants now have cachet, hence this book.

Eclectic is defined as "a person who borrows freely from various sources in forming opinion, taste, etc." and *eclectic* is the word for my choices in this book. The plants range from the common to the obscure; but, I hasten to add, there is a list of nursery suppliers in the back of

the book and I'll wager that more than ninety-five percent of the plants listed are available from sources somewhere in the country. For that other five percent, turn to the marvelous seed societies and dealers in rare native plants.

Phlox pilosa

Making Sense of Plant Names

Throughout this book I have used both the common and the scientific, or Latinized, names for the various plants being described. (There is no such thing as a "botanical" name; the correct word is "scientific.") I use both terms not to create confusion, but to ensure that author and reader are thinking about the same plants and to be certain that any plants the reader might decide to buy are the plants that they receive from the nursery. Many of the botanical names have a reasonable and often delightful history behind their creation, so I have included the translations of the original words used in creating their nomenclature.

Although it's true that many plants can be recognized by their common names, many more cannot. For example, there are five plant genera that use "mother-in-law" in their appellations: mother-in-law for *Kalanchoe pinnata*; mother-in-law plant for *Caladium* species and *Dieffenbachia seguine*; and finally mother-in-law's tongue for *Gasteria* species, *Sansevieria*

Helenium species

trifasciata, and *Dieffenbachia* species. All of these names are in general use. Now imagine the local variations across the fifty states and Canada. Then picture the additional confusion when someone in the order department of a major nursery, while perhaps suffering from a migraine headache, confuses one species of a mother-in-law plant with another that sits on a nearby bench and you see how you might end up with a plant completely unlike the one you ordered.

To prevent confusion, all known plants have been given scientific names—each unique—that are easily understood throughout the world, whatever native language is in use. In the 1700s, when the present system began, Latin was the international language of scholars and seemed the obvious choice to botanists. The words are derived from Renaissance Latin with a great many appropriated from ancient Greek. Carl Linnaeus (1707-1778) is the man primarily thought of as the founder of the system.

If you are concerned about pronunciation, don't be. Very few people can pronounce these names with impunity. The English, for example,

Solidago species

have rules for Latin pronunciation that are at odds with most of the rest of the world (remember, the English pronounce a migraine headache as a "meegraine" and Don Juan as "Don Joo-an"). Besides, you will probably only use the Latin names in written form.

A Guide to Names

Scientific names usually consist of four terms that are in general use: genus, species, variety, and cultivar (there are others but they are beyond the scope of this book). All reference books, most gardening books, nearly all responsible catalogs and nurseries, and even the majority of seed packets list the scientific name along with the common. In many cases the common names of popular plants are also scientific names that people use every day without realizing it: delphinium, geranium, sedum, and gladiolus immediately come to mind. In print, the genus and species are set off from the accompanying text by the use of italics. If the text is set in italics, the botanical name should be in Roman type. All publications follow this convention except *The New York Times,* which for some reason refuses to admit its existence.

Genus refers to a group of plants that are closely related, while the species suggests an individual plant's unique quality, color, or even habit of growth. Often, one of the names honors the person who discovered the plant. For example, the spiderworts are called *Tradescantia* after John Tradescant, one of the greatest and most adventurous of the English plant collectors. The genus can also be descriptive. The botanical name given to the popular spring bulb the snowdrop, for example, is *Galanthus,* from the Greek *gala* (milk) and *anthos* (flower), describing the white of the flowers. The species names include *byzantinus* for a type of snowdrop from south eastern Europe, *caucasicus* for another from the Caucasus, and *grandiflora* for one with larger flowers.

Usually the genus has an initial capital and the species is all in lowercase (at least most of the time). Although woefully out-of-date, one of the major references for botanical nomenclature used in this book is *Hortus Third*, and its authors will, on occasion, begin the species with a capital letter when it has been derived from a former generic name, a person's name, or a common name.

The third term is "variety." It is also italicized and usually preceded by the abbreviation "var." that is set in Roman or regular type. A variety represents a noticeable change in a plant that naturally develops by chance and breeds true from generation to generation.

The fourth term is "cultivar," introduced in 1923 by Liberty Hyde Bailey and derived from the words *culti*vated *vari*ety. Cultivar represents a desirable variation that appears on a plant while it is in cultivation and could result either by chance or design. The word is usually distinguished in print by being set in Roman type and

placed inside single quotation marks. (Copy editors take note: the last single quote appears before a period, semicolon, or comma.) Some references delete the single quotation marks and precede the cultivar name with "cv."

It should be noted that many plants listed in catalogs have scientific names that are woefully out-of-date. This is because the catalog writers know, for example, that the public recognizes *Oenothera missouriensis* as the name for one of our native evening primroses, but might be unfamiliar with the current and correct name of *O. macrocarpa*. So they use the old. I've indicated both names when possible.

Rudbeckia fulgida

THE WORLD OF PERENNIALS

Gardening with Native Plants

Right from the get-go, I've been interested in native plants and wildflowers, always making these stalwarts of the wild garden number one on my hit parade. True, I have a predilection for English gardens, but it's a passion more for the design involved than for the plants found in them.

I can't tell you the number of times I've been asked to help design an English garden and have disappointed the client by telling them that our climate in the Southeast is not really conducive to the delphiniums they want to include. They turn to another designer and wind up spending fortunes, not only in keeping exotic plants alive, but also in the necessary labor such plants demand.

Now, I must jump in to write that while native plants are tough, they are not the Superman or Wonder Woman of gardening. Even they sometimes have roots of clay (forgive the pun). In other words, when natives are planted out in the environment they were made for, they immediately settle in, hunker down, and perform like troopers. But if you insist on planting a trillium in unimproved clay soil in a hot, south-facing location, the plant will quickly perish.

I garden within the city limits of Asheville, North Carolina, officially rated as USDA Zone 6, but we're actually in Zone 7 two years out of three. The problem is that nobody knows which year is which! Herewith are a few thoughts about gardening with native plants.

A sunny border of native perennials includes, from front to back, purple coneflowers, blazing star, and coreopsis.

Mapping the Territory

Sketch a simple map of the area to be developed and planted with paper and pencil. The map need not be complicated or artistic because it's simply a starting point used to jog your memory about what may be coming down the line. Planning out a garden beforehand, whether it's on a grand scale or simply backyard potatoes, saves time, energy, money, and a lot of grief.

Solidago juncea

Only you can decide how much land is to be cared for and how much time you'll have for weeding and cultivating: Is your garden going to be a weekend pastime or a year-round pursuit?

On your map indicate the location of natural windbreaks, existing trees, the direction of the worst winter winds, possible obstructions to spring and fall sunlight, and all structures—whether already there or anticipated for the future. If you plan on raising some of your own native plants, leave a spot for a nursery bed (a temporary home for young and experimental plants) and a cold frame to winter-over selected specimens and protect seedlings in the early spring.

Checking the locations of natural and artificial windbreaks is very important, especially in the colder areas of the Southeast. You might find that you are in Zone 6 but within a protected spot, you can actually grow Zone 8 plants. Once you have that map, you can pinpoint the areas where the soil is always slightly damp, winter or summer, which might be perfect for moisture-loving plants.

Or, you might be lucky enough to have a natural (or manmade) swale within your garden perimeters and with a bit of work, bog and swamp plants would adapt with ease. As to sunshine, once you plot your map, you will know just how much sun will fall upon your garden. If you have just moved into a home built by an average developer (where every tree within reach is decapitated), start planting trees immediately. Check with your local Extension agent or do some Web research on fast-growing trees (hopefully natives), and begin the work even before you turn the dishwasher on for the first time. Even the smallest tree or bush can provide some shade. If you plant three trees in a triangle, it won't be long before you have a woodland garden with areas ranging from sun most of the day, partial shade, deep to partial shade, to deep shade all day long.

Wildflower Meadow

Microclimates

"The north wind doth blow and soon we'll have snow," goes the old rhyme, but if your garden is protected by some kind of natural or artificial barrier that blocks out said wind, you'll find you're able to sustain a number of species that would probably perish if left in the open. We garden on the side of a gently sloping hillside, with high, open oak trees above and Kenilworth Lake below. My friend Peter Gentling gardens on a higher slope overlooking the city of Asheville, with an elevation some 500 feet higher than our own 2,300 feet.

On those first really cold nights of early fall when the chill comes creeping down the mountainsides on cold little cat feet, it passes right over Peter's garden. At our place it's always a few degrees colder and that cold air settles in for the night. But once we enter true winter, nearby Kenilworth Lake moderates our climate and Peter, up on the side of the mountain, is always a few degrees colder than we are. Thus a few plants from a Zone 7 environment survive for us but perish up in Peter's garden unless protected by a mantle of snow.

I grow a healthy stand of our native climbing hydrangea (*Decumaria barbara*), a high-reaching woody vine with smooth, shiny leaves and aerial rootlets, sporting terminal clusters of white fragrant flowers, in an area where winter temperatures sometimes approach 0 degrees Fahrenheit. What saves it? The south-facing stonewall upon which it grows.

Things to consider in reference to microclimates include:

1. Buildings, because high or low, they deflect the winds.
2. Hills, for the same reasons. Sometimes they are actually warmer than valleys.
3. Valleys, as they provide shelter from the weather and hold the warmth or heat.

Wildflower Border

4. Watersides, because the larger the body of water, the more heat is holds, releasing it as the autumn advances.
5. Elevation, because the higher you go, the cooler it gets.
6. City versus rural, because the paved areas, buildings and their roofs, and all the lights of a city actually produce heat that is then reflected at night.
7. Sewer pipes prevent the ground from freezing in their vicinity due to their warm contents.
8. Walls, like buildings, also deflect wind and in certain ways concentrate the sun's heat.

Soil and Soil Types

The plants described in this book range from those delighted to have wet roots to those that demand perfect drainage in the driest of soils. So before you decide what you wish to grow, check your soil for its character: Is it solid clay,

Oenothera speciosa

rich loam, or a combination of both? Is it well drained or does the water stand in puddles even after a light rain?

Clay soils are sticky. If your soil forms a compact cylinder that doesn't break up when you roll a lump of wet soil between your fingers (as though rolling a cigarette in the old days), it's clay. Clay can become rock hard when completely dry, so instead of sinking into such soil, water simply rolls to the lowest level and sits. Sandy soil drains immediately; a soil that is rich, loamy and full of organic matter strikes a balance between the two. Unless a plant demands special conditions, try to prepare a garden soil that strikes a balance between clay, sand, and loam. In addition, the organic matter you add helps to provide food for healthy plant development.

There are many ways to improve the soil. You can add grit, pea gravel, organic boosters like various additives termed "Nature's Helpers," composted manure, shredded leaves, and even soil purchased from other places. You can make your own compost by maintaining a compost pile of grass clippings, weeds, garden and kitchen refuse (just never add any meat products to the pile).

And remember, if the soil set aside for your garden will not respond to any help you can provide, think about gardening in raised beds, where wood and stone provide the needed elevation.

A Few Other Things to Consider

Once your map is complete, think about garden helpers that might be needed down the line. I don't mean knowledgeable men lately retired

The field that ran rampant for more than twenty years was first scythed, then clipped again by Keith and his weed-wacker.

from tending classic English gardens, but things like laying underground pipes to bring water where it's needed most, or laying electric cable to allow for the installation of garden lighting or powering electric-powered equipment.

Our Own Garden

In the spring of 1992 we decided to clean up a section of our property that had not been worked for some twenty years. As the result of living on a hillside, the original owners had banked sloping soil with a handsome rock and mortar wall resulting in a three-foot-high wall

We install the concrete blocks to define the garden paths.

The pathways are seeded with grass and given a hay mulch. You can see reflections on Lake Kenilworth in the rear of the photo.

overlooking a ninety-by-thirty-foot plot. At one end of that ninety feet they even built the side walls for a set of six steps leading to the garden below—but never installed the steps. Below this rectangular plot and running the long measurement is another three-foot-high wall, this time with the land at its base gently sloping to Kenilworth Lake.

When you enter the garden, you pass through a grove of red oaks and dogwoods, a sourwood tree, plus assorted rhododendrons, mostly catawbas (*Rhododendron catawbiense*). At the far end of the garden shade is provided by a very mature dawn redwood (*Metasequoia*

We began garden work in March and the picture above was taken at the end of May. The tree in the foreground is the umbrella tree (Magnolia tripetala).

glyptostroboides), planted around 1955; a native white pine (*Pinus strobus*); and a most beautiful umbrella magnolia (*Magnolia tripetala*). There are also a few Canadian hemlocks at either end.

The hillside above is fairly steep and planted with various hydrangeas, goldenrods, asters, daylilies, and ornamental grasses.

So in that plot of land I have various areas of sun and shade, ranging from noontime brutal to morning and late afternoon pleasantries. Finally, there's a street light up above that overlooks the garden, at night becoming a sort of surrogate full moon. But enough description—there are photos accompanying this text—and on to the prep work we went through. Prep work that, over the long haul, added up to time and money well spent.

The garden in June of 1993.

Adlumia fungosa

Adlumia fungosa, the climbing fumitory, has been a personal favorite of mine ever since I saw my first rambling plant. The soft, leafy vines covered an old oak stump along the pathway that parallels the Laurel River in western North Carolina. The genus is named in honor of John Adlum (1759-1836), a plantsman who ran an experimental farm in Georgetown. The species is from the Greek word for sponge, referring to the spongy corolla that encloses the developing seedpod.

The leaves are fine and compound, divided and re-divided into many small, rounded segments on thin stalks. The clusters of pendulous pale-pink to white flowers, about an inch long, bloom from late spring into summer. The biennial vines form rosettes of foliage the first year, and the following year stems can ramble more than twelve feet by the time they bloom, twisting in and out of any support from stumps to the branches of shrubs and trees.

Provide a rich, well-drained—but moist—soil in partial shade. Propagation results from self-seeding and once started, you will have blooming vines every year. Seeds are usually available from the American Rock Garden Society.

USDA Zones 4 to 9

Allium cernuum, the nodding flowering onion, is a native member of the flowering onions that blooms in summer, sending up the blossoms from basal leaves that rise from the forest floor. The genus is the ancient Latin name for garlic; the species means "slightly drooping" as the flowers nod to one side.

If you're thinking that onions could hardly be valuable additions to the floral border, read on. These bulbous plants bloom with clusters of star-shaped blossoms of great charm starting in late spring and, depending on the species, provide color accents well into October. Except for ramps (see below), a mild oniony smell that's produced when leaves and stems are crushed is the only clue to their heritage. Many seedheads dry with great effect and make stunning additions to dried flower arrangements.

These bulbs sprout from the base with long, flat strap-like leaves to sixteen inches in length. The flower stalk can be up to two feet high and topped by up to forty rose to purple (sometimes white) star-shaped flowers that resemble skyrockets going off. In the fall, the seedheads dry and split, revealing shiny black seeds that look like Victorian jet jewelry. Cultivation demands are few: A reasonable soil that is loose enough to allow bulbs to expand, and sun to partial shade. When planting these onions, use at least five bulbs per planting hole to form small groupings. After a few years, when fewer flowers are produced, divide the bulbs in the fall and replant. Propagation is by seed or offsets gathered in the fall.

Allium tricoccum, or ramps, sometimes known as ramsons, give off the odor of leeks. The large flat leaves are up to a foot long with a reddish stalk, withering before flowers appear. In summer, clusters of small white flowers bloom on twelve-inch stems. Here in western North Carolina, the bulbs are collected for great ramp festivals. The species refers to the flower having a compound pistil.

USDA Zone 3 to 9

Amsonia tabernaemontana, known in the vernacular as the eastern bluestar, willow bluestar, or dog bluestar, came into my garden as a seedling offered by Bebe Miles, a great American wildflower gardener. The initial plant grew larger every year, eventually becoming a bush that in spring is still festooned with star-like blossoms in the almost unique garden color of pale blue (like the silk suit in Gainsborough's painting *The Boy in Blue*) and in autumn sports lovely butterscotch yellow leaves resembling tarnished gold. The

Amsonia tabernaemontana

plant was named in honor of Dr. Amson, an 18th-century Virginia physician, and 16th-century German herbalist Jakob Theodor Muller, who called himself Tabernaemontanus after a mountain near his place of birth.

Bluestars are bushy perennials with narrow leaves and those marvelous pale-blue blossoms on the tops of stiff branches that can reach a three- to four-foot height, blooming in spring. They are found in most of the Southeast ranging from the Virginias down to the Florida border.

In the true spirit of international gardening, one English book notes that these plants have too narrow leaves and the flowers sometimes droop. I suspect this is a problem with plants growing under weak sunshine and a lot of rain. Provide them with a well-drained, reasonably rich garden soil in full sun or partial shade, remembering that they seem to dislike the sun around noon. If the fading flowers of the first bloom are removed as they wither, there is usually a second round of blossoms, less abundant than the first, but welcome nonethe-

Amsonia hubrichtii

less. In my first garden, amsonia grew between some low-growing columbines and a big tree peony, where its bushy growth helped to camouflage the rough look of the peony's lower leafless stems. Propagation of bluestar is by division in spring or fall or by seed.

Recently some new cultivars have hit the market and not only is the species *Amsonia ciliata* or the fringed bluestar available, Tony Avent introduced the creeping bluestar, a beauty discovered in the sand hills of Central Georgia by Bob McCartney and given the unfortunate cultivar name of 'Pancake', hitched to *Amsonia ciliata* var. *filifolia*. Grown to advantage in a rock garden, the plants make a bright green mat of needle-like foliage that turns golden-brown in the fall and carries the beautiful pale-blue flowers at the tip of each branch.

USDA Zones 4 to 9

Anemonella thalictroides

Anemonella thalictroides, the common rue anemone, was once known as *Syndesmon thalictroides* then *Thalictrum anemonoides*, hence you get a rare glimpse into typical botanical wordplay in action. The genus means "little windflower" and refers to the resemblance of the blossoms to miniature anemones. The species alludes to the leaves aping those of meadow rues. Why windflower? The common name of anemone is derived from the Greek word for wind and relates to a myth in which a nymph beloved by the west wind, known as Zephyr, was changed to a flower by another jealous god. But another version credits the transformation of Adonis, who when he fell to the earth morphed into a crimson anemone.

Rue anemones are very delicate looking flowers of early spring that sprout up from small root-tubers, having prettily rounded fresh green leaves on wiry reddish-black stems. They bloom with one-inch-wide, five-petaled, white (or sometimes pink) flowers, the sepals surrounding prominent yellow stamens leading to blossoms of great charm—and they bloom for many weeks. Flowers eventually mature into little seedpods that are arranged in a whorl. The stems are usually between four and eight inches tall. They range from the northern borders of the Southeast south to Florida, Alabama, Mississippi, and Oklahoma.

A typical conservationist's heart might flutter a bit when reading the following words by Neltje Blanchan. The wife of Abner Doubleday, she was a formidable nature writer from early in the 20th century. "Pick them and they soon wilt miserably, " she wrote in *Nature's Garden*. "Lift the plants early, with a good ball of soil about the roots, and they will unfold their fragile blossoms indoors, bringing with them something of the unspeakable charm of their native woods and hillsides just waking into life."

Where there is some shade and well-drained soil, humusy, and on the acid end of the scale, these wildflowers should thrive. The plants live until the heat of summer when they sense uncomfortable times ahead. Then they slowly fade away only to begin again the following spring. To cover this eventuality, I grow them in the company of ferns whose fronds eventually hide the rue anemone's disappearance. Remember, in dry springs they need some additional water. Voles have been known to dine on the small and delicate tubers, so if they are a problem in your garden it might be a good idea to plant them within a hardware-cloth cage. For a delicate-looking wildflower, there are a surprising number of cultivars ranging from a semidouble form to a double pink and a double white. Propagate by seed and very careful division of the tubers.

Aquilegia canadensis, the American columbine, comes to my mind's eye as I think of spring, when its bright orange-red flowers fling themselves along the pathways of our garden. For many years I drove back and forth along a twisting two-lane highway that wound along the Delaware River between Callicoon and Port Jervis, New York. At one point a large flat-topped rock, probably left by a glacier 10,000 years ago, loomed over the road, and it sported a carpet of native columbines every spring. Imagine my surprise when I found the same tight little colonies in western North Carolina.

The genus *Aquilegia* is from the Latin *aquila*, for "eagle," whose claws are said to be represented by the curved form of the petals.

The common name comes from the Latin *columbinus*, or "dove," again referring to either the bird-like claws (or the beak-like spurs) of the flowers or the seedheads.

The compound leaves are attractive in their own right and often remain evergreen here in the South. If the leaves get surface tracings resembling unintelligible handwriting, it's the work of leafminers. These tiny insects tunnel their way inside the leaf. Ignore them, as they do not bother the plant. Hummingbirds will not pass up the flowers as they fly to the nectar at the bottom of the spurs. The plants grow up to three feet tall, but they are usually much shorter in the wild. They are almost ubiquitous in their range, being found from

Aquilegia canadensis

southern Canada south to Florida and Texas. That rocky slope along the Delaware River was a clue to the wild columbine's soil preferences. Given good drainage, it will adapt to most situations. Here in the South you must provide some filtered shade.

Because the flowers are attractive and bloom over long periods, columbines are excellent in both beds and borders. Extend the flowering season by deadheading spent flowers. Although most columbines are short-lived compared to many perennials, the flowers self-sow with ease. Older plants develop a tuberous-like root system that doesn't transplant well, but younger plants recover quickly. The various garden hybrids are bigger and blousier with their flowers but, because of hybridizations, usually do not come true from seed and frankly, do not compare to the delicate appearance of our native types. In addition to our own columbine there is *Aquilegia caerulea*, the Colorado columbine, which bears sky blue blossoms with white centers on wiry stems, growing to a two-foot height. Propagate by division of younger plants in spring and by seed.

USDA Zone 4 to 9

Arisaema triphyllum

Arisaema triphyllum, the common Jack-in-the-pulpit, likes the shade of the leafy woods and shuns open meadows or the edges of sunny trails. The common name assumes Jack to be the spadix, the column that bears the tiny flowers, and the spathe to be his hooded pulpit. The generic name of *Arisaema*, means "bloody arum" and refers to the red leaves of certain species. The species name, *triphyllum*, refers to the three leaflets usually overlapping the spathe. These are ubiquitous plants found from the northern borders of the Southeast, down to the northern border of Florida.

Just as there are differences in preachers, there are differences in pulpits, and sometimes the flowers will be a light green and sometimes a rich purple-brown. For years botanists thought the color indicated the gender of the flowers, but eventually one member of the scientific community looked carefully and it's now known that every blossom is unisexual with tiny male and female flowers sharing space at the base of the spadix, blooming at different times. Some authorities consider the different colors to be different species while others do not.

The flowers are not fertilized by bees because these insects are usually off foraging in the sunlight or at least in dappled shade, and overlook the flowers of most arisaemas. Bees are very fussy about their reaction to odors, hence pollination here is assisted by insects like fungus gnats, flies, or beetles. Fertilized flowers shed the spathe and by high summer the spadix is covered with bright orange-red berries. Amerindians would boil the berries along with the tuberous roots to remove acrid and mouth-burning juices, leave them to dry, then grind them into meal. One of the local names for this flower is memory-root, meaning that once bidden to bite root or berry, you'll be twice shy thanks to the hot shock to the mouth and tongue.

To entertain visitors, you can make the Jack emote a squeaking sound by taking the bottom of the spathe and gently rubbing it between your fingers. Provide the plants a shady spot and moist soil with added humus, preferably in a low spot near a source of water or a site accessible to the hose. Without these niceties, the plants will either refuse to flower or will disappear before producing the berries. And if you are a gardener with sensitive skin, handle the tubers carefully or wear gloves. Often these plants get to be quite large, assuming the stature of minor shrubbery. They are especially effective when under-planted with low and hardy ferns.

Arisaema dracontium, or the green dragon,

Arisaema dracontium, or the green dragon, is a similar plant that will grow in drier conditions. It's more of a garden curiosity than many members of the genus, the claim to fame being a spadix that sticks out five inches or more above the spathe. Like the Jack-in-the-pulpit,

Artemisia ludoviciana

green dragon has a chemical component, only in this case ingesting any part of the fresh plant can cause intense burning to damp skin and mouth parts caused by irritating calcium oxalates. It's not necessary to take plants of *Arisaema* species from the wild as they grow easily from seed. Collect the berries in the fall, crush them to remove the pulp, and plant immediately.

USDA Zones 5 to 9

Artemisia ludoviciana is one member of a plant family containing some 200 species of mostly aromatic, annual, biennial, and perennial herbs or shrubs native to the dry spots of the northern hemisphere. Like many plants that range over a large area, this artemisia has a number of common names, including white sage but also silver wormwood, wild sage, white mugwort, Louisiana sage, darkleaf mugwort, Mexican sagewort, Chihuahua sagewort, Garfield tea, and finally man sage. The artemesias were originally named in honor of Artemisia, the wife of Mausolus, a Persian governor who designed and eventually occupied the first tomb to achieve international notoriety—an idea that eventually led to the mausoleum. The species refers to a French king, and by extension to the state of Louisiana.

Like many plants of the Southeast, white sage was employed in many Amerindian rituals where it was often tied to smudge sticks and, like incenses, burned to ward off mosquitoes. It was obviously not used to great effect during the plague years of New Orleans as represented by Bette Davis in *Jezebel*. Man sage was the term Amerindians coined for this plant and included among the uses were a foot deodorant, a headache cure, and a medicine for horse wounds.

They also stuffed pillows and saddlebags with the leaves, again to ward off mosquitoes.

This particular species is grown for the masses of aromatic, evergreen, silvery-gray foliage that is extremely drought-resistant (making it a great candidate for xeriscaping), and one great silver-leaved perennial that stands up to the hot and humid weather of the Deep South. The silver-gray leaves are narrow and lance-shaped. Small flowers bloom in spikes at the top of the stems and add just a bit more drama to the plant. Plants soon reach a three-foot spread with a three-foot height.

Thanks to a wandering rootstock, allow enough room for growth, digging and dividing every few years to control its desire to invade and conquer. Provide average garden soil but it should be well drained. Water demands are average, and you should water with some regularly—but never overwater! In our garden I use the cultivar 'Silver King' in a stone planter some ten feet wide and only fifteen inches deep. I planted deep maroon caladiums within their ranks and the combination is spectacular.

USDA Zones 5 to 9

Aruncus dioicus

Aruncus dioicus, goatsbeard, wild spirea, or bride's feathers, is in full bloom in my garden today (June 10) and has been for almost a month. When approaching the white feathery wands of tiny blossoms, you immediately confront a host of insects—both large and small—chowing down on the sweet floral contents. So if you're interested in pollinators other than bees, be sure to bring a good hand-lens to the garden when enjoying the flowers.

The genus *Aruncus* is from an ancient Latin term for a goats beard and the species, *dioicus*, means "in two different households," a botanist's way of saying that male flowers and female flowers are found on different plants. Nurseries do not generally differentiate between the two. Upon examining the flowers and the foliage, the plant's relationship to both astilbe and spirea is easily noted. Goatsbeard would be grown for the foliage alone with its outspread branches of compound leaves, but add the showy plumes of tiny white flowers, on stems sometimes reaching a height of six to seven feet, and you have a wildflower winner.

While not generally at home in the hot and humid gardens of the Deep South, these plants range as far south as the higher elevations of Georgia and South Carolina, not to mention Alabama and Arkansas, then north to Pennsylvania and Quebec. They are at home in the moist to wet soils of rich woodlands, preferring partial shade or partial sun, depending on your interpretation of these terms. In the mountains of western North Carolina, you will often see goatsbeard reaching out from the sides of steep hills and down into the upper edges of drainage ditches. In our garden they line one of the bottom walkways, getting the full sun of morning, then shaded by lower branches of a katsura tree (*Cercidiphyllum japonicum*), a Japanese timber tree that should be found in more Southern gardens. Propagation is by seed or division in spring.

USDA Zones 4 to 8

Asarum shuttleworthii, the mottled ginger, has beautiful evergreen foliage that in colder areas develops a lovely purple tinge to the foliage in winter. The scientific name is derived from *Asaron*, the Greek name for the European ginger (*Asarum europaeum*) and the species name of this Southern beauty celebrates the

Asarum shuttleworthii

19th-century botanist Robert James Shuttleworth (1810-1874). Because it's evergreen, this ginger is often included in the genus *Hexastylis* (named from the Greek *hex* for six and *stylus* for style, referring to six styluses in a flower). The deciduous gingers, like the Canadian wild ginger (it's not limited to Canada but was first discovered there), are grouped in the *Asarum* genus.

The rounded, heart-shaped foliage of the mottled ginger is a lustrous dark green sporting marvelous dashes and dabs of silvery veining. In early spring, beige to purple "little brown jugs" open beneath the leaves, hugging the ground. They're pollinated by gnats, beetles, and the flies of March and April; no self-respecting bee is so active this early in the year. Plants slowly form large colonies with a general height of four to six inches. The rootstocks and sometimes the leaves (depending on rainfall) have a ginger-like odor and a hot spicy taste. Early settlers thought these plants were related to the tropical gingers.

One of the few cultivars of this ginger was developed by Callaway Gardens. It's small compared to the species, measuring in at a three-inch height. So far 'Callaway' has only been semievergreen, as it appears to be overly sensitive to winter cold snaps, not to mention summer hot spells. For all the gingers provide a good, humusy soil on the acid side in full or dappled shade. These gingers are great ground covers under shrubbery or along woodland pathways. The natural range is from the Virginias, south to Georgia and Alabama.

The Canadian wild ginger (*Asarum canadense*) is not evergreen and while a definite plus in northern gardens, hereabouts where snow is often lacking, winter dieback leaves much to be desired. But it is an excellent—if invasive—ground cover. Like the mottled ginger, I've found that it withstands dry conditions quite well. This wild ginger is most common in moist rich woods in light to dense shade. Under favorable conditions I've seen leaves as big as an outstretched hand. You have to get down on your hands and knees to see their pendulous "brown jug" flowers which hang down under the foliage. Propagation of gingers is by division in spring, root-cuttings, and seed.

USDA Zones 7 to 9

Asclepias exaltata

Asclepias exaltata, the white woodland milkweed, *A. incarnata*, the swamp milkweed, and *A. tuberosa*, the butterfly weed, are all first-class plants for the Southern garden. The genus commemorates Asklepios, the Greek god of medicine, and many members of this group have a long history of use in relieving chest complaints and supposedly had specific actions on the lungs.

Milkweed flowers are often fragrant and quite sophisticated in their methods of spread-

ing pollen. When insects alight, they find the flower's surface slippery and claw about for a foothold. As they struggle one or more of the sharp projections on their feet catches in the small clefts at the flower's base. Soon a foot is drawn into a slot at the end of the cleft where a little dark brown container holds masses of yellow pollen. As the visitor gives a final tug to free itself, the container goes along, firmly caught until the pollinator lands on another flower, where the container usually falls though another slot and fertilizes the flower. Sometimes it doesn't work with smaller insects and they wind up trapped.

Woodland milkweeds flower in dappled sunlight to medium shade, their pendant white flowers (sometimes tinged with lavender or a pale green) blooming in clusters atop three- to five-foot-high plants resembling bursting fireworks. This species is commonly called the poke milkweed because of a very superficial resemblance to American pokeweed (*Phytolacca americana*). After fertilization, the fading flowers produce six- to ten-inch vertical seedpods that last well into autumn. Both stems and leaves contain a milky sap. They need some shade and a good, moist—but not wet—woodland soil.

USDA Zones 5 to 8

Asclepias incarnata, swamp milkweed, grow between four and five feet high bearing long, opposite, smooth, lance-shaped leaves. Plants bloom in midsummer with many one-half-inch, deep pink flowers opening in small clusters about two inches wide. The eventual pods are from two to four inches long. Swamp milkweeds are perfect for the wild garden, meadow garden, and the back of the border. They prefer moist open areas, especially close to water.

USDA Zones 5 to 9

Asclepias tuberosa

Asclepias syriaca, the common milkweed, is great for meadow or wild gardens but it's really too rampant for the formal garden. It attracts monarch butterflies (the *Asclepias* genus is the only food their caterpillars will eat); as a result of that diet, both larvae and butterflies are toxic to birds and other predators. The species name comes from Linnaeus, who mistakenly thought this milkweed was imported from Syria.

Asclepias tuberosa, butterfly weed, has more common names than the rest, including swallowwort (*wort* is an Old English word for "plant"), chigger-flower, wind root, and pleurisy root. To my knowledge, it's the only milkweed lacking the typical milky sap. The flowers are both colorful and complex in form, blooming in large flat umbels with colors ranging from bright yellow to reddish orange—but usually just plain orange. While few blossoms form mature fruits, there are usually one or two pods on any plant, which eventually open to produce ranks of seeds, each with a powder-puff of silky threads, but much smaller than the pods of common milkweed (see below).

Because of their deep-thrusting roots, butterfly weed should only be moved when a young plant. Once established, you can forget most care because in addition to its other qualities, this plant is extremely drought-resistant. If grown in good garden soil, especially when it is laced with compost, they tend to grow taller than wild types but should only require staking in damp summers when there is a tendency to sprawl.

USDA Zones 4 to 9

Aster species represents a number of composites, or members of the great daisy family, the genus reaching its greatest complexity in the eastern United States. This fact is readily apparent to anyone who walks the autumn fields surrounded by blooming asters and goldenrods, carrying a wildflower guide. There are well over 250 species. According to *The New Britton and Brown Illustrated Flora*, thanks to the diverse construction of flowers in this genus and the insects of the field, asters hybridize with ease—you will always find something buzzing around the open flowers. These plants are all daisies, usually with a cluster of yellow disk flowers surrounded by ray flowers of many colors. The genus is named for the Greek and Latin words for "a star," referring to the lovely flowers.

There are so many asters that I'm only mentioning a few of the better-known plants. Like milkweeds and most goldenrods, they need not be pampered other than providing good drainage and full sun. Some are untidy or flop over, others grow straight as a rod, but those that do get too big can be cut back in late spring and they will bloom on shorter stems.

Planted in drifts either in the border or in the wild garden, with the smaller types used as edging, asters should be in every gardener's collection. They even succeed in a rock garden setting and, just as in the field, make especially attractive combinations when mixed with ornamental grasses. They are also great cut flowers. Propagation for all is usually by division, especially when you want to keep a particular color for the next season. Plants may be lifted and divided either in the spring or fall. Take softwood cuttings in the spring.

Aster azureus [A. oolentagiensis], the

heath aster, bears flowers of a rich and beautiful blue, with numerous blooms covering plants growing from two to three feet tall. Butterflies love them. They are common to the tall grass prairies and want average, dry to moderately moist, well-drained soil in full sun. They are native to meadows, open woods, and rocky divides from our northern borders south to Georgia, Alabama, Louisiana, and Texas.

USDA Zones 3 to 9

Aster carolinianus, the climbing Carolina

aster, grows with shrubby and arching branches often up to thirty feet long. These stems are grayish in color and covered in a fine down. The flower heads are at the ends of the leafy branches with pale purple or pink rays, less than an inch long. Unlike many wildflowers our long hot summers provide the impetus for great bloom in this aster and often in milder parts of the South, plants are virtually evergreen. The climbing aster is even a native plant in Florida. Provide this wandering shrub with a fence or some shrubbery to lean upon. Some gardeners note the flowers provide a smell of marzipan on warm autumn afternoons. The foliage colors up with dark red to purple tints in late fall. Never prune until after you see what lasts through the winter as this plant blooms on old wood.

Aster divaricatus, the white wood aster, is

unusual in that shade is preferred over bright sunlight. The small white flowers bloom above dark green, coarsely toothed leaves growing on purple-black stems. They light up the shadows. Height is about two to three feet and plants will sprawl, so the blossoms bend to touch their neighbors. Provide a good soil with plenty of humus, well drained but evenly moist. Range is from the Virginias south to west Georgia, Alabama, Mississippi, and westward.

USDA Zone 3 to 8

Aster lateriflorus, the calico aster, is usually

about four feet high but is represented in the trade by the variety *horizontalis*, a special favorite of mine. They grow wild around our property and fall would be a poorer time without them. Tiny panicles of lilac flowers bloom above horizontal branches with leaves that turn a coppery purple for fall. This plant is quite unusual because the species, sometimes called the starved aster due to the scarcity of leaves and pronounced stems, was introduced into English

Aster novae-angliae

gardens around 1829. It certainly takes a long time for an American beauty to return home to fame and fortune. 'Prince' is as appealing for its foliage as for its flowers, growing to about three feet and covered with tiny white flowers that stand out against the purple leaves. 'Lady in Black' is similar, but more open and airy.

Aster novae-angliae, the New England aster, often requires staking when grown in a garden setting. If your garden is closely planted, just let them sprawl. The two-inch-wide, deep violet-purple flowers bloom on three- to four-foot stems and every garden should have a few plants. They are native throughout most of the eastern United States.

⌣⌣⌣⌣⌣⌣⌣⌣⌣⌣⌣⌣⌣⌣⌣⌣⌣⌣

Astilbe biternata, the false goatsbeard, is the only species of this genus found as an American native plant. Other monikers include Appalachian false goatsbeard. It closely resembles the true goatsbeard (*Aruncus dioicus*) but differs both in flower structure (two pistils instead of three) and having a terminal leaflet on each leaf. Also, true goatsbeard is a member of the rose family and the false goatsbeard is actually in the saxifrage family. Plants are found from Maryland south to Georgia and Tennessee. It blooms from late spring to early summer.

Occasionally a scientific name comes along that is frankly not deserved. Such a name is *Astilbe* which means *a*, "without," and *stilbe*, "brilliancy." True the individual flowers are tiny, but because each flowering branch contains hundreds of flowers, the total effect is not only of brilliance but brightly so. Petals are white and small to the point of being insignificant and consist of a small cup with ten feathery stamens. But the flowers are quite

lovely when appearing as graceful sprays in many branched terminal clusters. Add the very dark green compound leaflets on plants up to six feet high and you have a garden winner.

These plants are especially attractive when used as a backdrop or massed in the shade garden and remain quite beautiful as long as the soil is not allowed to dry out in hot summers. Provide partial shade and the soil should be rich with humus and moist. Propagation is by division in spring and by seed.

USDA Zones 6 to 9

⌣⌣⌣⌣⌣⌣⌣⌣⌣⌣⌣⌣⌣⌣⌣⌣⌣⌣

Baptisia australis, the wild blue indigo, had a place in my first formal garden. Six of these plants stood in a row atop a bank, with hay-scented ferns carpeting the slope below, and a thin strip of mowed-lawn bordering the other edge. They never ceased to amaze, from the pea-like flowers of spring to the seedpods (known commonly as Indian rattles), to the unusual effect the foliage presented when it turned black with the first touch of frost. The

Baptisia australis

species *australis* is confusing because it doesn't refer to the country down under but simply means "to the south."

It's hard to believe that baptisias are native to America, first recorded in 1758. The genus is derived from the word *bapto*, "to dye," and thereby hangs a tale referring to the American South: In colonial times everyone thought these plants would lead to a substitute for the indigo dye obtained from the genus *Indigofera*—and fortunes would be made. It seems that over a long period of time the real indigo poisoned the gatherers; and while the English were never concerned about the health of colonials in places like India, here in the States it was a different problem indeed. Unfortunately, the color provided by baptisias wasn't fast and quickly washed out of all the linsey-woolsey used for clothing, and fortunes were lost!

This is a plant that calls for planning before setting it out. The root system becomes so extensive that old plants are not easily moved. In time, each plant will cover an area of several feet with their graceful foliage. Because they are legumes, baptisias will do moderately well even in poor soil and are excellent plants for holding banks in check and general erosion control. In the fall when the foliage turns black it's especially striking when planted with goldenrods and some of the ornamental grasses. To save the seedpods, cut them on long stems in early fall before they become too weathered. Place them upright in a cool, dry, well-ventilated spot and let them slowly dry.

The popular name of Indian rattle is well deserved. Thoreau noted in a February entry of his journal: "As I stood by Eagle Field wall, I heard a fine rattling sound, produced by the wind on some dry weeds at my elbow. It was occasioned by the wind rattling the fine seeds in those pods of the indigo-weed which were

still closed—like a small Indian's calabash." Plants range from the northern part of our range down to northern Florida.

USDA Zones 5 to 9

Baptisia alba

Baptisia alba, white wild indigo, is a herbaceous perennial that looks more like a shrub than a typical perennial. It grows into a nice round bushy shape up to four-feet high and nearly as wide. Because even in warmer areas this plant is dormant in winter, mark it carefully so you don't disturb it. In early spring, unique bare stalks with smoky-purple stems (looking a lot like asparagus stalks) appear bearing bunches of white, pea-like flowers hovering above the leaves. The foliage is blue-green. Provide plenty of sun and remember that this plant usually takes up to four years to become established. But once ensconced, it will be very long lived. *Alba* means white.

USDA Zones 4 to 9

Baptisia sphaerocarpa, the wild yellow indigo, is a native of Arkansas, growing up to three feet tall with yellow flowers blooming in early summer. Provide full sun in average garden soil. The species means "having rounded fruit."

USDA Zone 4 to 8

Boltonia asteroides

Boltonia asteroides, called boltonia or false chamomile, is a tall perennial with so many aster-type flowers it's easily mistaken for a member of that genus (and it is in the aster family). But one look at the cone-shaped, rather than flat, shape of the disk gives you an immediate clue that it is in a different genus. The plant is named in honor of James B. Bolton (1735-1799), an English botanist, naturalist and botanical artist who wrote and illustrated the *History of Funguses*. In nature boltonias are found in field and forest edge as far south as Florida then west to Texas. The species name refers to its resemblance to asters.

The plants have strong, five-foot-tall leafy stems that bear clusters of white aster-like flowers in early to mid-fall. They are not fussy as to soil and are exceptionally drought-resistant, hence are very suitable for xeriscopic gardening. Boltonias can be transplanted with ease as long as you provide plenty of water while they are settling into their new quarters. Remember, they can be pinched back in late spring to very early summer. In the nursery world boltonias appear to be fairly new on the garden scene but England's William Robinson wrote about the plant in the 1930s, and America's Norman Taylor told of their profuse blooms and suggested their use in autumn gardens.

Then in the 1980s, the cultivar 'Snowbank' hit the catalogs, and a new star appeared on the flower horizon with more and bigger flowers than the species and of a clear pure white—and mildew resistant, too. This seedling selection made by the New England Wildflower Society reaches a forty-inch height and plants are literally covered with three-fourth-inch blossoms. Other cultivars include 'Pink Beauty' bearing very large clear pink flowers on five- to six-foot stems; 'Nana' is a dwarf form with pinkish flowers on stems a bit over two feet tall.

Boltonias are attractive to bees and butterflies, and reported to be deer-resistant. They are very lovely plants when set out in drifts and look especially fine when set off against ornamental grasses in a rock garden setting. Propagate by division in spring or by seed sown directly out-of-doors in the fall.

USDA Zones 4 to 8

Camassia scilloides, the wild hyacinth, is not only a lovely flower, but is also a proper bulb to eat. Unlike the death camas, a plant with which it's sometimes confused, this plant was an important food supplement for the often hungry members of the Lewis and Clark

Camassia scilloides

these bulbs makes up for its short season by being so beautiful when in bloom.

When provided with a rich soil with plenty of organic humus, the bulbs increase naturally with offsets. When they begin to get too crowded, wait until the foliage fades, then dig, separate, and replant immediately. Propagation is by seed, though they take a few years to mature, or by division of offsets.

USDA Zones 5 to 9

Camassia leichtlinii

Expedition. The genus name is adapted from the Indian term *quamash* or *camass*. The species refers to the Latin word for "squill" (the genus *Scilla*) and the resemblance of this plant to that group of bulbs.

The native range of these bulbs is quite large, as they are found in moist open places from our northern borders south to Georgia and Texas. This is the only species of *Camassia* found in the east. There are a few other species in the west. I have a number of these bulbs planted in partial sun, surrounded by goatsbeard (*Aruncus* spp.) and Christmas fern, so there is plenty of interest to spark up that corner when the wild hyacinth flowers fade.

The basal leaves are grass-like, between eight and sixteen inches long, a little under one-half-inch wide, and somewhat prone to bending. The spires of six star-like, pale blue to white petals (really tepals) surround prominent stamens and each flower is about an inch wide. They begin to open from the bottom of the flower stem (or scape), which is between one and three feet tall. Although the leaves slowly fade away after flowers go to seed, a colony of

Cardamine concatenata, the toothwort or pepper-root, blooms on a slope that falls away from one of our neighborhood streets; in early spring the plants dot the virgin green earth with a narrow field of nodding white flowers. It once belonged to the species *Dentaria* because of angular ribs or teeth on the rhizomes, which are leaf scars left from last year's stems. But its name has been changed to *Cardamine*, an old Greek name for another, but today totally unknown member, of the clan. The species

Cardamine concatenata

name *concatenata*, means "to combine or link together in a chain," referring to the individual plants being joined by a wandering rhizome.

Found from our northern range down to the northern border of Florida, this wildflower is called a spring ephemeral. That's a plant that blooms and seeds before most spring leaves appear on the overhead trees and by late spring or early summer has disappeared from the scene.

Plants are from eight to fifteen inches high, with deeply lobed and irregularly toothed leaves whorled around the stem. The flowers have four parts and range in color from pure white to very pale pink or light lavender. This harbinger of spring does best in a wildflower garden or an area with ferns, where burgeoning leaves can cover up the absence of the toothworts in late spring. Provide a good, evenly moist woodland soil in a well-drained spot under partial shade. In time the rhizomes spread to form a sizeable colony but they are not invasive. These plants will not adapt to heavy clay garden soil so don't even try!

The roots have a peppery taste prized by the Amerindians and often collected by people today for salads and soups. Old recipes describe the roots being pickled or boiled like peanuts and eaten with salt. Propagation is usually by selecting individual plants from the colony or starting new plants from seed. The brown seedpods are called siliques and open to the dark brown seeds, usually mature about five weeks from flowering. You can collect them and use in pots or just scatter them around a well-prepared (and carefully marked) bed.

USDA Zones 5 to 9

Cassia marilandica, wild senna or sometimes the Maryland senna, has been growing in my garden for five years now, where it's located in front of some ornamental grasses (*Miscanthus sinensis* 'Gracillimus'). It's one of those bushy wildflowers that provides a good shrubby look and boasts interesting flowers. The genus is from *Kassia*, an ancient Greek name for a kind of spice and still used for *Cinnamomum cassia*. The species salutes the state of Maryland.

This erect perennial grows between four and seven feet tall, bearing alternate and pinnately compound leaves each with eight to sixteen leaflets about two inches long. The golden-yellow bunches of pea-like flowers bloom at the top of the stems and for the autumn garden form four-inch-long pods of seeds devoured by the birds. Long-tongued bees, like our favorites the bumblebees, usually pollinate the flowers. This plant is also the basic food source for two species of sulfur butterflies.

Plants can reach a height of six feet and have feather-like compound leaves that are very attractive, and those inch-wide flowers can bloom off and on throughout the summer. The leaf oil has been used in antiseptics, tonics, and remedies for intestinal gas. It may be dangerous if used. One of the most popular things about this plant is the tolerance of the roots to clay soil, especially if it's well drained. Once the plant is established it's quite drought-tolerant. Propagation is by seed, division in spring, and by soft-stem cuttings

USDA Zones 7 to 10

Chamaelirium luteum

Chamaelirium luteum, commonly called the fairy-wand (as are helonias, to which it is not related), blazing star, devil's-bit, drooping star-wort, and unicorn's horn, is another one of those wildflowers that exists in the paradoxical world of liking damp soil but it must be well-drained. The genus comes from a Greek word meaning "a lily on the ground." The species is from the Greek for "yellow" because while generally white, the male flowers have a yellow tint from the many stamens. Plants are found in open woods from southern New England south to Florida and Arkansas.

A rosette of basal leaves contains a number of entire leaves in the shape of an elongated oval, reaching a length of six inches. A long slender cluster of tiny white flowers appears in early summer, blooming on stems varying between one and three feet in length. Male and female flowers bloom on separate plants, with the wand of male flowers drooping at the tip and the female flowers coming to a blunt tip.

The Amerindians used the root of this plant to treat various disorders of the reproductive tract, including a boost to male potency. Provide a rich loam on the acid side, laced with plenty of humus, and a site in partial sun. The soil must be moist but the thick fleshy roots will rot in soil where water collects, hence the plea for good drainage. Propagation is by seed sown as soon as it's ripe. When dormant, dividing the roots is possible but it doesn't always work.

USDA Zones 5 to 9

Chimaphila maculata is known as spotted wintergreen, striped prince's-pine, spotted pipsissewa, or sometimes—in the rush to simplic-

Chimaphila maculata

ity—just pipsissewa. These woody herbs are members of the heath family, blooming in late spring to early summer. The reference to winter-green (*Gaultheria procumbens*) is somewhat confusing because they have no connection with this plant. The genus is from the Greek, *cheima*, for "winter," and *philos*, for "dear," referring to the common name of winter-green. Pipsissiwa is said to be from the Cree Indian name *pipsisikweu* meaning "breaks into small pieces," that name reflecting the plant's use in the treatment of gall and kidney stones. A leaf tea was used to treat rheumatism and as a diuretic. The species name of *maculata* refers to the leaf markings.

Pipsissewa was listed in the *US Pharmacopeia* from 1820 to 1916. Considered to be rare in parts of Canada and New England, it's protected by law in some states. Spotted wintergreen is at home in dry woods with very acidic soil from above the Virginias down to South Carolina, Georgia, Alabama, and Kentucky. It's also been reported in Florida's Leon County.

On the same day I went down to the garden to observe the goatsbeard (June 11), I stopped to see my small colony of spotted wintergreen, this year numbering fourteen plants, eleven with twin flowers, each shining like a minor galaxy, then like satellites, three new plants about three feet away, these sans flowers. The pipissewas send up shoots from a long-running underground root that changes direction when it meets an underground obstacle, hence the irregular shapes of the colonies found in the woods.

The lightly fragrant white or occasionally pink flowers have five regular parts and when fully open are almost an inch wide. They hang face down, usually in pairs but sometimes in threes. The toothed leaves are almost three inches in length, of a polished dark green and striped with an almost silvery-white, right down the midrib.

Common pipsissewa (*Chimaphila umbellata*) is easily distinguished because it lacks any leaf markings and the flowers are usually a pale pink. Both these species are refreshing when the leaves are chewed and those of *C. umbellata* were once used in the manufacture of root beer.

Unless the soil is very acidic, pipsissawas revel in shade. In our garden they grow beneath a low canopy of various azaleas and rhododendrons and a mid- to high canopy of oak branches. Bebe Miles has suggested their use in woodland terrariums for the winter months. Propagation by seed is not always easy and cuttings taken with enough of the root runner will sometimes succeed, but not always.

USDA Zone 6 to 9

Chrysogonum virginianum, golden star or sometimes green-and-gold, is a usually ever-green perennial wildflower once known only to garden purists. But in the past ten years or so this plant has hit the big time and is now often

Chrysogonum virginianum

found in large pots at box-store garden centers. Named by Linnaeus in 1753, the Greek *Chrysogonum* means "golden joint" and possibly refers to the blossoms rising from the stem nodes. The species points to Virginia as the first recorded location for the plant.

The scalloped leaves have tiny hairs and grow from creeping stems, the flowers being bright yellow, daisy-like blossoms with five petals. Plants are found from the north of the Virginias, down through Georgia and even in a bit of Florida. When golden star flowers first bloom they are only a few inches high, but the blooms may be on stems up to a foot high at season's end. The best show of flowers is in the spring, but when plants are in the right place, they will often bloom in summer then put forth more blossoms well into fall. In this case the right place calls for good drainage and added humus in moderately acidic soil. Use at least three plants spaced about a foot apart. In our garden, golden star is used as an edging plant with dwarf hostas to the left and right and a number of dwarf fescues behind. At the botanical gardens of Asheville, they grow along the base of an old stone wall in lightly filtered shade.

Two cultivars are sometimes available. The first, 'Allen Bush', grows more rapidly than the species and sports more flowers. It is named after the owner of Holbrook Farms, a well-known but not defunct nursery of Fletcher, North Carolina. The second is 'Mark Viette', a long-blooming form named in honor of the André Viette Farm & Nursery in Fishersville, Virginia. Provide ordinary but well-drained garden soil with added humus and when confronted by the noonday sun, provide some dappled or filtered shade.

USDA Zones 5 to 9.

Chelone glabra, the white turtlehead, is a native wildflower of great garden charm, especially where the soil is damp, with plenty of humus. The flowers are aptly named because when viewed from the side, they look just like a turtle with its mouth open. By lightly pushing the sides of the blossom, the mouth actually opens. The genus *Chelone* (it rhymes with baloney) is named in honor of a Greek woman who lived in a house by a river. She alone refused an invitation to the wedding of Zeus and Hera, so for punishment, she was pushed into the river with her house falling on top of her, and she became the turtle. The species means not having hairs of any kind. Sometimes called balmony, this species was used by the Cherokee Indians for treating worm infections and lowering fevers.

The large white flowers arise above the joints of narrow, opposite, toothed leaves and the square stems are quite sturdy. The better the home environment, the taller the plants grow, easily reaching three sometimes four feet, blooming in late summer into fall. They grow naturally along streambanks, in wet meadows, swamps, and marshes.

When moving them into the garden, find a low spot that's easy to water during periods of drought, a fairly predictable happening here in the Southeast. Use plenty of humus and mulch well to hold in the moisture. Partial shade is necessary, especially from hot afternoon sun.

If you want to keep the plants shorter, pinch back the stems to about six inches in early spring. They will quickly grow again but will be considerably shorter. For growing along the edge of a pond or even on a deck, turtleheads adapt quite well to containers, but be sure to keep the pot in a saucer so the water never runs out. Turtleheads make long-lasting cut flowers and are attractive to butterflies. Although a few websites say that deer dislike these flowers, the exact opposite is true and even rabbits have been know to salad-down on young plants.

Chelone lyonii

Chelone lyonii, the pink turtlehead, has foliage of a deeper green, topped in late summer with rose-pink blossoms. The square stems are red for most of the summer. There is a cultivar 'Hot Lips', another example of a poorly named variety that has brighter flowers than the species. The species name is in honor of William Scrugham Lyon, a late 19th-century nurseryman and orchid grower. There are other natives, including the red turtlehead, *Chelone oblique* and Cuthbert's turtlehead, *C. cuthbertii*, having purple flowers with a yellow beard.

Propagation of turtleheads is by division of the heavy rootstocks in spring and by seed.

USDA Zones 5 to 8

Chrysopsis mariana, the Maryland golden aster, is more closely related to the goldenrods than the asters but regardless, this is one great herbaceous perennial. The terminal clusters of one-inch-wide, golden-yellow flowers begin blooming in midsummer and continue, off and on, well into fall. The species was first described by Carl Linnaeus (1707-1778), the Swedish botanist from Uppsala and founder of today's system of binomial nomenclature, who penned the genus from two Greek words: *chrysos*, or "gold," and *opsis*, for "aspect."

The silky stems reach a height of one to two feet, and bear silvery oblong lanceolate leaves (without stalks). There are little sticky bracts below the petals (really ray flowers). They grow in dry, sandy places, often at the

Chrysopsis mariana

edges of pinewoods in New Jersey, and continue down into North Carolina, Kentucky, Tennessee, Georgia, Florida, Alabama, and Mississippi. These golden asters are truly drought-tolerant and very easy to grow. And for a plant that does well on sandy soil, it will do very well in moist soil, too. Provide a good, but very well-drained soil and place them in full sun.

These sunny flowers do exceptionally well in containers but don't overwater or fertilize. Maryland golden asters grow as a low rosette of leaves until late summer when its flowering branches lift the clusters of yellow, aster-like flowers a foot off the ground. I often find these flowers blooming on the beaches of Marco Island when visiting in December and it's amazing to me that they are not offered by more nursery centers. Even the fruiting heads are attractive. Propagate by division in spring and by seeds.

USDA Zones 4 to 10

Cimicifuga **species,** fairy-candle or bugbane, is a favorite plant for my or any garden. The popular name of fairy-candle is evident when the narrow racemes of white flowers bloom in a shady border. Bugbane refers to the supposedly disagreeable smell of the flowers found on *Cimicifuga racemosa*, but the odor, while a bit rank, is nothing to cause visitors to run in panic from the border. Among the repelled insects are bees and wasps, but supposedly flies are home free. *Cimex* is Latin for "bug," and *fugare*, "to drive away." They are found naturally from the Virginias down to Georgia and Tennessee.

The numerous small flowers have no petals and the bud covers, or sepals, fall away as the buds open. The flowers open from the bottom of the stalk, and soon the top foot or so of each six- to eight-foot stem is covered with clusters of glistening stamens, like shining, silvery white filaments. The very attractive toothed leaves emerge from the ground and are very large and divided. You could grow this plant for the foliage alone. Seedpods form and make a curious rattling sound, hence the other common names of rattle-top and snakeroot.

Where soil is continually moist, bugbanes will take some sun, but generally in the South shady sites are best, with sun limited to early morning and late afternoon. The soil should be on the acid side and laced with plenty of organic matter. Once planted they can be left alone for

Cimicifuga racemosa

37

years and all species spread seed about so there are always plenty of plants for neighboring gardeners. A shaded walkway between our garden and John Cram's next door is edged on the higher side with a long line of *Cimicifuga americana* with its tall spires blooming in high summer. The great English gardener, Graham Stuart Thomas, rated C. *racemosa* not only as a truly great garden plant, but also one of exceptional beauty. C. *americana* is the shorter of the two American species. Propagate bugbanes by seed sown in fall or by division of the roots in spring.

USDA Zones 3 to 9

Claytonia virginica

Claytonia virginica, the spring beauty, also answering to the wonderful common name of fairy-spuds, is, for many dedicated gardeners, the true harbinger of spring. Blooming in March and April, this member of the wildflower group known as the spring ephemerals bursts on the late winter scene before the leaves open on the trees above them, usually disappearing before those leaves achieve their full size. Linnaeus named this genus in honor of John Clayton (1693-1779), one of Virginia's first botanists, while the species refers to the colony of Virginia.

In early spring, the softly fragrant, starry pink flowers of spring beauty appear, their flowers gracing coiled stems that are often close to the ground. Each individual blossom is at best about a half-inch wide. But there is considerable strength in numbers and as many as a dozen blossoms top each stem, appearing to carpet the woodland floor with a flush of pink. This past spring I led a group of hikers along the banks of the Swannanoa River just below Warren Wilson College. We spotted literally hundred of thousands of these flowers growing in the moist soil of the riverbank, making a sunny April 21st unforgettable.

Each flower has two green sepals enclosing five petals that are usually a light pink, but are often almost white, with pronounced red veining. They bloom above thin, fleshy leaves up to six inches long. The flowers usually continue to open for two weeks or more but only in the full sun and, as the flowers fade, a small seed capsule develops. Then the plant seemingly disappears for another year, but leaves behind little underground tubers that resemble tiny potatoes, complete with eyes. Their natural range is from further north down to Georgia, over to Texas.

There is a second species, often found intermixed with the first, called *Claytonia caroliniana*, having wider leaves, each with a noticeable stalk, and sepals that come to a sharper point. The two species seem to hybridize with ease. Contrary to their delicate appearance, spring beauties are very tough and able to withstand a great deal of abuse. Just remember that the stalks break easily and once deprived of

Claytonia virginica

nourishment from the photosynthesizing leaves, the little tubers can quickly perish. The basic problem is, of course, losing habitat as development creeps on large caterpillar-like feet into every nook and cranny of our woodland heritage.

These plants like spring moisture and filtered shade is best. While adaptable to a number of soil types, some added humus is always welcome. Not only did the Amerindians eat the tubers with relish, it seems the boars of the Southern Appalachians follow the blooming plants, going up the valleys to the mountaintops, digging up the tubers as they climb. Propagate by seed and division of the tubers when dormant. If not planting seeds directly in a nursery area, remember to provide at least six weeks of cold in the refrigerator, not the freezer.

USDA Zones 5 to 9 (remember that spring beauties can only withstand two months of ground temperatures above 85°F)

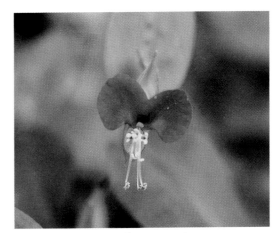

Commelina virginica

Commelina virginica, the Virginia dayflower, is not a showstopper as a single plant, but a small glade of these plants in bloom provides a host of lovely, three-petaled light blue flowers. Each flower is about an inch wide, blooming but a day. In the morning, astute gardeners find that the blossoms are open wide, their three petals supported by erect bracts at the rear of the flower. With that colorful display, the flowers are ready to be visited by neighboring bees and other insects. The activity continues till around noon. But after noon, as soon as pollination is complete, the lovely petals roll up, never to open again and quickly wilt into a shapeless puddle that, if touched, leaves a sticky blue fluid on your fingertips.

The top two petals are larger then the single bottom petal. Linnaeus, who had quite a sense of humor, named the dayflower after three Dutch brothers, two of which, Kaspar (1667-1731) and Johann (1629-1698), were botanists who published their works in the scholarly journals of the day. Unfortunately, the third brother was reported to be a cardsharp and ne'er-do-well.

Dayflowers range from southern New York, west to Illinois, then south to northern Florida and Texas and do very well in the mountains of North Carolina. The leaves are broad and grass-like, wrapping around the stems. Plants grow between one and three feet in height. The lovely blue flowers have three prominent stamens tipped with golden-yellow pollen. Dayflowers prefer a light, fairly dry, well-drained, humusy soil with added leafmold. Provide a generally sunny position with some shelter from noonday sun. Propagate by seed or division.

USDA Zones 5 to 9

Coreopsis species, are bright and shining daisy-like flowers that appear happy to exist in almost any conditions—but are saddled with an unfortunate scientific name. *Coreopsis* comes from the Greek *koris*, or "lice," and *opsis*, "a similarity," referring to the seeds, which were thought to resemble lice or ticks. One common name is tickseed. There are over 120 species from North and South America and Africa, including *Coreopsis tinctoria*, an attractive hardy annual that blooms in a number of bright yellows, pinks, and purples. But the most important garden coreopsis species are the perennials. Coreopsis are prized plants for the bed or border, the wild garden, the rock garden, and even hanging baskets and containers for the porch and patio. Shorter varieties are great as edging along paths and walkways. The flowers are also good for cutting.

Coreopsis tinctoria

Coreopsis verticillata

Coreopsis verticillata, the thread-leaved coreopsis, blooms with two-inch-wide yellow daisies on strong wiry stems, often to three feet high. The leaves are ferny. These are native Americans, originally from Maryland to Florida and west to Arkansas, and especially adaptable to hot and difficult places. 'Moonbeam' bears profusely blooming flowers of unusual light sulfur yellow. *Coreopsis grandiflora* hails from Kansas and Missouri, south to Florida, and bears two-inch-wide or larger flowers on two-foot stems. There is a double form called 'Sunray'. *Coreopsis rosea* is a creeping wildflower from the East Coast, fond of damp, sandy soil. It has a dense, bushy habit producing pink flowers on eighteen-inch stems and looks great in the rock garden.

Coreopsis auriculata grows about eighteen inches high with small yellow flowers. It spreads by stoloniferous roots. The dwarf form 'Nana', the bluegrass daisy, is a lovely form found near Maysville, Kentucky, by Dr. Lucy

Braun. It bears orange-yellow blossoms on foot-high stems. If deadheaded it will bloom from spring to frost. The variety 'Golden Star', although perennial, will bloom the first year from seed.

If you're looking for a flower to grace a hot, dry garden spot, this is one great group of plants. If the soil is too good, the plants sprawl instead of growing up strong and straight. So as for most of America, a lean diet is best. Cut off the spent blooms every few weeks to keep blossoms coming until frost. Propagation is by division in spring and by seed.

USDA Zones 5 to 10

Coreopsis grandiflora

Crinum americanum, the American swamp lily (or sometimes called the milk-and-wine lily, seven-sisters, and, rarely, the string-lily), is a native of the Southeast, doting on a wet environment and sometimes thought to be invasive in certain circumstances. Linnaeus based the genus *Crinum* on the Greek *krinon*, or "lily," because the flowers certainly resemble typical lilies. Other botanists claim the genus is based on the word *Crinos*, meaning "a comet" or "a hanging hair." The trailing tepals (an undifferentiated part of a blossom not distinguished as a sepal or a petal, as in lilies and tulips) of a mature blossom have small claws on their tips. In reality, these are drip-tips that apparently develop during humid weather, thus leading water away from the flower—consider that for hort engineering! Few early-day botanists had an opportunity to see specimens in flower, so for centuries, the reference to the drip-tips remained on the back burner.

Swamp lilies are perennial herbs with an onion-like bulb. The strap-like leaves start out growing erect and soon begin to spread, reaching an average length of three feet with a three-inch width. Flowers arise from a fleshy bulb on long flower stalks between one and three feet tall that are separate from the leaves. The sweetly fragrant flowers have three petals and three sepals, are white or white and pink striped, flaring from a six-inch-long floral tube that surrounds rosy stamens tipped with bright yellow pollen. They can appear throughout the warm seasons of the year and are followed by seed capsules about two inches thick. They grow naturally in wetlands, marshy creeks, pond borders, and the coastal plains, not to mention oceanside plantings in places like Marco Island, Florida, where they do far better in hotel gardens than many of the African bulbs brought in by landscape designers.

Crinums make great container plants. Use a pot one inch wider than the bulb diameter, and once planted, you can forget repotting for about five years. Although the bulbs like moisture, the pot must be well-drained using a potting mix of a good potting soil, sharp sand,

and dehydrated cow (or sheep) manure. Plant the bulb with the neck above the soil level, remembering to keep the soil level at least an inch below the top of the pot to allow for adequate watering. After they flower in the fall, hold back on water but not entirely, as the leaves are evergreen and should not dry out.

Outside in the garden, plant the bulbs at least ten inches deep in a well-prepared soil with a lot of added humus. The deeper they are planted, the fewer offsets the mother bulb produces and, in places like Asheville, the less worry about an occasional really hard winter. They will adapt to heavier soil and tolerate poor drainage. Provide a spot with at least four hours of sun a day, remembering the bulbs prefer partial shade or partial sun, the soil being drier as the sun gets more intense. Cut the spent stalks off to prevent seed formation unless you want to experiment with growing new bulbs from seed. Plant them on three- to four-foot centers to form a solid mass of leaves. Propagation of *Crinum* is by seed and offsets

In our Asheville garden I have overwintered and brought to bloom the cultivar ×*Crinodonna* 'Summer Maid' (actually ×*Amarcrinum memoria-corsii*), a hybrid of *A. belladonna* and *Crinum moorei*. Neither are native plants, but are often sold as such. The pink flowers appear in autumn and are sweetly scented and quite beautiful.

USDA Zones 7 to 11

.·.

Cypripedium calceolus var. pubescens,

the large yellow lady's-slipper orchid, is a wondrous plant to me because even though it's a native orchid of great beauty, it will do well in most gardens if given just a modicum of attention. The genus name is from the Latin *Cypris* (or Venus) and *pedilon*, for "shoe or slipper." The

Cypripedium calceolus var. *pubescens*

specific epithet *calceolus* is Latin for "a little shoe" in reference to the slipper-like shape of the labellum. The varietal name of *pubescens* is from the Latin for "downy or hairy" in reference to the hairy nature of the plant. The natural range is the foothills and mountains of the Carolinas, west to Arizona and north to Canada.

Everybody wants orchids in the garden though few gardens are up to providing the conditions necessary for their success. But the yellow lady's slipper is one that can survive in a number of conditions. This lovely plant arises from a rhizome and a number of fibrous roots, up to thrity-two inches high, with several to many stems. The three to five stem leaves usually sheath the flower stalk, are oval to lanceolate in shape, and from two to eight inches long and about half again as wide. One or two flowers bloom at the tops of the stems, having two twisted sepals and petals that are either green and streaked with brown. The lip that forms the slipper is a bright yellow pouch that is spotted with madder-purple dots within and is usually more than an inch long. Yellow lady's-slipper blooms from late April to June, then forms seedpods (with an estimated 10,000 dust-like seeds in each pod), finally becoming dormant with the heat of summer.

The yellow lady's-slipper is also known as the American valerian because of its calming effects. Root extracts were used during the 19th century as sedatives and pain relievers. Keep in mind that all of the lady's-slipper clan can cause contact dermatitis to susceptible persons. In nature these plants grow in rich, moist, hardwood coves and usually within spitting distance of rocks or underground ledges because they prefer some calcium in their soil. Plant the roots about an inch deep in a spot providing light shade. If your summer is too dry, you've got to take responsibility for some watering. A happy plant will slowly increase into a nicely sized clump. The variety *parviflorum* is also fragrant but is a smaller plant, happier in a cool climate. *C. acaule*, the pink moccasin flower, needs really acidic soil and is not as easy to grow as the yellow. Propagation of lady's-slippers is by seed (which can be difficult) and division in spring.

USDA Zones 6 to 9

Delphinium tricorne, also called wild larkspur, stagger-weed, or dwarf larkspur, is one of our native delphiniums. This lovely flower delights in growing on rocky steppes along the edge of the woods. Every year I watch a colony of these plants bloom along the Blue Ridge Parkway, just outside Asheville, the flowers nodding in the breeze generated by passing cars. The generic name is from a Greek word for an

Delphinium tricorne

ancient member of this plant group, while the species refers to the seedpod being divided into three parts. Alternate leaves are deeply lobed and divided. The flowers have four petals with two more petals fusing to make a curved spur. Flowers bloom on foot-high stems, their colors ranging from violet to deep blue to an occasional white. Seedpods follow and are divided into three sections, with each section having a tip that curls upward like a horn. Plants will fade in preparation for summer heat, so it's a good idea to mark the place where they grow in order to protect the dormant tubers. The range is throughout the entire Southeast, except for Florida. As wildflowers, they are under siege in Georgia from digging.

I take a clue about the conditions they need to grow from my observations of always finding these plants near rocky outcrops and have since learned of their preference for a

Delphinium exaltatum

slightly alkaline soil. In my garden I mulch with small marble chips. Larkspurs prefer a well-drained neutral to limy soil in partial shade. Because they disappear with the coming of summer, these wildflowers are often at an advantage when planted amidst a gathering of ferns. Just as the fern fronds unfold, the wild delphiniums are already showing ripening seed-heads. *Delphinium exaltatum*, the tall larkspur, can reach a height of six feet, while *D. carolinianum* is similar but blooms earlier in the spring. Propagation is by seed or by separating the dormant tubers.

USDA Zones 5 to 9

Dicentra eximia, fringed bleeding heart, turkey-corn, or wild bleeding heart, is a beauti-ful wildflower that performs a class act in the garden. If you have room for only one plant in a shady nook, this species, or one of the hybrids listed below, should be your choice. The genus name is from the Greek, *dis*, or "twice" and *centron*, "a spur," alluding to the two basal spurs on the flowers. The species name means "excellent."

The common names refer to the small cream-colored tubers and the belief that animals like turkeys and squirrels would root about and eat them like corn. Because members of the *Dicentra* genus in general are known to contain toxic isoquinoline alkaloids in the leaves and tubers, except for cattle eating leaves (hence a name of stagger-weed), they're usually left alone.

The leaves are bluish in color and fernlike in appearance, growing about six to eighteen inches tall. The heart-shaped flowers bloom as

Dicentra eximia

a panicle of hanging blossoms over the tops of the leaves, their colors a lovely dark pink. They are ever-blooming from May to September, or until cut down by a hard frost. Just never let the soil dry out and provide shade from the hot southern sun. The cultivar 'Alba' has smaller, white flowers but produces so many blossoms at one time that it's still very showy. 'Luxuriant' has deep pink flowers smaller than the species.

The eastern Dutchman's-breeches (*Dicentra cucullaria*) and squirrel-corn (*D. canadensis*) usually have white blooms but are known as spring ephemerals. The plants go dormant after spring, hence they are not as useful in the garden as the truly beautiful bleeding heart. For all *Dicentra* species provide a good, rich, moist, and well-drained soil as an added incentive for continued blooming. Propagate with seed sown in late summer and by division in spring.

USDA Zones 4 to 9

Dioscorea villosa, the wild yam, also billed as colic root and, in Turkish, *Yabani Hindelmasi*, is a deciduous and dioecious perennial vine. Deciduous means the leaves fall off for winter and dioecious means individual flowers are either male or female with only one gender found on any one plant. Both male and female plants must be grown for a crop of seed. The genus name is in honor of Dioscorides, a Greek naturalist of the first century. The species means "hairy" and refers to the leaf undersides of some plants.

Unlike many members of the yam family, this plant does not produce edible tubers; instead it has slender, but swollen, roots that are bitter to the taste. It's found naturally throughout the Southeast in woodlands and thickets, reaching down to the northern part of Florida. Amerindians and the early colonists used this plant to treat a number of female problems associated with childbirth, in addition to allaying the symptoms of various gastrointestinal problems; diosgenin extracted from these plants is used in the manufacture of modern steroids.

This climber can reach a length of fifteen feet, but I grow one male and one female vine on a tripod of eight-foot bamboo stakes in partial shade, so it never grows over ten feet in a season. The insignificant flowers are borne in clusters from the leaf axils and the fruits are about an inch long, mature in clusters, and have three broad wings. The leaves are truly

Dioscorea villosa

chordate, or heart-shaped, from two to four inches long, growing in whorls from a smooth stem that twines counterclockwise. In summer it's an attractive plant, a great background for other and brighter flowers; but in the fall, the leaves turn a beautiful golden-yellow and certainly brighten any corner. This vine is not fussy as to soil and will grow in sandy, loamy, or even clay soil, as long as it's well drained and evenly moist. Propagation is by seed or division of the tubers.

USDA Zones 6 to 9

Diphylleia cymosa, the umbrella leaf, has two species, one native to the Southeast and one, *Diphylleia sinensis*, native to Japan. The genus name is taken from a Greek word for "a double-leaf." The plant is similar in many respects to the May-apple (*Podophyllum peltatum*. Our native umbrella leaf was discovered and named by André Michaux (1747-1802), an extraordinary French botanist who roamed the Appalachian Mountains exploring both flora and fauna. It's one of some sixty-five plant species found in our southeastern mountains that match up with sixty-five closely linked species in Eastern Asia, resulting in what is termed "floral disjunction." This theory is based on the supposition that from the late Tertiary to the Quaternary periods of geologic time (65 to 1.5 million years ago and 1.8 million to 10,000 years ago, respectively), one continuous forest covered much of the Northern Hemisphere leading to this strange genetic link of various plants.

The range for umbrella leaf is damp woods and along the edges of steams from Virginia to Georgia along the mountain ridges and in higher altitudes. Plant height is about two feet, the foliage being a very attractive, single,

umbrella-like leaf that is deeply cleft and coarsely toothed on a non-flowering stem, often up to two feet across. From spring to early summer an umbel of small white flowers, each with six oval petals and six sepals, blooms above the leaves and is followed by small blue fruits. A root tea was used by the Cherokees to induce sweating.

"I grow the umbrella leaf in light shade in a moist swag with the companionship of the great hellebore (*Veratrum viride*)," says nurseryman Barry Glick. "It doesn't require as much moisture as the hellebore, but it appears to be very much at home and to have a wider window of acceptable growing conditions than most plants. Unlike its very close cousin, the May-apple, it doesn't hide its flowers from you." Propagation is by seed and by division.

USDA Zones 6 to 9

Dodecatheon meadia, the shooting star, has a number of common names including the American cowslip, Indian-chief, Johnny-jump, prairie-pointers, and pride of Ohio—this last being a salute to a flower that actually could be termed a statewide pride. The generic name is from the Greek *dodeca*, or "twelve," and *theos*, for "god," meaning that back in ancient Greece, the original primrose (the family to which the plant belongs) was under the watchful eyes of twelve gods. The species is named in honor of Dr. Richard Meade (1673-1754), physician to King George III, the king who kept an American flying squirrel in his linen drawer. The shooting star is also the trademark of the American Rock Garden Society.

Like the cyclamen, the individual flowers are held aloft on nine- to fifteen-inch stems and have reflexed petals, usually in white but

Dodecatheon meadia

Filtered shade is necessary especially in the Deep South and, again, good drainage is the rule. Propagation is by seed and, if left uncollected, you will soon find a grand colony of these plants ready to grace the departure of winter. Germination isn't difficult to achieve but plants take three years to bloom. They can also be carefully divided after flowering.

USDA Zones 5 to 10, perhaps 11

Echinacea purpurea, the purple coneflower (sometimes called the purple rudbeckia), represents a floral genus that, in addition to hosting stellar members, is well known in the pharmaceutical world for the number of extracts, cures, and treatments for infections, contributed by these plants. The genus name is in honor of

Echinacea purpurea

sometimes in shades of pink or lilac. The individual blossoms are borne in an umbel, and actually resemble a starburst of sky-tossed fireworks on the Fourth of July. The gray-green basal leaves range from three to twelve inches in length and are an elongated oval in shape. By mid-July the plants disappear from the garden but the seedheads remain.

Along the Woodland Trail at the botanical gardens at Asheville, the shootings stars are planted along the edge of a three-foot-high wall in fertile soil so they enjoy excellent drainage and late-spring shade. Along the Mountains-to-the Sea Trail above the Fold Art Center of the Blue Ridge Parkway, the plants again do beautifully among huge boulders that provide only thin layers of soil for the roots. To me this means that while many authorities say acid soil is needed, plants do better with a bit of lime leached either by a wall or rocks. Bebe Miles would mulch her plants with marble chips.

echinos, the hedgehog, because the receptacle that holds the flower parts is very prickly. The cone-shaped heads are a rich bronzy-brown and are surrounded by petals (really ray flowers) that begin horizontal but soon droop (the botanical term is reflexed). Colors vary but are predominantly in shades of rose-purple. The blossoms open on top of very stout stalks, from two to four feet high, and, will continue to bloom until frost when deadheaded. The simple and alternate leaves are very rough to the touch.

Echinacea purpurea is the plant usually offered by nurseries and seed companies. John Banister, an English naturalist, sent the first seeds from America to the Oxford Botanic Garden sometime in the mid-1680s. Some cultivars include: 'Magnus' with almost non-reflexed petals of rose-pink, 'White Swan' bearing white flowers, and 'Bright Star' with maroon flowers.

Echinacea pallida

There are many others. *Echinacea pallida* has narrow reflexed petals on three- to five-foot stalks, with pale purple petals, and a taproot that enables it to survive most contingencies in the garden. The Amerindians of the Northern Great Plains used this coneflower to treat more ailments than any other plant. It doesn't take to heat like the common coneflower, growing in USDA Zones 4 to 8.

Coneflowers are especially beautiful when massed either in the formal border or the wildflower garden—in fact, the more the better. They make excellent cut flowers and are able to withstand drought conditions. Plant in ordinary but well-drained garden soil in full sun; they will withstand partial shade but are never at their best when sunlight is diminished. There's a garden up the street where a large batch of purple coneflowers grows right up to the asphalt's edge, shining up to hot sun that would bend most people, and blooms until frost. Propagate by division in spring or by seed.
USDA Zones 4 to 9

Eryngium yuccifolium, rattlesnake master or button snake-root, is both an interesting and unusual flowering plant native to the Southeast. This wildflower ranges from the northern borders of Florida and west to Texas up to Pennsylvania. Other common names include yucca-leaf and snake-button. The genus is taken from the Greek word *eruggion*, an ancient name of one Old World species. The species refers to the leaves resembling those of a yucca.

I first ran across the plant a few years ago while visiting the Ventnor Botanic Garden on the Isle of Wight, a garden that displays a wide variety of exotic plants, shrubs, and trees gath-

Eryngium yuccifolium

In a place warmer than Asheville, this wildflower is in leaf all year, blooming in midsummer to early fall. The flowers are pollinated by bees, flies, and beetles. The plant is self-fertile.

Plants prefer a light, sandy or a well-drained soil rich with humus but will survive in poor soil as long as it's well drained. While acid soil is preferred, they do survive in alkaline soils, too. While preferring full sun, the plants will adapt to partial shade. They resent being disturbed, so when planting be sure to choose a spot where they won't be touched for a few years. The up to four-foot stems of spiky, yucca-like foliage surround three-foot-high stems of white, prickly, rounded heads made of very small, off-white, individual flowers. In addition to a root tea once used to treat snakebite, the plant has also enjoyed a history of medicinal uses ranging from respiratory problems to the treatment of social diseases. Propagation is by seed, or root division in early spring, using the minimum of disturbance when dividing them.

USDA Zones 5 to 10

ered on a world-wide basis. There, in a group planting of various wildflowers requiring good drainage and noted for unusual foliage or interesting flowers, a four-foot-tall *Eryngium yuccifolium* was blooming. Following a bit of careful praise about both the garden and English history, the botanist in charge also admitted that more than a third of the most fascinating plants in their collections came from the United States—a fascinating admission from any English gardener.

I'm also familiar with this plant because it's one of a handful of natives that grows at Shuffletown Prairie, a remnant of the Piedmont prairies that once existed along the Catawba River in the central part of North Carolina. There in the company of the federally endangered Schweinitz's sunflower, there is a colony of rattlesnake master.

***Erythronium* species**, the trout lilies (because the leaves look like the markings on brook or brown trout), adder's-tongue, dogtooth violets, or fawn lilies (this name because the leaves echo the look of a spotted fawn), are perennial wildflowers that grow from a deep and solid corm, having one leaf when mature and then two leaves until they grow up to flowering stage. The leaves are mostly oblong, tapering to the base, fleshy, mottled with brown on a green background, about eight inches long with hardly any visible stem. The genus name is from the Greek *erythros*, or "red," first given to the purplish-flowered European species.

Erythronium americanum

three to four inches deep, but to place a stone underneath to encourage blooming. The range of this plant is from our northern borders south to Maryland, Alabama, and Oklahoma. *Erythronium americanum* also loves to form colonies and will do well even in a fairly wet soil, as long as the acidity is to its liking. The petals are yellow and the anthers are yellow or red. These wildflowers are found throughout the eastern United States. Propagation of trout lilies is by seed but it takes a few years before plants reach flowering size.

USDA Zones 3 to 9

Depending on the species the nodding flowers are white or yellow solitary bells, a few inches high, on a stem (or more accurately a scape) four to eight inches tall, always blooming when there is a single-leaf on a mature plant. They require rich, moist, woodland soil with filtered shade in summer. These plants form colonies over time. And they persevere. My next-door neighbor has a bevy of trout-lily leaves to the left of the entrance to his Japanese moss garden, but this patch of *Erythronium americanum* never produces its yellow blooms; it only sends up a mass of leaves without flowers every spring. This is because the soil is so acidic (though the mosses love it).

Erythronium albidum, the white trout-lily, loves to form a colony and has a strong dislike of acid soil. The reflexed petals are bluish-white, striped with a pale brown on the outside and may have a touch of yellow at the base. Bebe Miles mulched her plants with marble chips and advised gardeners to plant the corms

Eupatorium species includes the Joe-Pye-weeds and their relatives, and it's a mighty group. The members are, on the whole, late summer and fall flowers, not spring flowers. Using any of these plants in your garden will brighten everything from mid-August on. Centering in the American tropics, some 500 species spill over into the Southeast. I'm only going to cover a few of those most important for the garden. The genus is named in honor of Mithridates Eupator (132-63 B.C.), King of Pontus, who is recorded as using one species from this genus in medicine. Like the goldenrods and asters, there are many difficult-to-discern hybrids. Most of the members found in this genus have leaves in pairs or in circles, with some fused or wrapped around the stem (hence in boneset, the plant was thought to knit bones), and a few species bear single leaves. Generally, the heads contain tubular flowers, without petals, and many are clustered in such a way they make a flat or round-topped inflorescence.

Eupatorium capillifolium, dog-fennel, is best described as a coarse perennial from three to seven feet tall having hairy stems and opposite leaves towards the bottom and alternate above, averaging about three inches in length. The species means "having thread-like leaves." The inflorescence is a long panicle with many small greenish-white flowers without petals. Close up the flowers are rather unimpressive but seen from a few feet away, the plant becomes quite beautiful. You will see it in the wild ranging from open woods to fields to roadsides, generally throughout the Southeast. I was one of its detractors until I saw it planted in part of the herb collection at the Atlanta Botanical Garden, and since then it's always been in my garden, blooming in late summer. There is a cultivar called 'Elegant Feather' with leaves even more willowy and needlelike, with the pink-tinged, generally white flowers just icing on the cake. This unusual perennial, the very definition of "fine textured," is an elegant addition to the garden with willowy, relaxed needlelike leaves, which cloak upright and branched, fuzzy white

Eupatorium capillifolium

clumping stems. Bright green new growth gains hints of red in maturity, and pink-tinged white flowers top the stems in late summer. Provide ordinary, but well-drained soil.

Eupatorium coelestinum

***Eupatorium coelestinum* [*Conoclinium coelestinum*]**, mistflower or the hardy ageratum, is another one of those great native garden perennials that has never received good press but deserves it. The natural range is from New Jersey west past the Mississippi, and south to Florida and Texas. The species name refers to the seed structure. Looking just like an annual ageratum on steroids, flat-topped clusters of soft fluffy violet-blue flowers bloom on three- to four-foot stalks. There are cultivars with white and blue flowers. In damp garden soil it spreads with stoloniferous roots so you have to be inclined to pull it up where not wanted; in drier soil progress is much slower. These plants will tolerate poor drainage. Provide partial shade to full sun. Deadhead old flowers and plants will continue to bloom until cut back by frost.

USDA Zones 6 to 10

Eupatorium fistulosum

Eupatorium perfoliatum, the white bone-set, has leaves that are fused at the base and the stem hence they were important to Amerindians who used boneset to treat break-bone fever (dengue fever), with infusions also used to treat colds, not to mention the treatment of malaria, pneumonia, and muscular pain. The species refers to the stem going through the leaves. While a bit too rough for the formal garden, when massed they are great in the wild garden, and because they do well in swampy or poorly drained areas they are perfect for fall color in such places. They are found naturally through-out our range down to the Florida Panhandle.

USDA Zones 4 to 9

Eupatorium purpureum, Joe-Pye weed, is a stunning plant for large gardens with its big heads of lovely flowers. It is a genuine butterfly magnet, not to mention attracting an incredible number of other insects, ranging from beetles, bees, wasps, and other smaller, nectar-lovers of all sorts. There are at least two other species: *E. maculatum* has spotted stems and *E. fistulosum* has smooth and purple, hollow stems.

It is, to me, the most important member of the genus. The green or purplish stems are from three to ten feet (occasionally more) with whorls of three to six (usually four), oval to lance-shaped, saw-edged, thin and rough leaves on short stems (or petioles). When crushed the leaves have a slight vanilla scent. The flowers are a pale or dull magenta or lavender-pink, slightly fragrant, terminal clusters of many tubular flowers, often up to eighteen inches across. Joe-Pye weed was named after a North American Indian called Joe Pye, who walked the streets of Boston, selling a cure for typhus, using an elixir of this plant to induce profuse sweating, thus breaking the fever.

There are plants of moist fields and pastures, and especially abundant along back-road ditches and summer streams. Believe it or not, English garden books featured these plants in the 19th century, though America is still finding out about these wild beauties. They do best in full sun because plants grown in partial shade reach for the light and get too tall, sometimes falling over. Provide plenty of water. Plants survive in dry sites, sometimes classified as being drought tolerant, but are never as showy when grown without abundant water. Several cultivars have been named, including 'Atropur-pureum' with purple stems, leaves, and flowers; 'Album' has white flowers; and 'Gateway' is smaller, usually staying about five feet tall. Propagate by division in fall.

USDA Zones 3 to 9

Eupatorium rugosum [Ageratina altis-sima], the white snakeroot, also known as the American ageratum and the through-wort, is unlike others in the clan because this plant likes a dry location. I've had one snakeroot growing right next to the trunk of a cannon-ball viburnum, rarely watered, with rain usually missing it thanks to the leaves above, but thriving year after year. Cows that eat white snakeroot produce poison milk but it took the death of Abraham Lincoln's mother from drinking the same to promote a bit of research, after which cows were kept away from the plants.

Opposite leaves are sharply toothed, about seven inches long and five inches wide on stout stalks, between two and four feet tall. The flowers bloom in dense, somewhat flat-topped clusters of fluffy white flowers. During a summer drought these plants will sometimes droop but given a bit of water, they once again stand up straight. They are great cut flowers. And they do well in almost any well-drained soil in partial shade. There is a very attractive cultivar called 'Chocolate' with reddish chocolate-brown foliage on purple stems and tiny white flowers, blooming in the fall.

USDA Zones 3 to 10

Filipendula rubra, queen-of-the-prairie or prairie meadowsweet, has flowers that look so much like cotton candy, that they lack only clowns and a Ferris wheel to be the complete package. The common name does not refer to meadows but mead, because the European species (see below) was used for flavoring herbal beers. When crushed, the leaves have the fragrance of sweet birch. The scientific name is derived from *filum*, or "thread," and *pendulus* or "hanging," in reference to root tubers that hang off the fibrous roots. The species name is the Latin word for "red."

These are plants of the low woods, wet prairies, and meadows from New York to Minnesota then south to North Carolina and Kentucky. They were actually introduced to European gardens in 1765. Amerindians used this plant not only to treat heart problems, but for love potions. The plant is also an astringent and was once used to wash wounds. Foliage is large, lobed, and jagged with uneven teeth, attractive even when the plants are out of flower. The clusters of tiny flowers are often confused with the genus *Spiraea* and upon close examination are easily recognized as relatives of the rose family. A large clump in bloom is a showstopper and a magnet for innumerable tiny bees and flies. The roots spread by rhizomes and can, over time, become a great specimen plant. Plants will usually not bloom until the second summer after transplanting.

The queen, while surviving in drier soil, does not do so with grace. Moist to wet soil is

Filipendula rubra

required for a full show of flowers and the plant is perfectly suited for a bog or the edge of a pond or pool. The cultivar 'Venusta' (often called 'Magnifica') produces six- to eight-foot stems covered with bright pink flowers blooming in midsummer. Propagate by seed and by division.

USDA Zones 3 to 8

Gaillardia × grandiflora

Gaillardia × grandiflora, the blanket flower, is a hybrid plant developed from a cross between G. *aristata*, a perennial that is rarely grown today, and G. *pulchella* (Indian blanket), an annual wildflower that graces many Southern gardens. This is one of the few situa-

tions when new is indeed bigger and better, for this hybrid is far more attractive than its counterparts and, if properly sited, a blooming delight. The genus is named in honor of M. Gaillard de Marentoneau, an 18th-century French magistrate and patron of botany.

This short-lived perennial hybrid of two American natives bears dark red flowers with yellow borders that blooms throughout the summer. The gray-green, eight-inch-long leaves are mostly hirsute (hairy), a characteristic that helps to shield them from the sun's rays. It is not a particularly attractive plant. But four-inch-wide daisy-like flowers are glorious in the garden, with (depending on the cultivar) those bright ray flowers circling a yellow to brown center. Height varies from one to three feet.

This plant dotes on full sun and is especially useful for dry soils that are not very rich. In fact, moist and fertile soils are the worst thing for blanket flower to have great blooms and healthy plants. Even under the best circumstances, blanket flower is a short-lived perennial that is susceptible to powdery mildew and aster yellows. Propagate by seed, root cuttings, or an annual division that should be a project every spring.

Among the many cultivars look for 'Baby Cole', an eight-inch dwarf plant bearing the typical blossoms; 'Burgundy', thirty inches high with three-inch-wide, wine-red flowers; 'Dazzler' bearing yellow flowers with maroon centers on sixteen-inch plants; and 'Goblin', a very free-bloomer with yellow-edged red flowers on foot-high stems.

USDA Zones 3 to 10

Galax rotundifolia is commonly known as galax, in addition to the charming name of wandflower. It is also known by the less attractive names of beetleweed and skunkweed, salutes to a faintly unpleasant scent to the flowers. Galax is an evergreen ground cover of stellar attractions found throughout the Southeast from our northern borders down to Georgia and Alabama, apparently rebelling against Florida's heat. There is but one species in the genus *Galax*, from the Greek *gala* or "milk" (referring to the color of the flowers). The species describes the rounded leaves. Plants were once classified as *Galax aphylla*.

This is a plant with a fascinating history. Once considered rare in parts of the Southeast, it began to make a comeback. Now, once again, galax is facing a decline as the florist industry—at least here in western North Carolina—continues to collect the leaves because they are long lasting in flower arrangements. The town of Galax, Virginia, is named for this plant.

Basal leaves are rounded, roughly heart-shaped and edged with small rounded teeth. They are a beautiful glossy green that turns reddish-purple as winter advances, with new leaves appearing every spring. Usually between three and four inches across, there are forms that exhibit polyploidy, where the chromosomes are doubled and plants may exhibit leaves twice the normal size. Galax flowers are tiny, blooming in a narrow raceme up to twenty inches tall, appearing in late spring and early summer.

When walking the woods on humid summer days, you may discern a distinct foxy odor like that of boxwoods but a bit stronger. As you turn a bend in the trail, you may find a large colony of galax. This is also the plant that led to the discovery of Oconee-bells (*Shortia galicifolia*), the famous lost flower of American botany. Unfortunately, though its existence has been proven, it is hampered by dry air and heat so it is beyond the parameters of this book.

Provide a full to partially shaded location for galax. You will generally find it growing in both small and large patches (rarely singularly), luxuriating in an open and dry forest environment, often in rocky, well-drained soil. In areas with hot and dry summers, plenty of acid humus will not only help in retaining moisture, but provide the low pH the plants require. In carefully prepared soil, galax will quickly spread into those great masses of attractive foliage. Propagate by seed in late spring or the fall, and division in the spring.

USDA Zones 5 to 8

Gaura lindheimeri, white gaura or, sometimes, wild honeysuckle, is a native perennial

Gaura lindheimeri

55

plant with the genus pronounced "gar-ruh." Although the flowers are small and certainly not showy, the plants have an airy charm and blossoms that might be butterflies fluttering in a summer zephyr. The generic name of *Gaura* comes from the Greek word *gauros* meaning "proud," referring to the charming flowers. The species is named in honor of Ferdinand Jacob Lindheimer (1802-1879), the Father of Texas Botany, the first serious scientist. It's estimated that he collected between 80,000 and 100,000 specimens in a life of study. The plants are native to Texas and Louisiana and down into Mexico.

White gaura is a great perennial that grows in a bushy clump about four feet tall with a three-foot spread. Leaves are spoon-shaped, from one to three inches long with toothed margins, on slender and wiry stems that easily move in the wind. Flowers bloom on erect spikes up to three feet long; the individual blossoms are about an inch across with four reflexed petals. They open in early morning as white and fade to pink by day's end. Only a few flowers are open on the stalks at one time, resulting in a delicate appearance. Here's a perennial meant for hot, dry climates and, because it has a long taproot, it will stand up to drought. While wanting full sun, in the Southeast plants will adapt to partial shade. Propagation is easy by seed and by dividing clumps in spring.

Cultivars include 'Corrie's Gold', which bears leaves with golden-yellow variegations; 'Swirling Butterflies' is smaller than the species at two feet in height, flowering more profusely; and 'Siskiyou Pink' has light pink flowers.

USDA Zones 5 to 10 (but mulch is often needed in Zones 5 and 6)

Gentiana andrewsii, the bottle gentian, is a wildflower of the fall, sometimes blooming when woodsy ferns already have a touch of gold and the angle of the afternoon sunlight tells gardeners that short days are coming. The genus is named for King Gentius of Illyrica, credited with discovering the medicinal value of some gentian roots, though not this particular species.

One- to two-foot, stout stems bear opposite ovate to lanceolate leaves with clusters of small, balloon-shaped violet-blue flowers in the upper leaf axils. The common name refers to the rounded bottle-shaped flowers that never really open. Flower color is variable but the flowers are usually more purple than blue, and some forms have pure white flowers. While never as abruptly showy as other fall-blooming flowers, you will immediately spot their bright colors in your garden; a patch in bloom is really quite beautiful to see.

The way this flower is pollinated, even though it never truly opens, is a great lesson in natural history. The agent is not the usual insect, certainly not the lightweight and immigrant honeybee, but our native bumblebee. Only she is heavy enough to push her way into the floral interior by thrusting her tongue between the five overlapping tips of the blossom. This visitor chooses younger flowers (identified by a bit of white that shines against the rest of the flower's gentian blue), throwing body weight against the flower's tip. Once inside with only hind legs and abdominal tip sticking out into the autumn air, she will back out of the flower, brushing golden dust from her head and pollen baskets, then buzz off to another flower.

In the wild garden the bottle gentian wants an acid soil and partial shade, along with soil that has plenty of humus and never dries out.

There's a spot in our wild garden where some sumacs have formed a mini-grove and hay-scented ferns grow in combination with oak seedlings (I cut them for a short-term hedge), making a shadowed dell. It's a perfect backdrop for clumps of white wood asters (*Aster divaricatus*) and my autumn crop of bottle gentians. Propagation is by seed and division of plants in the early spring.

USDA Zones 5 to 9

Geranium maculatum, the true wild geranium, is not the common blousy bloomer that glows in shades of hot reds and tropical oranges, planted in pots and window boxes from American small towns to cemetery

Geranium maculatum

plots (those are hybrids of the South African genus *Pelargonium*). No, these geraniums are native hardy plants best suited for the perennial border or the wild garden. It has garnered a number of common names, including alum bloom, alum root, American cranesbill, crowfoot, dove's foot, old maid's nightcap, shameface, spotted geranium, and stork's-bill. And it has often been used for medicinal purposes. The scientific name is derived from the Greek word *geranos* or "crane," and refers to the similarity of the seedpod to a crane's bill. When the pods mature they eject the seeds far from the parent plant. These wildflowers are found in most of the Southeast, with the exception of Florida.

Nothing beats this native geranium, from its attractive leaves to its great blossoms. Loose clusters of pink to lavender-purple, five-petaled flowers sit atop one- to two-foot stalks, which are hairy and slender. The leaves are finely cut.

There are a growing number of cultivars and a white form called 'Album' that is not too common. Spotted geraniums prefer partial shade and a humus-rich, well-drained soil. Where winters are not too frigid, the basal leaves are usually evergreen. They grow from a tough rootstock, so plant individuals about a foot apart—and once planted let them be. By judicious mulching the plants will be weed-free and eventually form a large colony of plants, making them a great ground cover. Both the leaves and the roots have a long history of use in folk medicine and because the leaves and rhizomes contain tannin, the early pioneers used them for tanning hides.

USDA Zones 4 to 9

Gillenia trifoliata, bowman's root, has other common names including Indian physic, American ipecac (ipecac is a powerful laxative), and Indian hippo (hippo being short for hippocras, a cordial made of wine and spices). The genus is named in honor of Arnold Gillen, a 17th-century German botanist. Back in the beginning of the 20th century, the genus name *Gillenia* became more commonly used for this plant than *Porteranthus*, but now, 100 years later, the genus has switched back to *Porteranthus*. The alternate genus name is for the botanist Thomas Conrad Porter (1822-1901), an American of the 19th century, the man who in 1874 first described the prairie wild rose and wrote the *Flora of Pennsylvania*. *Anthus* means "flower." "Bowman" does not refer to a particular person in history but instead means "a man who held a bow." Why this name is applied to this plant, I do not know.

Gillenia trifoliata

Bowman's root is a perennial herb common in most of the Southeast, ranging from north of Pennsylvania down to Georgia and Missouri. Inch-wide white flowers (rarely with a pinkish tinge) sport five twisted, narrow petals that bloom in a loose cluster on top of three-foot stems, opening from late spring to early summer. The slender leaves are almost without stalks, divided into three sharply toothed segments with a pair of small stipules at the base of each leaf. Both the leaves and stems of this charming plant exhibit a slight red tint.

These delicate and beautiful flowers really show up when backed by shrubs or bushes with dark green leaves and they move about in the slightest of garden breezes. Going up Town Mountain Road in Asheville, the bowman's root blooming between the rocks on the hillsides are tossed and turned with every passing car. The dried root of this wildflower has long been used for its medicinal properties, including those of an emetic, a cathartic, and an expectorant. The Amerindians used it, as did the early colonists. American ipecac or *Gillenia stipulata* (*Porteranthus stipulata*) is very similar yet grows just a bit taller.

Bebe Miles often said this plant grows as well in clay as in woodland soil, but always does best when humus is added and the pH is on the acid end. And if the first blossoms are deadheaded before seeds form, there is additional bloom. As they age, the clumps get larger. Just remember the key to survival for this plant is to water during hot and dry summers and provide light shade with morning sun. Propagation is by seed and division in early spring or fall.

USDA Zones 4 to 9

Helenium autumnale is called sneezeweed by some, Helen's flower by others, and swamp sunflower by a few—it's all in your point-of-view. There are about forty species of this genus native to North and South America. The scientific name refers to Helen of Troy, but the original plant that celebrated her glories is unknown. One story reports these flowers springing up where her tears fell upon the death of Hector. The most popular common name refers to the heavy yellow pollen easily seen falling from the flowers and the unfortunate fact that like goldenrod (another plant that gets undeserved bad press), it blooms at the same time as the notorious ragweed (*Ambrosia* spp.). The species name points out the autumn bloom time.

Sneezeweed is found growing on moist, low ground from Quebec to Florida, then west to Arizona; in fact, a USDA map shows this plant being recorded in all the states of the union except Maine and New Hampshire. The whole plant is said to possess errhine (nasal-clearing) properties, with the disk florets being the most active. The round flower heads of small yellow disk flowers are surrounded by bright yellow, triple-scalloped, turned-back ray flowers on usually stout stems that can reach six feet. Plants have evergreen basal rosettes in most of the South.

This cosmopolitan plant has great beauty both in the perennial border and the wild garden. Just provide a rich, moist soil in full sun—although in the Deep South it will take some shade. If the soil is poor, amend it to prevent weak stems and flopping flowers. Cutting back in early spring leads to shorter plants. Cut back after flowering, too. It's probably a good idea to divide the plants every two or three years. They also do well in containers; remember to fertilize lightly every month or so of

Helenium autumnale

active growth. During periods of drought, give sneezeweed extra water; doing this in midsummer means more flowers in the fall.

A number of cultivars of great beauty are available including 'Butterpat' with clear yellow flowers, 'Bruno' with mahogany red flowers, 'Kugelsonne' (or "sun sphere") with bright yellow two-inch petals around a chartreuse disk, and 'Moerheim Beauty' with petals of a beautiful bronzy-red. *Helenium flexuosum* (*H. nudiflorum*), the purple-headed sneezeweed, has a very dark-colored disk surrounded by the typical yellow ray petals. This is a more compact species usually not topping three feet in height. The flowers distinguish purple-headed sneezeweed from other species of sneezeweed, which have yellow-green disks. Increase flowering by cutting back the plants by at least one-third in early summer. Plant in full sun to dappled shade in loosened, humus-amended soils. Propagate sneezeweeds by seed and by division in the spring or fall after blooming.

USDA Zones 3 to 10

***Helianthus* species**, the sunflower, is another one of those American plants European gardeners consider coarse, rough, and weedy. The plants appear that way to eyes accustomed to the regimentation of European floral displays and the implied peacefulness of age-old shady walkways. Sunflowers are, instead, akin to many American originals: tough, rugged, and, like the American skyscraper, tall and bold. The scientific name is from *helios*, "the sun," and *anthos*, "flower."

Usually when sunflowers are mentioned, beginning gardeners think of the giant annual species (*Helianthus annuus*), that produces foot-wide flowers with disks crowded with seeds arranged in patterns following the theories of Fibonacci. Fibonacci, called Leonard of Pisa, was an Italian mathematician who discovered a mathematical relationship between the spiral of seeds on a sunflower disk or in the screw-like arrangement of leaves around a stem. These familiar sunflowers are grown commercially for oil and their edible seeds. They are also grown by many gardeners to see just how tall they can grow. But there are a number of perennial sunflowers perfect for the garden, providing bloom during the waning days of summer and on into the fall.

Their wants are few: ordinary soil and full sun. In return, they will bloom until cut down by a killer frost. Although some are best in the wild garden, others become welcome additions to the back of the border, and one, the willow-leaved sunflower, adds elegance that few other plants provide.

Helianthus angustifolius, the swamp sunflower or the narrow-leaved sunflower, grows in sunny spots in moist soil from southern New York to Florida, west to the Ohio River valley, then south to southern Texas. The specific name means "narrow-leaved." As suggested by its common name, this plant likes to be in swamps and wet pinelands, including coastal salt marshes. Blooming time is from late September into October with two-inch-wide flowers that crowd the tops of eight-foot-high plants; even the leaves are attractive. Although plants do well with damp feet, they adjust to

Helianthus annuus

ordinary garden soil but need additional water when rain is wanting. If pruned in late spring, the plants will be bushier.

USDA Zones 6 to 9

Helianthus decapetalus, the thin-leaved sunflower, is found in the wild from Maine to South Carolina, then west to Wisconsin. The specific name of *deca*, "ten," and *petalus*, "petals," refers to there being ten ray petals on each flower, something that is not always true. Once again European nurserymen have taken a particular plant and developed a number of radiant cultivars. Look for 'Capenoch Star', developed in Germany back in 1938, which gives you four-inch-wide bright yellow flowers from August into October. 'Flore Pleno' is sometimes listed as *Helianthus × multiflorus* and was derived from a cross between *H. decapetalus* and the annual sunflower. The result is a plant reaching a height of four to six feet that blooms in late summer with five-inch-wide bright yellow double flowers on three- to four-foot stems. This is a stellar plant, great in the open border, or spotted here and there as an accent to other fall-blooming plants.

USDA Zones 4 to 9

Helianthus giganteus, the tall or giant sunflower, blooms from midsummer until frost. According to Neltje Blanchan in *Nature's Garden*, for many years the origin of this flower, which was known for its splendor in European gardens, appeared to be in doubt. Then, towards the end of the 19th century, botanists learned that back in the mid-1600s, Champlain and Segur visited the Indians on the eastern shores of Lake Huron and found them cultivating this plant, plants in turn carried from their native prairies beyond the Mississippi. It seems the plants furnished the Indians with a textile

Helianthus angustifolius

fiber, fodder from the leaves, and a yellow dye from the flowers. The tubers were edible, and the seeds were a very special food—and a hair oil! This is a tall and elegant plant with stems often topping twelve feet. The leaves are narrow, tapering at both ends while the deep yellow flowers, two to three inches wide, are among the latest sunflowers to bloom. 'Sheila's Sunshine' bears soft, pastel-yellow flowers on ten-foot stems, again blooming in the fall.

USDA Zones 6 to 8

Helianthus grosseserratus came to me as seed offered by the American Horticultural Society in the early 1980s. Like its annual relative, this particular perennial can reach a height of thirteen feet when given that happy combination of full sun and a good, well-drained soil.

Blossoms are over two inches wide and up to twenty of them can top a nodding stem, blooming in early October, and smelling deliciously of cocoa. The leaves are usually (but not always) edged with coarse teeth, hence the species name. The Meskwaki Indians of Kansas used a poultice made from the flowers to treat burns.

USDA Zones 3 to 8

Helianthus salicifolius, the willow-leaved sunflower, first came to my attention in a 1975 book entitled *The Personal Garden* by Bernard Wolgensinger and José Daidone. Unfortunately, due to a problem with translations, the plant was not identified. Then, five years later, I picked up a used book, *Garden Guide* by Ludwig Koch-Isenburg, and there, in a small black-and-white photograph, the same plant graced the corner of a small garden pool. This is a must—the graceful bend of the five-foot stems adorned

Heliopsis helianthoides

with such elegant leaves becomes a foil for any garden design. Small sunflowers bloom in late September and are but icing on a lovely cake.

USDA Zones 5 to 9

Heliopsis helianthoides bears a number of common names, including ox-eye or false sunflower, sun glory, or orange sunflower. It's a close relative of the true sunflower, the differentiation being that the ray florets of sunflowers are not fertile as are the florets of this genus. The scientific name comes from *helios*, or "sun," and *opsis*, "like," while the specific name again refers to this bloom being the flower of the sun.

It is described as being large and coarse, with coarse referring to the plant's lack of any delicate characteristics. Originally a plant of the tall-grass prairies and savannas, today it's often found growing along railroad tracts. Found throughout the Southeast it apparently draws the line at South Florida but is known for

Helianthus salicifolius

its resistance to both heat and drought. The leaves were often used in folk remedies, especially for lung congestion or fever reduction.

The thin, opposite, three- to six-inch, dark-green, ovate leaves feel like a fine-grain sandpaper, both top and bottom, and also have toothed margins. From July well into autumn, the plants burst with two- to four-inch-wide flowers on stout stems, each blossom with ten to sixteen pointed yellow ray flowers surrounding orange disk flowers that mature into smooth, four-angled seeds. The flowers are excellent for cutting. Not only are they undemanding but bloom the first year from seed. Floriferous is the adjective to use in describing floral output. If the spent flowers are removed, ox-eyes will continue to bloom until a hard frost.

Plants do their best in a good, well-drained loam but will actually tolerate clay soils as long as water doesn't stand. Over time the plants form large clumps. Every few years lifting and dividing the plants keeps them in good shape. During dry summers provide some extra water; in the South they will sometimes droop around noon. While insect pests are negligible, use a strong burst from the hose to dislodge visiting aphids. Like most prairie plants they are late to emerge in the spring, so mark them well if your memory is short. They enjoy full sun but in the Deep South will tolerate partial shade.

The most widely available cultivar is 'Sommersonne' ("summer sun"), a cultivar of *Heliopsis helianthoides* var. *scabra*. The dark green foliage is topped with profuse numbers of golden-yellow flowers on plants about thirty inches high. 'Ballerina' is a compact plant bearing semidouble flowers. 'Golden Plume' and 'Gold Greenheart' are both double flowering. Propagation is by seed, which is very, very easy and division in spring or early fall. Plants will self-sow and while some gardeners consider them invasive, they are easily

removed when young. Frankly, I'd rather see these glorious salutes to the sun as opposed to vast acres of unnecessary lawn.

USDA Zones 3 to 10

Hepatica nobilis represents two varieties, the first being the round-lobed hepatica, once *H. americana*, now called var. *obtusa*, and the sharp-lobed hepatica, var. *acuta*, once called *H. acutiloba*. Common names include hepatica, liverwort, kidney liver-leaf, or squirrel cup and celebrate one of spring's first flowers. *Hepatica* is the Latin word for the liver. Sometimes hepaticas bloom through the snow, their lovely, sometimes fragrant, half-inch-wide flowers snuggly wrapped in fuzzy hairs until opening. Hepatica leaves have three lobes, their scientific name referring to The Doctrine of Signatures, a

Hepatica americana

theory that if a plant resembled an organ of the human body, it could be used to treat any illness of that organ. These wildflowers are found from our northern borders south to Georgia, Alabama, and Missouri.

The mostly evergreen leaves survive the winter but by the time of blooming, they are old and weatherworn, turning shades of maroon and brown. New leaves are rounded, leathery, and sometimes mottled with blotches of reddish-purple, spreading out on the forest floor from a common center. Furry stems about six inches long hold high the blue, lavender, purple, pinkish, or white flowers, that are occasionally, but not always, fragrant. These wildflowers shun the sun and need full to partial shade and a deeply organic, well-drained soil. While adapting readily to an acidic soil, wildflower watchers note that in nature, they adapt to neutral to limy sites. Use plenty of organic matter when preparing the site and mulch the plants with pine needles or leafmold.

As to being a medicinal plant, hepatica tea has been used for bronchitis, liver congestion, and gallbladder problems, but I've been told that the sap of freshly cut stems can be irritating to the skin of some people. Propagation is by division in spring after flowering or by seed.

USDA Zones 3 to 9

Hesperaloe is a small genus belonging to the Agavaceae, and of the three species recorded, two are interesting perennials for the Southeastern garden. Like the yuccas, they form grass-like clumps of long narrow leaves, the margins lined with threads and, also like the yuccas, they are pollinated by moths that live in the deserts of the Southwest. *Hesperos* is Latin for "western" and *aloe* refers to the family

resemblance of these plants to the aloes. The species means "small-flowered." The red yuccas were originally found from the Texas Rio Grande area down into northern Mexico.

Hesperaloe parviflora is often called the red yucca. The leaves can reach a height of three feet with the plants making a four-foot spread. In midsummer, four-foot-tall spikes appear, lined with nodding, bell-like flowers that are usually pink, but often glow with darker shades of red. As evening approaches, the flowers slowly turn up to the sky but their color is such that, except on moonlit nights, it would be better if the flowers were white—but I've yet to find that particular cultivar. It is extremely hardy to frost and a great plant for the sunny garden in temperate and subtropical areas. This

Hesperaloe parviflora

species makes a great container plant and is also a great plant to attract hummingbirds. Recently, a yellow-flowered form has been introduced on the market. After blooming, a distinctive ping-pong-ball-like seedpod appears, full of flat black seeds stacked like bread slices in a loaf. In time and given the needed room, these plants can reach a height of six feet.

Hesperaloe nocturna is truly a nocturnal plant, opening its inch-long flowers as the sun sets and the desert sky turns a flaming purple. These flowers are a greenish purple with a white interior especially suited to guide a moth's tongue deep inside the floral tube.

Both species are true desert plants and have a tendency to rot their roots in excessive water or damp soil. My one plant of *Hesperaloe parviflora* is set in a narrow space about eighteen inches wide, formed by a four-foot-high walled planter where our garage door once stood. You must provide full sun and a very well drained soil. Propagation for *Hesperaloe* is by the easily collected seed or by division of clumps in early spring.

USDA Zones 7 to 10

Heuchera species

***Heuchera* species**, the coral-bells or alum-roots, are a genus of about fifty perennial herbs, most originating in the U.S. The genus includes *H. sanquinea*, a plant with bright coral-colored flowers and the most popular plant for gardeners, native to New Mexico and Arizona. The English name of alumroot refers to the astringent quality of the rhizomes. The genus is named for the 18th-century German physician and botanist Johan von Heucher (1677-1747), while the species is taken from sanguine or blood.

The coral-bells have been extensively hybridized both in America and in Europe with many of the resulting hybrids better choices for a garden setting than our originals. But our eastern species are known for their beautiful leaves ranging from a lovely purple to marbled leaves alternating with green and white, the coloration a result of air spaces between the layers of leaf tissue.

Several of our eastern species, including *H. americana* and *H. pubescens*, often exhibit these colorations, many arising from hybridizing accomplished by Nancy Goodwin at Montrose Nursery in North Carolina. *Heuchera americana* is our Southeastern coral-bell, a wildflower that ranges over a large area from our northern borders southward to Georgia, Alabama, and Arkansas. Like any plant that's at home over such a broad expanse of land, this species exhibits many variations, with leaf edges that range from being lobed to toothed, and a wide

Heuchera villosa

the leaf stalks are covered with reddish hairs, meaning they are villous. The flowers appear in late summer and, when open, are no more than one-eighth-inch long with white, or sometimes pink, petals. In autumn the leaves turn a rich bronze. They are generally at home on rock outcrops and wooded slopes, from West Virginia, then south to Georgia, Alabama, and Arkansas.

These plants need a well-drained, humusy soil in partial shade. Every few years remember to divide the more mature plants to prevent their being crowded out. Propagation is by seed and by division in spring and in fall.

USDA Zones 4 to 9

variety of leaf colors, although most are generally reddish. The pale-green flowers are about one-fourth inch in length and are never as interesting as the leaves. They usually bloom from April to June.

Heuchera pubescens, the downy alumroot, has smooth leaf stalks and stems even though the species means "downy." The leaf blades are deeply lobed and the flowers grow in a conical inflorescence that is wide at the base and tapers to the top. This species is at home from Pennsylvania south to North Carolina, and west to Kentucky.

Heuchera villosa, the hairy alumroot, has deeply lobed, sharp-pointed leaf blades and often

Hibiscus coccineus, the scarlet rose hibiscus, sometimes called the Texas hibiscus, is a big and beautiful wildflower that deserves to be more widely used; it's really native to swamps and wetlands from Florida, west to Alabama and Georgia, Louisiana and north to the Carolinas. The genus is taken from the Greek, *hibiskos*, named for the original marsh mallow that grows in boggy conditions in Europe. The species refers to the brilliant scarlet red color of the petals.

In other parts of the world, the hibiscus species are used for fiber, food, or to make medicinal products, but here in the U.S.A., they are usually relegated to ornamental horticulture. *H. cannabis*, or Indian hemp, makes the greatest rope in the world and ceased to be classified as a hallucinogenic back in the 1930s, but it's still only approved for agricultural purposes in some twelve states, a few in the South.

In mid-July I visited the High Museum of Art in Atlanta. Outside the ground floor cafeteria is a small garden under the shadow of a great Alexander Calder mobile. There amidst some summer annuals were three or four blooming

Hibiscus coccineus

scarlet hibiscus, over nine feet tall and boasting more than ten stalks, each topped with the striking flowers. Even the developing seedpods are handsome additions to the garden scene.

Stout vertical stems that rarely need staking sport large, dark-green, palmate (like the fingers on a hand) leaves, separated into three to seven narrow, pointed, serrated lobes, up to eight inches wide. The stems get a bit woody as the summer passes. The five-petaled flowers are brilliant crimson red, about six to eight inches across, with each flower lasting but a day. But there are always plenty of developing buds, and new blossoms continue to open until late in the fall.

This is one southern wildflower that takes the sun. The plants will tolerate a bit of shade but never more than a bit. Soil should be moist and the plants will tolerate poor drainage. The scarlet hibiscus could be listed with plants that really like water but these wildflowers will adapt to normal garden soil—just remember to

water during dry summers. Propagate by seed and by division in early spring and fall.

USDA Zones 7 to 10

Hymenocallis species, the spider lily, sometimes affectionately called the swamp lily, blooms in ditches, along pond edges, and the banks of slow-moving rivers and streams, where the exceptionally beautiful flowers are a joy to see. When you see the blossoms the genus name is evident, easily recognized by the three petals, three sepals, and six stamens joined by a membrane or hymen. The species is from the Greek, *lirion*, or "lily," and *osme*, for "odor or smell," referring to the sweet fragrance.

Hymenocallis is in the amaryllis family. The species have long (up to eighteen inches), attractive, sword-like leaves arising in midspring; they may die back by late summer or in dry weather. They have clusters of usually six flowers (sometimes less and sometimes more). *Hymenocallis caroliniana* (*H. occidentalis*) is a stunning plant with icy-white flowers that not only takes to water, but does well in moist soil. It ranges from the Carolinas, Tennessee, western Kentucky, Missouri, and Arkansas, to north of the Ohio River into southern Illinois. Flowers appear in late summer or autumn. These brilliant white blooms are, from petal-tip to petal-tip, up to seven inches across while the stamen cup is about two inches in diameter.

The stem (really a scape) that holds the flowers aloft ranges from one to two feet in height. Grow these plants in a good, fertile, moist to wet soil, in sun or partial shade. Remember, this plant needs hot summer days with temperatures in the 80s for best flowering. The powerfully fragrant flowers open at dusk and bloom all through the night until the morning sun announces a new day. It's a great plant for the sunny bog.

Hymenocallis caroliniana

Hymenocallis palmeri, the alligator-lily, has one to four flowers and green sepals. They are found in the prairies and Everglades of southern Florida. *Hymenocallis coronaria* has four or fewer flowers in a cluster and the edge of the membrane is toothed like the edge of a saw.

Hymenocallis liriosome, the Texas spider lily, has moved to the western borders of the Southeast and is the one plant often offered for sale by nurseries and bulb suppliers. It grows along the Gulf Coast from Texas to Florida, making its home on beaches and along the shores of rivers, where it can occur in such abundance as to be overwhelming, especially on cloudy days or in late afternoon to early evening when the fragrance is the most powerful.

Set plants or bulbs into wet or boggy areas; they will adjust to a few inches of shallow stand-ing water. If growing them in drained soil, remember the soil must be kept moist. The only chore is to eventually divide crowded clumps. Spider lilies may be planted in two-gallon containers using rich soil, the pot then set in up to six inches of water, providing sun or partial shade.

USDA Zones 7 to 11

Hypericum species, Saint John's-wort, represents over 300 species of ground covers and sprawling shrubs to upright bushes, all blooming with their trademark golden flowers, with many species useful for gardens in the Southeast. The genus refers to the Greek words *hyper*, or "above," and *eikon*, or "picture," which collectively translates to "over an icon." Wort is the Old English word for plant. Originally St. John's-worts were associated with St. John the Baptist and were hung over his image on St. John's Day. In addition, the flowers often bloom around his day (June 24), and because they exude a red pigment like blood, were again associated with this saint. Many of the various species contain the chemical compounds hypericin and hyperforin and today the plant is involved in a great deal of medical research with doctors warning patients not to take herbals that contain it in conjunction with some medicines prescribed for nervous disorders.

Unfortunately for a book on native plants, a number of the most popular hypericums have arrived on our shores from China and the Far East, including Aaronsbeard (*H. calycinum*), goldflower (*H. × moseranum*), and the typical St. John's-wort (*H. patulum*). Luckily, there are a few very beautiful native members of this genus. There is the coppery St. Johns-wort, *H. denticulatum*, first described by Thomas Walter (1780-1861), an English botanist who lived in South Carolina. I have only seen this plant in a garden once, but you should search it out because it's such a great plant. Our native hypericums will adapt to most soil conditions, and do well in full or partial sun. They respond to a top-dressing of composted manure every two or three years. Propagate by seed, the shrubby kinds by soft-wood cuttings, and the ground covers by division.

Hypericum densiflorum, the bushy St. John's-wort, is one of the taller members of the family reaching between four and six feet tall and three to four feet wide. This native is found throughout most of the Southeast. The two-inch-long leaves are very narrow and the inch-wide golden yellow flowers bloom on and off most of the summer. Although they are often found in the wild growing along the edges of streams, these plants will adapt to good, well-drained garden soil. They make a great garden hedge. The cultivar 'Creel's Gold' is a semiev-

Hypericum densiflorum

ergreen shrub, up to six feet tall and four feet wide, but densely branched, with really bright yellow, one-inch flowers, the entire plant having a fountain-like appearance.

USDA Zones 5 to 9

Hypericum kalmianum, Kalm's St. John's-wort, is a very hardy native shrub originally from the North but proving most valuable in the Southeast. The species is named in honor of Peter Kalm, a Swedish botanist. When planted in groups, this plant gives the impression of being a mounded ground cover; height is between two and three feet. The opposite blue-green leaves are a little over two inches long, their color being perfect to set off the golden yellow of the one-inch-wide flowers. The stems exhibit a peeling bark. These plants are drought-tolerant and adapt with ease to various soils, and do well in full sun or partial shade. Prune old wood in early spring as flowers bloom on new growth—which is rapid. These minishrubs are great as a path edging or foundation plantings. They make a fine low hedge. Often evergreen in warmer areas.

USDA Zones 6 to 8

Hypoxis hirsuta, yellow star grass or hairy yellow star grass (referring to little hairs that edge the leaves), is a member of the amaryllis family and one of the longest-flowering plants for the garden. The genus is from *hypo*, "beneath," and *oxys*, "sharp," referring to the base of the floral capsule. The species means "hairy" of course.

In the summer of 2004 I spoke at the Cullowhee Native Plant Conference and was fortunate to hear a presentation on replacing the gravel and tar of traditional flat roofs with soil and native wildflowers. Described was an old meatpacking plant in north Nashville that was renovated and a new 2,600 square foot green-roof installed. The plant list included the yellow star grass, among other natives. The inspiration for this particular planting of a green-roof came from the endangered Cedar Glade plant community, endemic to a 60-mile radius in central Tennessee. Cedar Glades are a harsh environment with community plants growing in full sun and a shallow nutrient-poor soil with a limestone base. The rains come and go, so a periodic inundation is followed by extended drought. Now there's a place to look for tough plants.

This lovely wildflower blooms from spring to fall, with small clusters of six-pointed yellow or whitish stars, the petals and sepals alike arising from basal leaves that are narrow and grass-

Hypoxis hirsuta

like, up to a foot long. In nature the plants are found in open woodlands and meadows from Maine and the Canadian border south to Florida and Texas. To encourage the long bloom, remember to snip off the spent flowers from time to time. Although sometimes found in boggy spots, they do their best in humus rich garden soil and shaded from the noonday sun. To get the full effect of this charmer, plant the tiny bulbs (about an inch deep) in a decent-sized patch. They will self-sow. Propagation is by seed and by division of offsets in fall.

USDA Zones 4 to 9

Ipomoea pandurata, the wild potato vine, is sometimes known as man-of-the-earth or mecha-meck. It is a favorite of mine because it blooms every year in late summer, winding its way through a shrubbery border with the giant tuberous root located about eight inches from the edge of the macadam on Lakewood Drive as the road curves around the edge of my garden. The genus name is taken from the Greek *ips*, "a worm," and *homoios*, "resembling," pointing to the twining habit of the stems. The species refers to the heart or fiddle shape of the leaf, a pandura being an ancient mandolin. This plant is naturally found at the edges of dry woods or thickets from our northern range southward to Florida and Texas.

The leaves vary a bit in shape but are usually about five inches long, heart shaped with a pointed tip. The large, funnel-form flowers are typical for the morning glories, including the five-pointed stars made by the folding creases of the blossom. They have purplish centers two to three inches long and about as wide. The large tuber can weigh over twenty pounds and be several feet long. Amerindians used these

Ipomoea pandurata

tubers as a food, but unless you have the correct recipe, don't try it because the uncooked root is listed as a strong purgative. Vines can grow to a length of over twenty feet. Provide a well-drained, slightly moist soil in full sun, and be sure there are shrubs or bushes in the area for the vines to climb through.

USDA Zones 6 to 9

Iris species—the members of the great iris family include native plants that run the gamut from the Louisiana irises of Southern bayous to the charming wildflowers that creep along the woodland floor. The genus is the Greek name used for the plants by Theophrastus (born c. 372 BC) and means "rainbow."

Irises have distinctive flowers, each with three sepals usually matching the color, but not the shape, of the three petals, with the sepals (in most species) curving to the ground and the petals to the sky. In addition, the sepals sport a beard, crest, or a furry ridge, often of a bright

color and surrounded by dark lines that lead insects to the nectar within the bloom. The grass-like leaves are folded lengthwise along their midrib and, in turn, each enfolds a younger leaf, a process Linneaus called equitant. The fairly common yellow flag (*Iris pseudacorus*) is actually not a native but an Asian import. Propagation of irises is by seeds or division.

Iris cristata, the dwarf crested iris, blooms earlier in the spring than do most irises (April and May), has attractive foliage that lasts through the summer, and lavender blue flowers about two inches across on six-inch stems. The sepals have a yellow crest. Crested iris creeps with thin rhizomes that run almost at the soil surface. The narrow leaves form a fan usually about six inches high. Because of their traveling nature, a colony will slowly move outward, so every few years the gardener should reposition the rhizomes into an attractive clump. Provide well-drained, humusy soil in partial shade. The natural range is from Maryland to Indiana and Missouri, then south to Alabama,

Iris cristata

Mississippi, and Oklahoma. There are a few cultivars including the white form 'Alba' and 'Skylands' with slightly larger flowers.

USDA Zones 4 to 8

Iris verna has slender rhizomes on the surface, with leaves often more than a foot in height but less than a half-inch wide. The flowers are violet and instead of a raised crest, have an orange or yellow band with nectar lines on the sepals. Compared to the crested iris, this species prefers a very thin, acid soil.

USDA Zones 6 to 9

The Louisiana irises include the following species: *Iris brevicaulis*; *I. fulva*; *I. giganticaerulea*; *I. hexagona*; and *I. nelsonii*. These species grow in different geographic locations because of environmental preferences, including light, soil types, pH (degree of acidity or alkalinity), and the salt content of water. *Iris brevicaulis*, the lamance iris, grows about sixteen inches high, prefers dry land but is often found in pastures and next to stream banks. The medium-sized flowers range from lavender to white.

Iris fulva

Iris fulva, the copper iris, bears small flowers ranging in color from red to scarlet, on stems to three feet high. It grows in sunny swamps and is often found in roadside ditches. This species will not grow in salt-tainted water and wants full sun.

Iris giganticaerulea, the giant blue flag, is aptly named, having plants that can reach a height of six feet. The fragrant flowers range in color from pure white to a variety of blues—and even to pale pink. The plants grow along the coast of Louisiana in sunny marshes and swamps. Insects and birds delight in the flowers but it will spread about a bit. Thanks to its moisture demands this iris is great for bog and water gardens. Parts of this plant are poisonous. In some places it is a protected species. *Iris hexagona* has deep violet sepals with a yellow crest, the petals slightly smaller and, except for the height of only up to four feet, resembles *I. giganticaerulea*.

Iris nelsonii was discovered by Mr. W. B. MacMillan around the early 1940s in a swampy region south of Abbeville, Louisiana. The leaves are a yellow-green and droop at the tips. Both the sepals and the petals droop and, due to the beautiful red color, were originally called the Abbeville reds. Other colors included yellows, purples, and shades of brown. The original plants have led to countless hybrid forms.

The Louisiana irises are easy to grow but in areas of really hot weather, it's normal for the plants to become dormant with yellowing leaves. At that time it's a good idea to trim the unattractive foliage and to divide the plants. Dan Gill and Joe White, writing in the *Louisiana Gardener's Guide: Revised Edition* (Cool Springs Press, 2002) extol the virtues of these irises and say: "The hybrids bloom best with at least six hours of sun and when planting these Louisiana irises in traditional garden beds, till the soil to a depth of 6 to

8 inches, spread a 2-inch layer of organic matter and a sprinkling of general-purpose fertilizer over the soil, and till it in. Or place potted Louisiana irises into aquatic gardens with the water's surface a couple of inches above the pot's rim."

USDA Zone 8 to 10

Iris species

Isopyrum biternatum, the so-called false rue anemone (a terrible common name), is one of those charming wildflowers with little or no press that is a terrific ground cover in a number of garden situations. The genus is from the Greek, *isos*, or "equal," and *pyros*, "wheat," because the fruits somewhat resemble grains of wheat. There is a move to change the scientific name to *Enemion biternatum*, this time with the genus referring to an Old English spelling of anemone. The species refers to the divisions of the leaf. The plants are found in the woods ranging from our northern border southward to Florida and Texas.

This plant would be valuable as a ground cover and the white flowers that appear about the time that bloodroot blooms are icing on the cake. The leaves are divided into three segments on a long stalk with each leaf again divided into three rounded segments. The flowers have five white sepals, with numerous stamens also having flat, white stalks. The roots are joined with small, scattered tubers. Plants are about a foot high. The seeds are shot from the pods, giving them a great claim to nearby territory.

This is an easy-grow plant when provided with a rich, acidic, evenly moist soil with plenty of humus mixed in. For light try to provide dappled shade. Barry Glick says: "The foliage reminds me of a *Corydalis* species and appears to be resistant to insect damage or deer browsing." Reason enough. Propagate by seed or division.

USDA Zones 3 to 8

Jeffersonia diphylla, the twinleaf, is that rarity, a native wildflower named for a president, in this case Thomas Jefferson. It's a two-species genus with the other (*J. dubia*) native to Japan and northeast Asia. The dedication of the plant took place at a 1792 meeting of the American Philosophical Society with American botanist Benjamin Barton making the presentation. The species name refers to the two-parted leaves. Based on plants collected in Virginia, Linnaeus first named this plant *Podophyllum diphyllum*, making it a sister species of the May-apple (*Podophyllum peltatum*), as both belong to the barberry family. Other common names include jeffersonia, rheumatism-root, helmet-pod, ground squirrel-pea, and yellow-root.

The rhizome was used as a medicinal treatment of various muscular ailments including rheumatism. Twinleaf is at home in the rich, fertile woods of the Northeast, reaching down to North Carolina, Tennessee, Alabama, and

Jeffersonia diphylla

Georgia. Palmately veined and palmately lobed, eventually six-inch leaves arise from a tangled root and in very early spring twine around eight-inch stems each topped with a small, white, eight-petaled flower, looking a great deal like neighboring bloodroots (*Sanguinaria canadensis*). Upon maturity, the ripening ovary forms a capsule that closely resembles a helmet or the kind of capped pipe smoked by Bürgermeisters in Rembrandt's paintings. Each flower lasts but a day but the leaves alone make this a worthy garden addition.

Plants are easily grown from seed and will often self-sow around the garden. Twinleaf also transplants well and is a garden natural, when provided with good light but summer shade, plenty of humus in the soil, and moisture when rains are sparse. Allow at least three years from seed to flower. Propagation is by seed and by division of the rhizomes in the fall.

USDA Zones 6 to 8

Liatris scariosa, blazing star, or sometimes called button snake-root or gayfeather, is one of a number of species in this genus native to North America and flowering in late summer to early autumn. Botanical authorities register the derivation of the genus as unknown. The only reference I found was in the *Webster's New International Dictionary* (1925) as being New Latin. One wishes it were the name of a beautiful Indian princess who was lost during a buffalo hunt and later went off to charm the kings of Europe, like an Annie Oakley of the prairies. The species refers to the roughness of the stem and leaves.

This is a tall and stately garden plant for bed or border. The flowers, unlike most plants, bloom from the top down, which makes them a valuable addition to bouquets. At one time the corms of this and other *Liatris* were thought to cure rattlesnake bites, obviously untrue or every snake herpitorium would have it growing just outside the front door.

The flowers are composed of tubular florets ranging in color from white to pink and shades

Liatris spicata

Liatris species

grows near exposed rocks and balds provided with near perfect drainage. The floral stalks are best described as being dainty and rarely top two feet. Grow in USDA Zones 5 to 8. *Liatris pycnostachya*, the Kansas gayfeather (the species here is Greek for a stem densely crowded with flowers), grows from three to five feet tall with spikes of violet-lavender to rosy-purple flower heads that are really beautiful, especially when the plants are massed. The flowers are also fine for flower arrangements, both fresh and dried. The plants are found from our northern borders south to Florida, Louisiana, and Texas.

USDA Zones 3 to 10

of purple, while the thin, soft and hairy leaves are described as being punctate or covered with resinous dots. Branched stems reach heights up to five feet. In nature this plant extends from Pennsylvania and West Virginia south to Georgia and Mississippi.

When planting liatris remember to provide full sun and well-drained garden soil; it cannot adapt to wet earth. Taller varieties sometimes need some staking. These plants look their best when in a xeriscape setting combined with other prairie and desert plants like the yuccas and a selection of the larger ornamental grasses. These plants are attractive to the three B's: birds, butterflies, and bees.

Propagate by seed and stem cuttings in the spring after growth has started (remember, these seeds must be subjected to at least a six-week chill for stratification), and by gathering little stem tubers that sometimes appear. There is a cultivar called 'Gracious' that bears huge clumps of white flowers and comes true from seed.

Liatris microcephala, the dwarf liatris, is a plant of the southern Appalachians, where it

Lilium canadense, the Canada lily (not the Canadian lily, just like you wouldn't say Canadian geese), numbers among the great native plants of the Appalachian Mountains and the Southeast. While not always easy to grow, this is one plant that's worth the effort. The genus is from the Latin name of the plant and the species refers to the place where it was first reported. These beauties are found from the northern range south to Missouri, Georgia, and Alabama.

Flowering plants consist of candelabras of nodding yellow or reddish bell-shaped blossoms, on strong stems from four to sometimes ten feet tall, bearing ten to twenty (or more) three-inch flowers of great beauty. The leaves are lanceolate in shape, whorled on the stems, often six inches in length. The bulb looks like a white artichoke because of the overlapping scales. When mature, the bulbs often send out runners and eventually there's a lily colony in your garden.

My next-door neighbor, John Cram, takes care of a very large garden, full of native plants brought in by his efforts and those of predecessors, including a stand of these lilies. They bloom in late summer, shaded by tall oaks and at the back of an area of grasses that slopes down to a creek that flows year-round. Hence their location corresponds to the usual requests that these lilies should grow in open moist areas, in a good and rich damp loam, but one that is well-drained. Should your garden not have such soil, good, humusy garden soil will do, but you must be prepared to water in dry summers. It's also a good idea to provide a mulch to keep the bulbs cool. Plant the bulbs six inches deep. Remember, mice and voles (not moles, as they are meat-eaters) love lily bulbs so it's a good idea to plant yours in a hardware-cloth cage.

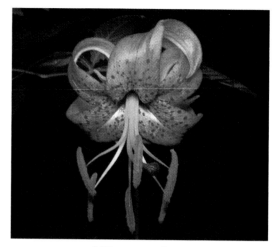

Lilium superbum

Lilium canadense

Lilium superbum, also known as the Turks-cap lily (from its resemblance to a fashion statement from medieval Turkey), is another eastern lily of great beauty. The species means "superb." The flowers are orange and yellow with darker spots and bloom on ten-foot stems, appearing first in midsummer. There can be up

to forty blossoms on a mature plant. The Turks-caps are found from our northern borders south to the Florida panhandle, then west to Arkansas. Provide deep, fertile, moist—yet, well-drained—soil in partial shade. Propagation of both species is by seed (but it takes years to get a blooming-sized bulb), by propagating individual scales from a bulb, and by offsets.

USDA Zones 4 to 9

Lupinus perennis, the wild lupine, or sometimes old maid's bonnet or the wild pea, belongs to a jumbled genus of plants containing over 200 species, with many of them found in western North America, but luckily in the Southeast the species number is smaller and plants are easier to recognize. The genus is from the Latin word for "wolf." Lupine roots contain nodes that support colonies of nitrogen-fixing bacteria, enabling the plants to thrive in nutrient-poor sand. Years ago, when early settlers first saw lupines they assumed these wildflowers had caused the sparse soils they grew in by "wolfing" all the nutrients, rather than the opposite. The species denotes a perennial status; this plant should not be confused with the Texas bluebonnet (*L. texensis*), an annual.

As to the jumbled genus reference, as part of developing the Russel Hybrid lupines, the wild lupine was mixed with the taller (and blue) *Lupinus polyphyllus*, originally from the Northwest, resulting in the possibility that if grown from seed you might get other colors besides blue, usually red, yellow, and sometimes bi-colors. Wild lupines are the most widely distributed lupine in the Southeast. Two-foot-high plants bear dense spires of lightly fragrant, typical pea-like blossoms of blue or slightly purplish flowers. Palmate leaves are divided into seven to eleven segments. The fruits are a broad, flat, hairy pod about an inch-and-a-half long, holding four or five seeds. Plants are found in fields at the edges of open woods, not to mention sand hills, from our northern borders south to northern Florida and west to Louisiana.

Note that while not all lupines are poisonous (usually to cattle), it's very difficult—even for many botanists—to distinguish between nontoxic and toxic species, so here, as with many plants, discretion is the better part of valor; although these plants are rarely involved in human poisonings.

While many gardens consider wild lupines to be a bit on the wild side, a well-grown cluster of these plants is very attractive and the flowers attract butterflies, bees, and hummingbirds. They are also interesting plants because they go to sleep at night by folding many of their leaves, hence one of the lesser-known common names being the sun-dial. Provide average, but well-drained, dry, sandy, acidic soil, remembering that these plants have deep taproots making them very difficult to trans-

plant. They also do well in containers as long as you provide full sun and a well-drained soil.

USDA Zones 4 to 10

Manfreda virginica [*Agave manfreda*],

the false aloe (although there is nothing false about it), the American aloe, or rattlesnake master (not to be confused with *Eryngium yuccifolium*), is a true succulent and one of the few such members of the agave family to be at home in the Southeast. The genus is named in honor of Manfred, listed as an ancient Italian writer, and I haven't the foggiest notion as to the reasoning. The American aloe grows naturally from West Virginia south to the Carolinas and Florida, and west to Ohio, Illinois, and Missouri.

The plant exhibits a basal rosette of fleshy, dark green, succulent, pointed leaves up to sixteen inches long. The rosettes spring from a wandering underground rhizome; if appreciative of their surroundings, they eventually make a colony of plants. The pale-green flowers are between one and two inches long and bloom along a four- to six-foot stalk.

A number of references point to reports of the floral fragrance, a fragrance that varies from that of spicy honey to vanilla to a whiff of Easter lilies. Most writers admit to missing the experience, which is because the flowers produce these scents only in late afternoon to early evening. In appearance, this plant is close to another member of the agave family, the time-honored houseplant, mother-in-law's tongue (*Sansevieria trifasciata*). So be sure to grow this plant close to the house so it can surprise you on warm summer evenings.

Amerindians used the root of this plant to treat dropsy, and like so many other plants, snakebite. In nature this plant delights in limestone cliffs and rocky ledges where the soil is dry and well drained and the sun is bright. It's worth a spot in the Southern garden for its fragrance alone! Propagation is by seed and division from mature colonies.

USDA Zones 6 to 11

Manfreda variegata

Manfreda variegata, the variegated *huaco*, is another interesting member of this family found only along the Lower Rio Grande River and in Tamaulipas, Mexico. Its succulent leaves are spattered with liver-colored spots and grow in a basal rosette. In late spring or early summer the rosette sends up a fascinating floral stalk, sometimes up to a height of six feet and bearing an eight-inch-long, five-inch-wide flower cluster of light yellow blossoms turning red with age. While great for massing as a desert-type

ground cover, because growth is slow this plant is perfect for containers, as long as the soil and pot have perfect drainage. Provide full sun to partial shade. Propagation is by seed and division of rhizomes.

USDA Zones 9 and up

Marshallia grandiflora, or Barbara's buttons, is a very beautiful flower, a member of the daisy family, and an endangered plant in many Southeastern states. Giving it a place in your garden helps to keep the plant in circulation. One would think the genus was named in honor of the marsh where this plant delights in growing, but it's named for an 18th-century plant lover and botanist, Dr. Moses Marshall. The species celebrates the stunning flower.

Marshallia grandiflora

In 2002, The Center for Plant Conservation reported that Barbara's buttons was endangered in Pennsylvania, Kentucky, and Tennessee, and threatened in West Virginia. It added that all historically known populations in North Carolina and Maryland are now extinct, the result of development and the accompanying destruction of wetlands where populations were known to exist. Bebe Miles introduced me to this charmer and it endured for seven years in my garden, then disappeared towards the end of the drought we suffered in western North Carolina, a drought that persisted from about 1997 to 2002.

Barbara's buttons forms ten-inch clumps of glossy, bright green, usually evergreen leaves. From late spring to early summer, tubular pinkish-mauve daisies from one to two inches across bloom on top of one- to two-foot stems, lasting for a couple of weeks.

The lush green foliage holds up most of the summer as long as plants have a good, humusy soil and partial shade. And don't forget water. In most of the Southeast this plant is found in floodplains where it delights in plenty of moisture. When planting, keep the crown above the soil, gently firming the soil around the roots. Botanique, a nursery specializing in bog plants and insectivores, suggests a soil of one-third sand and two-thirds peat moss, although many soils can work as long as they are acidic, hold moisture, and drain. Keep the plants moist to wet but not flooded as this can cause rot. Propagate by seed and by division.

USDA Zones 5 to 9

Mertensia virginica, Virginia bluebells, sometimes called the Virginia cowslip, Roanokebells, or the smooth lungwort, is a very

Mertensia virginica

beautiful wildflower, blooming in mid-spring with funnel-form pendant flowers that begin as pink but then turn blue as the flowers continue to open. The genus is named in honor of Francis Karl Mertens (1764-1831), a professor of botany at Bremen. The species honors Virginia.

Early on this lovely flower made the trip to Europe, where it quickly became a regular in English gardens. William Robinson, in his important book *The English Flower* (London: John Murray, 1881) said of this plant: "There is something about [this family] more beautiful in form of foliage and stem, and in the graceful way in which they arise to panicles of blue, than in almost any other family and handsomest of all is the Virginia cowslip. In many gardens it never makes the slightest progress; but a sheltered, moist, peaty nook is the best place for it. It is a charming old garden plant, and one which unfortunately has never become common."

Not to be topped by English writers, Neltje Blanchan, writing in *Nature's Garden* (New York: Doubleday, Page & Co., 1904), said: "A great variety of insects visit this blossom, which, being tubular, conducts them straight to the ample feast [and] occasionally one finds the cowslips perforated by clever bumblebees." The leaves are large, entire, and alternate and often begin as a dark purple but quickly change to a pale bluish gray. The fruits are four seed-like little nuts, leathery and wrinkled when mature. Their natural range starts at our northern borders and travels south to South Carolina, Alabama, Arkansas, and Kansas.

The critical factor in success with this plant is plenty of moisture, something quite surprising when you note that the thickened, dark, twisted roots certainly don't look as though they can put up with a lot of water. These plants are spring ephemerals dying back by the end of June, so plant something in the area to take over after the bluebells fade. In my garden, they are planted next to turtleheads (*Chelone glabra*) and a number of native ferns. A pure white form called 'Alba' is sometimes listed and worth the search. Propagation is by seed or division after the flowers fade but do so before the leaves disappear entirely—or you won't find the roots.

USDA Zones 4 to 9

Mimulus ringens, the Allegheny monkey flower, is a delightful little flower (on a tall stem). One look at the two-lipped blossom— the erect upper lip and a lower lip directed downwards—and you can see it is a member of the snapdragon family. The genus name is from the Latin *mimus*, or "a buffoon," while the species means "gaping" and again refers to the shape of the blossom. The plant ranges from our northern borders southward to Georgia, then west to Texas. Using that wondrous prose found in horticultural writing of the late 19th century, Neltje Blanchan said of this plant's flower: "Imaginative eyes see what appears to them the gaping face of a little ape or buffoon in this common flower whose drolleries, such as they are, call forth the only applause desired—the buzz of insects that become pollen-laden during the entertainment."

The plants have square, erect, usually branched stems from one to three feet high, bearing opposite, lance-shaped to oblong, saw-edged leaves. The flowers are light blue to white, usually striped with deep blue or purple, and bloom in summer. Gardeners often set these plants in one- or two-gallon containers of good, humus-rich soil, then cover with one-half to two inches of water. Monkey flowers delight in growing in damp or wet soil at the edge of a swamp or beside streams and ponds. Propagate by seed or by division.

USDA Zones 4 to 10

Mitchella repens, the partridge berry, sometimes known as the twinberry or the squawberry, is a low, evergreen creeper that trails along the woodland floor. When growing in conjunction with mosses, it's truly a class act as a ground cover. Linnaeus called this diminutive beauty *Mitchella* in honor of his doctor friend John Mitchell, who was not only a plantsman and a cartographer, but also developed a means of treating yellow fever. The species means it's a trailing or creeping plant. The stems often root at the nodes. Plants grow

Mitchella repens

most outdoor perennials must have a season of chill in order to survive, and that goes for ferns and ground covers, too. When planting, use lots of pine needles and water well, providing them with full shade and an evenly moist, humusy soil. Propagation is by seed, planting the berries in the fall in damp peat and sand, or rooting cuttings.

USDA Zones 3 to 9

Mitella diphylla, the miterwort, is often described as nothing much when it comes to flowers, an opinion best exemplified by *Wild-flowers of the United States: The Southeastern States* in the entry: " . . . scrawny, unattractive little plants with minute flowers—but a hand magnifier reveals unexpected delights." Linneaus named the genus not for the flower, but for the seedpod, using *mitella*, a Greek word for "a little cap," because young pods somewhat resemble a bishop's miter.

The tiny flowers are white, about one-eighth-inch across, but a number of eighteen-inch (or taller) stems dotted with these minute blossoms looks like a bit of unfinished lace especially when moved about in a gentle spring breeze. The metaphor is only enhanced when you take a hand-lens and see that each of the five petals are deeply cut so the flower is seen as another bit of lace embroidery. The foliage on the flower stalk consists of a single pair of heart-shaped, three-lobed, toothed and stalk-less leaves halfway up, hence the species designation. Basal leaves are up to three inches wide and resemble maple leaves.

Blooming in late April and May, this elegant woodland wildflower grows low to the forest floor, requiring a soil rich in humus. It's a member of the saxifrage family and, like others

naturally from our northern borders south to Florida and Texas.

The opposite, small, rounded leaves are a shiny deep green and grow along a rambling stem up to a foot long. In late spring two lovely four-petaled white flowers appear, each attached to the same calyx. The flowers are *dimorphous*, meaning they occur in two forms: In one flower the pistil is short and the stamens are long, in the other it's the reverse, thus neither flower can fertilize itself and both must be fertilized in order to produce one bright red berry. Upon close examination, each berry will exhibit two eyes, the result of two flowers for one fruit. If not eaten, berries will remain on the plant for an entire season.

Not only will this creeper delight in the garden, plants set into a well-planned terrarium will last for a year until they must be removed and set out into the garden. Remember that of the group, these plants can grow in only a few inches of soil, especially when they are close to water seeping from stones. Propagation is by seed or division.

USDA Zones 4 to 8

- -

Monarda didyma, or bee-balm, sometimes called Oswego-tea, fragrant-balm, and horse-mint (not to be confused with M. *punctata*, also called horsemint), is a most attractive member of the mint family, easily recognized as such by its square stems. The genus is one of seventeen North American species, commem-orating Nicolas Monardes (1493-1588), a Spanish physician and botanist. The species means "divided into two lobes" referring to the two-lipped mouth. Their natural range is from New York south to the uplands of

Monarda didyma

Georgia, North Carolina, then west to Tennessee. One of the more interesting bits about this plant concerns its mention as "monardes didymes" by Jules Verne in his wonderful book, Mysterious Island.

The aromatic leaves are opposite, dark green, oval to oblong lance shaped, and saw-edged, often hairy beneath. The scarlet flowers bloom in clusters arising from a solitary, termi-nal, rounded head with leafy bracts below. Individual flowers are often two inches long. The leaves have a long tradition of use in brew-ing a mint-flavored tea reputed to be an excellent easing for fever, stomach problems, plus promoting a deep and restful sleep. The name Oswego tea was bestowed by John Bartram, who refers to the plant's popularity in the Oswego Indian territory of upstate New York, near the shores of Lake Ontario. Another of its common names hearkens back to British colonial days and the fragrant resemblance of the leaves to the bergamot orange, a cultivar of that fruit whose rind is used in making perfumes and flavoring Earl Grey tea, not to mention Constant Comment®.

Note that this plant is attractive to the three B's: birds, butterflies, and bees. Most of the members of this genus suffer greatly from powdery mildew and in areas with hot and humid summers, the leaves eventually get that gray color reflecting the presence of the various fungal causes, chiefly mildew.

Monardas are spreaders and when passing rural fields where these and other rambling wildflowers bloom, you will note their presence over large patches of land. In your garden it's usually necessary to divide in order to conquer but this action always leads to healthier plants. Provide any reasonable garden soil but remem-ber monardas like moisture, so during dry summers it helps to provide additional water.

Monarda fistulosa

As Neltje Blanchan wrote: " . . . they look as if they might be placed in a glass cup and make an excellent pen-wiper."

Monarda punctata, or horsemint, is a short-lived perennial, often grown as an annual, with terminal clusters of small, unusual yellow and cream-colored flowers with purple spots. The small flowers are surrounded with colorful bracts and because they are about three feet tall, make excellent additions to the rear of the border, either formal or wild. Homelands range from our northern borders southward to Florida, then west to the Mississippi, and beyond. Provide full sun in well-drained, sandy soil of average fertility.

USDA Zones 4 to 9

While performing well in partial shade, the various funguses are worse there, so put these plants in full sun, allowing for plenty of air circulation, and they will stand straight and tall without staking. There are many garden cultivars available with flowers in shades of pink, white, red, purple, rose, and colors in between. Some are billed as "mildew-resistant." Propagation is by seed and division in early spring or in fall.

Monarda fistulosa, the wild bergamot, has extremely variable—and smaller—flowers ranging from purple to lavender, to rose, and finally magenta. They are found naturally in open woods, thickets and along dry, rock hills, ranging from our northern borders south to the Gulf of Mexico. Unlike bee-balm, the flower heads only open a few flowers at a time.

Oenothera fruticosa, or the sundrops, is a species of native plants included in one of two groups: the evening primroses and the day-bloomers known collectively as the sundrops. Unfortunately they both share the common genus *Oenothera*. The name is derived from the Greek words *oinos*, meaning "wine," and *thera*, "to hunt," because of confusion regarding these flowers and still another genus of plants with roots possessing the aroma of wine. The species means the plants are shrubby or bushy, which they are.

Today many evening primroses are found around the world, but originally they were all Americans, their range stretching from the deserts of the Southwest to the Eastern Seaboard. In 1729 Parkinson noted that evening primroses were exported to England from Virginia. The common evening primrose (*O. biennis*), a biennial, was introduced into gardens sometime in the 18th century as a root vegetable called yellow lamb's lettuce or German rampion.

For many years we took care of a sloping bank in the front of our old farmhouse that was covered with wild daylilies (*Hemerocallis fulva*), but between the lilies and the lawn we kept a long, narrow bed of sundrops (*O. fruticosa*).

Oenothera fruticosa

Memories come and go, but I suspect that no matter how many years pass, the sight and smell of a summer garden after a morning rain will remind me of these bright, golden-yellow flowers. The plants have simple leaves and are easily missed in the garden until coming into bud and bloom usually in high summer. Then the unassuming plants, usually under two feet in height, are topped with clusters of bright red buds and golden-yellow, four-petaled flowers, each over two inches in width. Basal rosettes are evergreen in the South.

This species is perfect in the wild garden and even at the edge of a meadow they can hold their own—no mean feat under the threat of advancing meadow grasses. For the formal garden, the cultivars are best, having even bigger and brighter flowers, but a bed of any sundrops in bloom is as close as you can get to a pool of molten gold. The plants spread rapidly, but being shallow-rooted, they are easily pulled up when not wanted.

The cultivar 'Fireworks' exhibits upright clumps of bronzy-red foliage and the blossoms open to a clear lemon yellow, 'Yellow Moonlight' is as it's named, 'Silvery Moon' shows an even lighter yellow; all are quite beautiful. Care is minimal. Sundrops ask only for full sun and well-drained soil; dryness is no problem. Gathered in early winter, the seedheads make interesting additions to winter bouquets. Propagation is by seed and division after blooming.

USDA Zones 4 to 10

Opuntia compressa, sometimes botanically designated as *O. humifusa*, is commonly called the prickly-pear or the Indian fig. Local names include bunny-ears or beavertail cactus. (With more than one plant they are called cactuses, not cacti because cacti is the Latin plural, not the English.) Joseph Pitton de Tournefort (1656-1708), a French botanist, bestowed the original scientific name based on cactus-like plants he saw in a Greek town. The species refers to the flattened stems. Cactuses are really woody plants, not herbaceous perennials, and would ordinarily be in a book dedicated to them alone. Few gardeners make the distinction, however, so here they are.

Opuntia compressa

plump up again like sponges. The Amerindians removed the outer skin from these segments and used the remaining pads to dress wounds, as they are not only cooling, but sterile, too. When it comes to planting, cactuses will survive in clay soil but you must amend it with gravel or stones. This is especially important in the winter because most plants die from having roots touching cold, wet soil; if drainage is good, they usually survive. If you're worried about having to dig and alter too much soil, try raised beds. Full sun is necessary. Propagation is by seed or breaking off a joint then propping it up with a few stones with just the bottom edge touching soil and it will root.

USDA Zones 8 to 10

There are possibly 300 species of prostrate to treelike, mostly jointed cactuses native to the New World. The plant body is made of thick, succulent segments, or joints, usually covered with spines, the spines often growing in clusters. These spines easily detach and stand ready to cause trouble with both man and beast. There are few, if any leaves, most falling away as soon as they develop. The flowers are quite beautiful, consisting of many sepals and petals, arising from a sort of cup that also holds many golden stamens. Blossoms are followed by fruits, which are bigger than cherries, and turn a rosy-red with maturity. Luther Burbank gambled that the American public would eat thornless cactus fruits but lost the game. Now with the rise of regional cooking, these fruits have finally come into fashion. Plants can be up to three feet high.

The succulent segments begin to shrivel with cold weather, then with the spring rains

Pachysandra procumbens, or Allegheny spurge, is an American native and a surprisingly aesthetic member of a genus that numbers five species, with the other four coming from Asia, including the plant that box store garden cen-

Pachysandra procumbens

ters delight in selling, Japanese pachysandra (*P. terminalis*). It's one of the most widely sold ground covers in the hort business and most of these dealers have no idea of the quality of plant available here at home. The genus is from the Greek *pachus*, or "thick," and *aner*, or "man," referring to the stout floral filaments. The species is taken from the Latin word for "falling forward," alluding to the plants' growth habit. This plant is found in rich woods and is native to West Virginia, down to Louisiana and across to Florida.

The plant is a semi-evergreen ground cover, the two- to four-inch leaves remaining through the winter in areas with mild weather. In colder areas the plants become herbaceous perennials. The simple alternate leaves are coarsely toothed in the distal half and clustered at the tips of the shoots. They grow in whorls, with most of the basal stems lacking foliage, spreading by rhizomes, the branches intertwining and the plants reaching an average height of between six and ten inches. The showy, fragrant, white flowers (sometimes with the faintest flush of pink), usually with four sepals, bloom in two- to four-inch spikes. In the cold of winter, the leaves show a marbled, silvery mosaic pattern, the background color changing from a dark green to deep brownish-red.

Allegheny spurge wants a moist, acidic, well-drained soil laced with humus and a location in partial to full shade. Until it covers its assigned area, you should remove any invading weeds, but once established this plant cares for itself. Do not use heavy clay soils unless properly amended. 'Eco Treasure' is a Georgia selection featuring more boldly marked leaves. Propagation is by cuttings and is very easy.

USDA Zones 4 to 10

Parthenocissus quinquefolia, Virginia creeper, is in reality a vine but it's a perennial vine so I'm sneaking it into this book. Although it's able to climb a tree or trellis in almost a single bound, where no support is available or where support has been denied this vine turns into a magnificent ground cover, wandering about its area, holding the foot-wide clusters of leaves on foot-high stems. The genus is Greek for "virgin ivy," and the species name means "having five leaves or leaflets."

I found the ground cover trait by accident when I happened to cut down a poorly placed white pine at the edge of my woods that was acting as host to a Virginia creeper. Not wanting to lose the vine, I carefully pulled the tendrils away from the tree's bark and laid it on the ground, intending to eventually transplant it to another spot. Later I returned to find the vine wandering over the ground and taking root. So allow me to introduce the creeper as a

Parthenocissus quinquefolia

ground cover and not a climbing vine, although it does this second job with great gusto. And the glory of it all is in the autumn when the creeper's leaves turn a brilliant scarlet-red, quite unrivaled by anything else except perhaps the sour gum (*Nyssa sylvatica*) or the stag-horn sumac (*Rhus* spp.). This vine is also resistant to salt spray, making it a natural for the seaside garden, and birds love the berries. Finally, once established, it's quite drought-resistant.

Virginia creeper is a deciduous, perennial vine that climbs and holds fast, with tendrils having adhesive tips. The large palmate leaves are divided into five leaflets. Inconspicuous white flowers mature into small black berries. The foliage is a brilliant scarlet in autumn. Although able to climb masonry walls, its hold-fasts are relatively weak and may be pulled from the wall by strong winds. Provide ordinary, well-drained garden soil in full sun or partial shade. Propagation is by division or layering where stems touch the ground.

There are cultivars: 'Engelmannii' has smaller leaves that still are brilliant in the fall, the leaves of 'Saint-Paulii' have deeper lobes, 'Hirsuta' has especially striking color, and 'Murorum' has shorter branches. Finally, there are variegated forms that are less vigorous, the most popular being 'Star Showers'.

USDA Zones 6 to 9

Passiflora incarnata

Passiflora species, the passion flowers, were discovered by a Catholic friar in Mexico in the early 1600s. Because the elaborate floral parts suggested the Passion of Christ in symbolic terms and because it was found in heathen territory, the flower became a *cause célèbre*. The Church interpreted the find as a message from the Lord asking that the natives be converted to Christianity. The natives already used the plant in folk medicine and as an aphrodisiac, attaching a different meaning to the plant's new name. *Passiflora* is the Latin name for the original flower. The ten petals represent the apostles, without Peter and Judas; the filaments of the corona are either the crown of thorns or a halo; the five anthers are the wounds; the styles are three nails; the three sepals on the floral stem are the Trinity; and the whips of persecution are seen in the coiling tendrils of the vine.

Passiflora incarnata or Maypop, is the native to the U.S., a climbing or trailing vine with soft, hairy stems sometimes reaching a length of twenty-five feet. The six-inch leaves are palmately lobed into three sections. The blossoms are about three inches wide, with whitish sepals and petals; the corona is lavender. The fruit is greenish-yellow, edible, and makes a very good jelly. It's found throughout the Southeast, from southern Pennsylvania south. The species name means "flesh-colored" and refers to some of the floral parts. Maypop is the official state wildflower of Tennessee.

Passiflora lutea is a much less traveling plant, with stems usually around fifteen feet long. The blossoms are about a half-inch wide, the flowers have narrow whitish-green petals, a yellow-green corona, and are not as showy as Maypop. The fruit is a small black berry. The species name refers to the color yellow.

Passion flowers should have as much sun as possible to guarantee flowers, and with luck a new vine will sometimes bloom the first year if seed was started in late winter.

These are great container plants. Use a six- or seven-inch pot for a few years, fertilizing with a weak solution of plant food every three or four weeks during the summer. If you wish to overwinter the plant, make sure you keep the pot where the roots get at least six weeks of 40-degree temperatures. They will not survive if kept in a warm greenhouse. Before spring, cut back about a third of the canes, stopping just before a lateral bud. Propagation is by division, stem cuttings, or by seed.

USDA Zones 6 to 10

Pedicularis canadensis

Pedicularis canadensis, wood betony, or for gardeners with more style, the Canadian lousewort, gets its second common name from the old belief that cattle grazing the European species would become infested with lice, that belief easily traveling from the Old World to the New. The genus is the Latin word for "pertaining to lice." The species signifies the plant's initial discovery in Canada. Pliny once reported that the first common name of betony was vettonica, named for the Vettones, a people of Spain. But present-day neologists claim betony to be the correct name, from the Celtic *bew* ("a head") and *ton* ("good"), referring to medicinal uses for complaints of the head.

Amerindians are reported to have used the leaves in soup or as a salad green, while young men carried a bit of the root when they went to meet a potential lover. Mrs. M. Grieve wrote of an old Italian proverb in A Modern Herbal: "Sell your coat and buy Betony," marking the great value placed on the medicinal properties of wood betony. Antonius Musa, chief physician to the Emperor Augustus, wrote a long treatise demonstrating it was a certain cure for no less than forty-seven diseases.

In the South, plants usually bloom in early to mid-spring, sporting dense swirls of flowers resembling throaty snapdragons, in yellow, white, or reddish-brown. The alternate, lightly cleft leaves are almost fernlike in their elegance, the plants ranging from six to about fourteen inches in height. Wood betonies often form large colonies, the foliage starting out a rich wine color, and turning green with the advance of summer. In the botanical gardens at Asheville, wood betony not only has formed a large grouping of plants, it also has started to spread slowly along the edge of the trail. The flowers are especially attractive when seen from above, looking like colorful pinwheels ready to move in the slightest breeze. Even the seeds are attractive.

Plants prefer full to partial shade in moist, acid, woodland soil, and are often found growing along the edges of streams. They range from Maine and Canada, south to Florida, Texas, and even Mexico. Wood betony wildflowers occur naturally in acid soils on dry open woodlands, ridges, prairies, and along mossy slopes bordering streams. Swamp lousewort (*Pedicularis lanceolata*) is a similar plant but lacks the little hairs, has opposite leaves, and blooms in the fall. Propagation for wood betony is by seed or division in spring.

USDA Zones 5 to 10

Penstemon species, the beardtongues, belong to a genus that includes over 250 species, all but one native to North America, that one stranger being from Southeast Asia (*P. frutescens*, native to Japan). While the majority of the penstemons are chiefly found in the western states, we do have a few native to the Southeast. The genus is named from *pente* or "five" and *stemon* or "stamen," referring to the presence of a fifth stamen that in many species is tipped with a little beard made up of a tuft of hairs. There are about fourteen species native to the Southeast and, in addition, so many of the western species will do well in the Southeast that gardeners could spend their lives just growing these plants. Be reminded that penstemons do not like a combination of

cold and damp soil, especially in the winter, so be sure your soil is well drained and in as much winter sun as possible. Propagation is by seed, cuttings, or by division in spring or fall.

Penstemon digitalis, the foxglove beardtongue, has flowers that arise on two- to five-foot stems above a rosette of oblong basal leaves from four to six inches long. The species in this case refers to the flowers resemblance to the foxglove or digitalis. The floral stems have paired leaves topped with a terminal inflorescence consisting of mostly white flowers. This is a great choice for the rear of the border as it blooms in midsummer and makes a good backing for shorter plants. The individual flowers are tubular and open out to five spreading lobes, with the inside marked with purple lines or nectar guides for visiting insects. It does seed

Penstemon species

about, so if you don't want more penstemons, cut back the plants after flowering. Although delighting in sun, this species will adapt to partial shade here in the Southeast. The Perennial Plant of 1996 was a cultivar of this species called 'Husker Red'. This plant has lovely white flower clusters that stand about eighteen inches above deep bronze-purple leaves. Plants prefer slightly acidic soil and do well both in full sun and light shade.

Penstemon hirsutus, the hairy beardtongue, produces clusters of lavender and white, tubular flowers about an inch long on eighteen-inch stems. The basal foliage is evergreen. It is found naturally from our northern borders south to Virginia, Kentucky, and Tennessee.

USDA Zones 3 to 9

Phlox is a genus of all sorts of plants ranging from garden perennials to stars of early spring

Phlox paniculata

wild gardens and rock gardens. Every country home worth its salt had the original garden phlox in the border because it grows in open woods and bottomlands from New York to Iowa and Kansas, then southward to Georgia, northern Mississippi, and Arkansas. Its scientific name is *Phlox paniculata* and plants have escaped from gardens—then back again—for centuries. The genus is taken from the Greek word for "flame," referring to the bright colors of some species. The species means the flowers bloom in terminal panicles. It has mostly paired leaves, undivided and un-lobed. The plants usually reach a height of three to five feet. Flowers have a bell-shaped corolla, or tube, that flares into five lobes, like a trumpet with an attitude. Flowers vary greatly in color, from white to pink, and a bright purplish-pink, but if mixed in with cultivars the color range eventually expands. Because this is ostensibly a book on native species I will not list the many garden forms now available on the market.

Garden phlox wants full sun to light shade and well-drained but moist garden soil, best produced by working in added humus. Because the leaves of most varieties are prone to powdery mildew, keep the individual plants at least two feet apart to provide good air circulation, and look for the mildew-resistant cultivars. Divide the plants every three years to keep them vigorous, and deadhead to prolong bloom and prevent unwanted seedlings, of which there can be many. Thin the weaker shoots on plants every spring, and pinch back the front shoots for lower flowers and a better display. Use garden phlox for cutting—we always keep additional plants in the cutting garden so the border isn't disturbed. The sweetly scented flowers (some people find them a bit too fragrant) attract butterflies during the day and nocturnal moths when the sun sets.

Phlox amoena, the hairy phlox (not really as bad as it sounds—it's no Cousin Itt) bears two-inch lance-shaped leaves that sport long hairs, with even the attractive flowers having a bit or down. Color is usually lavender. Since height is under a foot, this is an effective ground cover. 'Cabot's Blue', named for Lucy Cabot of Atlanta, is said to bloom about four months if provided with full sun to bright shade and average soil (even clay), but the drainage must be good. Plants do well in containers. The species means the plant is beautiful.

USDA Zones 6 to 9

Phlox amplifolia, the large-leaved phlox, is found in most of the Southeast except in Florida and areas with high heat. Plants are about five feet high and grow naturally on wooded slopes and banks. This could be a great garden plant, if more widely available. The flowers are usually lilac to pinkish. The species means "large," referring to the leaves.

Phlox carolina, the thick-leaf phlox, blooms in open woods and thickets throughout the Southeast and bears pink or purplish-red flowers in round clusters. A number of garden cultivars have developed, generally flowering during July and August. Colors range from white to pink, mauve, then crimson and purple. They are perfect in rock gardens.

USDA Zones 4 to 8

Phlox divaricata, the blue phlox or wild sweet William (an unfortunate common name, as the sweet-Williams are really pinks, or *Dianthus*, in another plant family) is a beautiful native phlox found in woods and fields from the Northeast to the Southeast, from Florida west to Texas. If grown in full sun they must have a moist soil, but prefer a shaded spot, at least dur-

Phlox subulata

ing noonday heat. When heat is intense they have a tendency to go dormant, so mark their locations well. The species name refers to the sometimes-bent stems.

Phlox floridana is found in open woods and along the edges of bogs and swamps in northern Florida, then west to Mississippi and Georgia. Height is between one and three feet, with some leaves being three inches long and the flower color ranging from pink to purple.

Phlox pilosa is a small phlox between eight and twenty-four inches in height, growing throughout most of the Southeast. This species prefers dry open woods, thickets, and prairies. The sometimes-white flowers usually bloom in various shades of purple-pink, opening from April to July—but they sometimes exhibit sparse bloom in the fall. The species name refers to the downy stems.

Phlox stolonifera, the creeping phlox, is a fast-growing wildflower that marches across the ground with leafy stems. Height is generally between six and twelve inches, with plants forming low mats of leaves. The pretty flowers range from white, to pink, purple, and violet. Plants are found in the mountain woods of Pennsylvania and Ohio south to Georgia and Tennessee. Provide light sun to light shade in a slightly acidic soil. They are heavy feeders so lace the site with humus. The species name refers to the creeping stems.

USDA Zones 3 to 9

Phlox subulata, the moss-pink, is not a moss or a pink. Unlike most of the phloxes, the leaves on this species are needle-like, growing from stems generally reaching a height of about six inches. They bloom from April to July and cover the plants with flowers that range in color from white to lavender, lilac, and blue, in addition to the vibrant colors found at most garden centers. This is originally a native phlox growing from Maine, west to Michigan, then south to North Carolina and Tennessee but has escaped from garden cultivation and is now widespread. This plant is especially effective when it flows naturally over the edge of a wall or rocks in a rock garden. The species refers to the fine-pointed leaves.

USDA Zones 3 to 8

Physostegia virginiana [Dracocephalum virginianum], the obedient plant (sometimes mistakenly called the false-dragonhead), is, like most members of the mint family, best described as a robust grower. Obedient plant is native to eastern North America from our northern borders then south to Texas, Louisiana, Alabama, and Georgia. It's also one of those plants usually described by nurseries as being "easy to grow!" The scientific name is from *physa*, or "bladder," and *stege*, "a covering," referring to the inflated floral tube. The common name of obedient plant is well deserved. Move each blossom back and forth or up and down and it will stay where it's placed. Flower arrangers have long known about this oddity, and children are also amused by this seeming power over a flower. In nature this ability allows the blossoms to face away from a storm. Because insects, like bees or bumblebees, land against the wind, the flowers have this advantage for pollination. Once moved, the flowers keep their position because of friction between the flower stalk and the surrounding bracts; remove the bracts and the flowers are limp. Obedient plant overwinters as a basal rosette of willow-like leaves

Square stems hold opposite, thick, lance-shaped leaves, irregularly but sharply toothed.

Physostegia virginiana

Terminal spikes of usually rose-pink flowers like small snapdragons bloom atop stems, often over three feet tall. The flowers appear from mid-summer into fall. Obedient plant does well in either sunny or lightly shaded areas, but is at its best with some shade and soil on the dry side, and a spot in full sun where soil is damper.

Physostegia virginiana 'Alba' has white flowers and there's a plus. The plants are easier to control and this type also doesn't demand the damp soil preferred by the species. 'Summer Snow' is a named variety. There is also a variegated, pink-flowered form called 'Variegata' and, like the white form, this, too, lacks some of the strength necessary to take over nearby land. 'Rose Queen' is about two feet high with rose-pink flowers, 'Bouquet Rose' grows about three feet tall with shell-pink flowers, 'Rosea' reaches four feet with pink flowers, the flowers of 'Pink Bouquet' have rose-colored flowers, and 'Summer Glow' has flowers of a rich rose-crimson color. 'Miss Manners' is a less aggressive grower.

Because obedient plants are aggressive, moving around with creeping roots, they naturalize with ease. But if they do transgress, simply pull them up. They are beautiful when massed in a formal border or allowed to wander in a wild garden. Because they do wander, plan on dividing plants every three years. Propagation is by seed, but remember that cultivars will produce seedlings with flowers of various colors, and by division in spring or late fall.

USDA Zones 3 to 9

Podophyllum peltatum, the May-apple, or sometimes the hog-apple, mandrake, or wild lemon, is a herbaceous perennial long grown by Southeast gardeners and a plant with a history that goes back to being named by Linnaeus. Supposedly he saw a resemblance between the leaf and a duck's foot and so called it foot-leaf, with *Podo* being Greek for "foot" and *phylum* meaning "leaf." However, Neltje Blanchan writes that equally imaginative American children called them green umbrellas. This plant, too, has an Asian relative known as *P. hexandrum*, at home in the Himalayan Mountains, with pink flowers and elongated red fruit.

Podophyllum peltatum

Many years ago at the Bronx Botanic Garden, where a grand dinner party honored the Garden Writers of America, Bebe Miles and a number of other prominent wildflower advocates, were having a spirited discussion about tough plants. "You could kill a May-apple if you planted it in full sun and very dry soil," Bebe said, "but otherwise, I'll bet on the plant." And how right she was. May-apples, if properly planted in a friendly environment, become a very attractive ground cover.

The large, deeply divided leaves are usually some nine inches across, sitting on top of a foot-high stem, with leaf overlapping neighboring leaf. The nodding white flowers, which generally display six white petals (but occasionally can have nine), only bloom on plants that have two leaflets, with the flowers being hidden beneath the leafy canopy. As the summer advances a fleshy, yellowish, egg-shaped fruit, about two inches long appears, again hidden by the leaves. The fruit is edible when ripe, but all other parts of the plant are toxic. The roots produce a toxic action on cell division and have been used in anti-cancer therapies. But when eaten with abandon the plant can lead to death. Amerindians made an insecticide from powdered roots.

Sometimes, usually by midsummer and after periods of rainfall, the May-apple leaf becomes infected with a rust or fungus known as *Puccinia podophylli*, with the leaf's upper surface becoming spotted with orange-yellow spots. Some attentive gardeners will also note that one colony of plants might be infected and a nearby colony completely free of this disease. There is no treatment and the plants easily recover.

May-apples do well in any good garden soil that has added organic matter and partial shade or filtered sunlight. As a ground cover, May-apple is superb and soon covers problem areas of bare earth, even slopes where erosion is a problem. Over a few seasons the plants will merge. Propagation is by seed and the rootstocks, which can be divided almost any time.

USDA Zones 3 to 9

Polemonium reptans, American Jacob's ladder, sometimes known as Greek valerian, is a wildflower that blends pleasant flowers with very attractive foliage. The common name is a reflection of the religious leanings of many settlers of early America, the regularly ranked leaflets reminding them of a ladder to heaven. The genus is said to be named in honor of Polemon (A.D. 150), an early Athenian philosopher. Found in moist woods from New York to Minnesota and south to Georgia, Alabama, Mississippi, and Oklahoma, this is a native plant that moved to various gardens, then escaped back to the woods again.

The leaves are alternate but each is pinnately compound with one terminal leaflet and three to eight leaflet pairs. The flowers are a little over a half-inch long, cup-shaped, and vary in color from lavender to white, each with five lobes and prominent cream-colored stamens. Use plenty of humus and find garden soil that is evenly moist or plan on occasional watering in dry summers. This is a lovely plant for partial shade, doing beautifully when mixed with ferns, but if there isn't enough water the leaves will continually wilt. Propagation is by seed and division in spring.

USDA Zones 4 to 8

Polemonium reptans

Polygonatum biflorum

Polygonatum commutatum, sometimes listed as *P. giganteum*, is truthfully the great Solomon's-seal and a stunning wildflower addition to any garden border. In the wrong place it won't survive because hot sun and dry soil are a deadly combination. But given a spot in the shade with moist soil, this plant is in it for the long haul. The genus is very old, derived from a name used in ancient Greece, *poly* meaning "many," and *gonu* translating to "a knee joint," referring to the many-jointed rhizome growing beneath the soil's surface. The species means "changeable" and reflects the movement of the parent rhizome, as year after year the floral stems come up in a different place. The common name hearkens back to the religious background of most settlers to America and describes the seal-like scars that are left each season on the underground rhizomes where the flowering branches originated. These scars resemble the wax impressions used to ensure the authenticity of ancient documents.

In nursery catalogs, *Polygonatum commutatum* is often listed as *P. canaliculatum*, although *P. canaliculatum* is actually another name for a shorter species, properly called *P. biflorum*. To add to the confusion, there is a theory that the great Solomon's-seal is a form of *P. biflorum* working with four sets of chromosomes. The rhizomes have been utilized in folk medicine for centuries, especially as an astringent, a tonic, and for pulmonary complaints. And no matter what the future scientific name, this is a striking perennial, with tall arching stems that often reach a height of eight feet, the top half bearing alternate oval leaves with pointed tips and prominent veining that makes them appear to be pleated. Even without flowers this plant would be a noteworthy addition to any garden setting, especially in the fall.

Each single flower stalk arises from a leaf axil, usually bearing one, two, or sometimes three pendant flowers. These tubular flowers are lobed at the tip, greenish-white or yellowish-green, about one-half inch to just under an inch in length. Eventually fruits resembling little grapes develop; in reality they are bluish-black berries. The leaves turn a stunning golden-bronze in fall.

When planting the rhizomes use plenty of humus. If summer rains are sparse, remember to water these plants in order to keep the foliage fresh and green. Plants can sulk after moving, so give them a year to recover unless you begin with container-grown nursery plants. Also be aware that the variegated Solomon's-seal is in reality a variegated form of the Japanese *Polygonatum odoratum* that comes true from seed and does seed about. A good under-planting for the great Solomon's-seal would be any of the shorter native ferns, including lady fern (*Athyrium filix-femina*), maidenhair fern (*Adiantum pedatum*), or Christmas fern (*Polystichum acrostichoides*).

Polygonatum biflorum, smooth Solomon's seal, is a smaller version of its great sister, seldom topping three feet in height. *P. pubes-*

cens, or hairy Solomon's-seal, is so named because the leaves are downy underneath. Propagation for the Solomon's seals is by seed or division of the rhizomes in early spring.

USDA Zones 4 to 8

Rhus typhina, the staghorn sumac, is one of my favorite native trees and I am sneaking it in this collection of plants by calling it a very large perennial. American nurserymen and some gardeners usually think poorly of this tree (not to mention various state highway departments), but it deserves far better shrift than it gets. *Rhus* is an old Latin name for the genus and the species refers to a tea made from the densely hairy berries (really drupes) or the leaves to treat fevers and sore throats. First cultivated in the early 1600s, the staghorn sumac is a small tree with few demands. It grows so quickly that you do get immediate gratification and it is quite beautiful throughout the

Rhus typhina

garden year. Sometimes called a shrub, it has an ultimate height of about thirty feet.

The look of the tree is decidedly tropical. The pinnately compound leaves have between eleven and thirty-one leaflets each. The flowers are insignificant but over the summer develop into terminal cones of dark crimson fruits that persist through the winter. When the leaves fall, the felted stems resemble those of a stag "in velvet." The hairs on the branches change from pink to green the first year and are shed by the time the bark is about three years old. Our old friends, the English gardeners, say this tree is unsurpassed in fall when the leaves turn a glorious and brilliant orange and scarlet, giving the garden a fiery sunset glow in the backyard.

The most imaginative use of this tree that I've ever seen is in the Wild Garden at Wave Hill, a public garden located in the community of Riverdale in The Bronx, New York. There a fifty-year-old tree has generated a multitude of smaller trunks, and all have been allowed to twist and turn either naturally or by shaping and pruning so they've become a bower with a look more likely to appear in Brazil than overlooking the Hudson River just above Manhattan.

To qualify as an addition to a list of perennials, let me add that this sumac can be used as a living hedge by cutting its tropical foliage to the ground in early spring and only allowing it a year of growth before cutting it again. You can do the same with a single tree by cutting it back every fall and creating a tropical fountain of green. Propagate by cuttings or rooting the suckers that arise around the mother tree. There is a very attractive cultivar called 'Laciniata', with the individual leaflets finely cut and, in addition, it's a much shorter plant.

USDA Zones 3 to 10

Rubus odoratus

Rubus odoratus, the purple-flowering raspberry or Virginia raspberry, is technically not a perennial but a shrub. It's such a valuable addition to the garden landscape either as a specimen plant or a living background for other perennials, however, that I include it here. The generic name is taken from the Latin *ruber*, for "red," referring to those members of the clan that sport luscious red fruit. Found throughout the Blue Ridge Mountains from our northern borders south to the mountains of Georgia.

Many years ago while leading an elder hostel tour on a back road near the Laurel River, we walked along a mountain trail and came to one of those ever-changing and always restful waterfalls that ripple down from mountains on high. There, next to the bursting spray and glistening rocks, were a number of purple-flowering raspberry bushes, full of flowers, their light purple petals bright against the maple-like leaves. "But where the bright blossoms of the Virginia raspberry burst forth above the road-side tangle and shady woodland dells," wrote Neltje Blanchan in *Nature's Garden*, "even those who despise magenta see beauty in them where abundant green tones all discordant notes into harmony."

The shrubs are usually six feet or more in height, with large five-lobed, maple-like leaves, those at the bottom sometimes being almost a foot across and downy underneath. Flowers are fragrant, up to two inches across, and bloom most of the summer, often producing until cut down by frost. There are many yellow stamens but when fertilized, the flowers mature into dry and tasteless berries completely unlike that delicious fruit produced by many other members of the genus. The bark of the mature stem exhibits loose peeling.

Don't look for this plant at fancy nurseries; as with many of our American natives, the management often considers these shrubs too coarse for the gardening public. But those firms devoted to furthering the cause of our native flora usually carry the flowering raspberry. As to nurture, all that is needed are a good garden soil on the moist side, plenty of sun to just a bit of light shade, and watering until the plant is established. Propagation is by seed, by division (sometimes a tough job), and softwood or hardwood cuttings.

USDA Zones 3 to 7

Rudbeckia species, members of the coneflowers or black-eyed Susan clan, are flowers of the field and nonstop summer-to-fall bloomers, being as American as hot dogs, root beer, and the dog days of summer. They all have black disks surrounded by bright yellow to orange petals (really ray flowers); the plants are easily identified by their varying heights. The genus name is a salute to Olaf Rudbeck (1660-1740) and his son, both professors of botany at Upsala University in Sweden. All are tough, drought-resistant plants that revel in full sun and seem to bloom forever. In the past decade, the popularity of the coneflowers has continued to grow, especially because they work so beautifully with the many popular ornamental grasses. Whether in the formal border or the wild garden, these are workhorse flowers. They range throughout most of the Southeast. Propagation is by seed for the species and division in spring for cultivars of *Rudbeckia*.

Rudbeckia fulgida, or the orange coneflower, is a reverse carpetbagger that journeyed up to the North from the South. It's a variable perennial up to three feet tall, moderately hairy, and very stoloniferous, leading to the formation of large colonies. The flowering heads are about two inches wide, and they are very common in fields, the edges of woods, and along ditches. American goldfinches and Carolina chickadees delight in their seeds. *R. fulgida* var. *sullivantii* 'Goldsturm' has large golden-yellow flower heads from three and a half to five inches across, blooming on two-foot-high plants. This cultivar

Rudbeckia fulgida

was named the 1999 Perennial Plant of the Year. The species means the flowers are shining and brightly colored.

Rudbeckia hirta is a short-lived perennial usually from one to three feet tall, with leaves from two to seven inches long and blooming with very showy bright yellow or yellow-orange flowers with a dark brown disk. It is common to pastures, fields, abandoned land and the roadsides over much of the U.S. and southern Canada. It's well suited for the wild or meadow garden. The very popular gloriosa daisy is an offspring of this plant. The species name means "hairy," referring to the stems and leaves.

Rudbeckia laciniata, the cut-leaf coneflower, grows up to ten feet tall, having a smooth stem freely branched above and bearing two- to eight-inch leaves deeply divided and toothed. The seeds are also attractive to birds, so this species is another valuable addition to the wild garden. The bright yellow flowers can be five inches across. This native was first described way back in 1753 and is often found around old farmhouses and in abandoned gardens. The double-flowered cultivar 'Golden Glow' still survives, having been in cultivation since around 1913. Often reaching seven feet, this plant might need staking in a wet summer. There's another cultivar, introduced in 1951, known as 'Goldquelle', which rarely tops thirty inches and is not invasive. The species describes the cut leaf of this plant.

Rudbeckia triloba, the branching coneflower or the brown-eyed Susan, has two-inch blossoms of golden yellow ray flowers surrounding brown centers on stems from two to five feet tall. Again, these are short-lived perennials, often biennials, sometimes treated as annuals, that seed mightily and are excellent for naturalizing in the wild garden or at the edge of a meadow. The species name refers to the usually three-lobed leaves.

USDA Zones 4 to 11

***

Ruellia caroliniensis, the wild petunia, sometimes called the smooth ruellia, is not always at the top of the list when it comes to plant suppliers, but native plant nurseries and various seed indexes usually have one of this and the other species mentioned below. Superficially, the flowers do resemble petunias but on much taller stems. The scientific name salutes Jean Ruelle, a 16th-century French herbalist. This particular wildflower is noted here because it not only grows well in my neck of the woods but does well in the rest of the South, too. Despite its species name being a salute to the Carolinas, it's also a native of Florida. In fact plants grow naturally from New Jersey west to southern Indiana, then south to Florida and on to Texas.

Plants grow from six inches up to a foot in height with a two-foot spread. The leaves are a light green, opposite, and a little over one-half inch in length. The flowers are showy, tubular or funnel-form in shape and light purple in color. Their nectar is a favorite of butterflies. Occasionally, the gardener will spot holes bitten in the floral tube, the damage usually traced to bumblebees, which apparently delight in finding the easy, backdoor way to the nectar within.

While not described as being invasive, wild petunias do well even growing under adverse conditions, with plants adapting to partial shade and disliking full sun. Soil should be acidic and moderately moist, but the plant does best in sandy soil. If your soil is clayey, be sure to add some humus for this plant. Although having a predisposition for sandy soil, they are intolerant of salt spray and so are not meant for seaside gardening. They are moderately tolerant of drought and are found planted along stone pathways in our local botanical gardens at Asheville, as they make excellent edging plants, especially when mixed with ferns. They also adapt to hanging baskets or containers in general. Propagation is by seed, cuttings, or division in early spring or fall.

Ruellia humilis, the glade wild petunia, grows about two feet tall and has longer leaves (a little over two inches), than the species described above. *R. ciliosa*, the hairy ruellia, is similar, has a more lavender color, and really prefers a dry, sandy spot with perfect drainage and full sun.

USDA Zones 8 to 11

Ruellia caroliniensis

Salvia azurea [*S. pitcheri*], the blue sage, azure blue sage, or pitcher sage, is a relative of the sage used in cooking (S. *officinalis*), but is an erect perennial from two to five feet tall merely used for garden ornament. This genus is distinguished by flowers that bloom in a so-called "interrupted spike," that is, a number of floral clusters encircle the stalk, all occupying the upper part of that stem. The genus name is the old Latin word for "sage." The species name means "blue" and refers to the flower color. The

Salvia azurea

leaves are downy and minutely hairy, lanceolate in shape and from one to four inches long. The racemes have six to twenty flowers per node, having a slightly hairy calyx, and a corolla that varies from azure blue to white.

Plants range from Florida (except the southernmost part) to Texas, then north to North Carolina and as far west as Nebraska. As a wildflower it grows from four to six feet tall but can be pinched back to keep it shorter. It's also an excellent butterfly attractant. Plants

grow well in any garden soil with full sun or partial shade, but if your soil is un-amended clay, this sage may winterkill due to a dislike of wet, cold feet. This is also one of those plants that will not emerge until it's sure that warm weather is on the way, so be certain to mark its position well. Propagation of blue sage is by division in spring or fall, but plants are slow to recover. Cuttings from three to four inches in length can be taken in early summer.

'Nekan' is a cultivar named for a population found north of Lincoln, Nebraska, having larger flowers and a tougher constitution. As Nebraskan nurseryman Harlan Hamernik is quoted as saying: "If it'll grow in Nebraska, it'll grow anywhere!"

USDA Zones 3 to 9

Salvia lyrata, the lyre-leaf sage, is a favorite wildflower of mine. Here in the mountains it blooms along the sides of country roads, turning boring grassy areas to a sea of blue. It also usually means spring has arrived, and summer just might be down the pike—plus the flowers are very attractive. The plant was so named because the leaves are shaped like an almost forgotten musical instrument, an ancient Greek stringed instrument similar to the harp called a lyre (or sometimes, the tail feathers of a lyre bird). Unfortunately, the leaves on this plant do not really look like a lyre.

This ubiquitous plant prefers sandy soil—hence it does well on the roadside—and is found from Connecticut to Missouri and southward to Florida and Texas. The basal leaves of this plant are from four to eight inches long on stalks up to four inches long, pinnately cleft with the end lobe the largest. The terminal raceme is from six to twelve inches long and the flower clusters are set apart with, on average, six flowers per node. The inch-long corolla is tubular, and varies in color from a pale blue to lavender or sometimes white. Propagate by seed.

USDA Zones 4 to 9

Scutellaria incana, the downy or hairy skullcap, is one of a dozen or so species in the Southeast. The flowers can't be missed or misidentified since the calyx (the outer whorl of sepals covering the petals) has a hump or dish on the upper side often compared to a *galerum*, or leather skullcap worn by the Romans. The genus is named for the Latin term, *scutella*, for that dish or hump, while the species means "hoary or white," referring to the fine whitish hairs that cover the stems and leaves. This species of skullcap grows in open woods, in savannas, and along roadsides from New Jersey and New York, south to Florida and Alabama. The square stems are indicative of the mints but unlike most members of that family, the skull-

Scutellaria incana

caps have no aromatic properties, although many were used in various herbal remedies.

This skullcap reaches a height of two to four feet, bearing opposite, ovate leaves, scalloped or blunt-toothed on the margins, up to five inches long and about three inches wide, with those minute hairs on the leaf undersides. Tubular flowers are narrow, violet in color, with the upper petal having a concave cap-like structure with two smaller petal lobes. The bottom petal lobes are fused into a hanging lip. The flowers bloom in loose spikes or branched, terminal racemes. Every year this species of skullcap blooms along the wooded trails of my neighbor's garden, just below his sundial garden. They occur naturally in rocky sites, preferring a good, organic, partially shaded location with well-drained soil. They are especially beautiful when planted in drifts, a situation that has occurred naturally over at John's next door. Propagate by seed or division in spring or fall.

USDA Zones 3 to 9

Sedum ternatum, the mountain stonecrop, shepherd's-cress, or the three-leaved orpine, belongs to the Crassulaceae or live-forever family, a group known for succulent leaves and small, star-like flowers. Many species are also called live-forevers because their leaves contain so much water that in a drought they can remain viable for so long a time. The genus name is from the Latin *sedere*, "to sit," alluding to the ability of many species to exist and grow on tumbled rocks and old stone walls. The species means "having three," referring to the lower leaves, usually occurring in whorls of three. While in the North full sun is a necessary condition, here in the Southeast many sedums do quite well in the shade. And while mountain stonecrop does spread by creeping stems that root along the way, it's not at all invasive. The plants range from New York to Michigan then south to Georgia and Tennessee.

In spite of one of its common names, the leaves do not generally grow in threes; there is a cluster of about six leaves at the base of each erect branch, usually obovate (rounded ovals) and evergreen. These branches, usually prostrate, are seldom higher than six inches. The flowering stems rise above the succulent leaves, have alternate leaves that are thin and pointed, and are topped with white blossoms having five white petals, the stamens usually twice as many as the petals.

In our garden, most of the stone walls that run through shady areas are carpeted with these lovely plants. Not only are they valuable for their year-round texture, they're among those few garden denizens that I call marvel plants because they're always there, visible from the corner of your eye, and in late spring, ablaze with those starry flowers, becoming a trailing Milky Way in the garden! Any well-drained, humusy soil will do, but a rocky ledge is a plus. Propagation of sedums is by seed or division in spring or in fall.

I might mention a few more sedums that are generally not on the market but worth a search: First, *Sedum nevii*, a wildflower from the Virginia mountains with white flowers and neat little leaves is always a delight. Then, although it's an annual, look for the elf orpine (*S. smallii*), generally having red stems, little red leaves, and white flowers. And from California, *S. purdyi* [*S. spathulifolium*], having white flowers held about four inches above flat leaf rosettes, forming mats with red stolens.

USDA Zones 4 to 8

Senecio aureus

Senecio aureus, the golden ragwort, also called swamp squaw-weed, cough-weed, or grundy-swallow, is one of the first bloomers of spring not only in the garden but sometimes (it seems) in every free space the ravages of winter have opened up. The common name is not as foreboding as it sounds, because it merely means a plant with ragged leaves, and *wort* is an Old English word for "plant." Ragworts also have interesting histories, especially the belief that small fairies used ragwort stems or twigs instead of a witch's broomstick. The genus is from the Latin *senex*, for "an old man," referring to the hoariness of many species or the white hairs around the flower buds. The species name means "golden yellow."

These early spring wildflowers are found in fields, gardens, wet meadows, and the edges of swamps from our northern borders down to

Florida and Texas. Golden ragwort is a smooth perennial from one to three feet tall with long-stalked, blunt, heart-shaped basal leaves up to four inches long, often with a blue cast in early spring. The handsome flower heads are golden-yellow and about an inch wide, each flower having about eight to ten ray petals. These plants also have a long history both in folk and herbal medicine. Propagation is by seed and division.

USDA Zones 3 to 9

Silene virginica, the fire pink, sometimes called the red catchfly or the crimson campion, is a showy native wildflower of such brilliant color you can spot one bloom from a far distance. It's one of over twelve species in the genus *Silene* found in the Southeast, the rest generally having pale white flowers of the evening. The "pink" in its common name does not refer to the flower's color, but to the shape of the petals, which are often notched or "pinked." Catchfly alludes to the sticky stems that often trap small insects, thus possibly preventing undesirable insects from interfering with pollination. The genus is a salute to the mythological Silenus, the foster father of Bacchus, a name adopted by Linnaeus from earlier researchers. The species, of course, cites Virginia as the first state where this plant was cataloged.

When walking at Chimney Rock, North Carolina, in late spring, you can see sudden flashes of the hottest red stars standing out against rock backdrops, especially vibrant after a rain. The same habitat is found at the botanical gardens at Asheville, where these plants cling with great tenacity to large boulders. That's because open woods and rocky hills are the natural habitats of this extremely showy wildflower.

The weak stems have five to eight pairs of broadly lanceolate to nearly round stem leaves, about four inches long. At the top of the stem the inflorescence opens with a few tubular flowers an inch across, each blossom having five petals. In the home garden provide a well-drained, humusy soil, with "well-drained" emphasized because if the soil is cold and wet during the winter, the roots begin to rot. It's probably a good idea to mix some large stones and gravel into the soil mix. Propagate by seeds and by stem cuttings after blooming is finished.

USDA Zones 4 to 8

Sisyrinchium angustifolium, or blue-eyed grass, is one of some seventy-five species of perennial plants in this genus that are native

Sisyrinchium angustifolium

to the Western Hemisphere, closely resembling grasses but really members of the iris family. The genus is taken from an old word used by Theophrastus for "a bulbous plant," which this is. The species means the plant has narrow leaves. Those leaves are glaucous to dark green, stiffly upright, and fine in texture, usually growing to a length of four to eight inches. The flowers are six-petaled, varying in color from a pale blue to violet—rarely white—about one-half-inch wide. The fruits appear in summer. These plants do best in full sun to partial shade, preferring good, moist, well-drained soil.

When massed, they are attractive in leaf but even more charming in bloom. Naturalizing with ease, blue-eyed grasses look great in the rock garden or the wild garden, gracing the border, or allowed to naturalize in the lawn—thus cutting back on mowing. The cultivar 'Lucerne' bears larger flowers—three-fourths-inch wide—of a rich bluish-purple, flowering from May to July. Plants are eight inches tall. Propagation is by seed or division.

USDA zones 5 to 10

Smilacina racemosa, often called the false Solomon's-seal, should really be known as Solomon's-plume, as there is nothing phony about this plant. Other common names to choose from are the wild spikenard and Solomon's-zig-zag. It's not only tough, but it's also beautiful in flower and in fruit. The genus name is adapted from *smilax*, a term used early in the 1700s by Joseph Pitton de Tournefort (1656-1708), a French botanist who developed a theory of botanical classification based on the shape of the flower, which was superceded by Linneaus. The species means the flowers bloom in a raceme.

This lovely wildflower ranges from Quebec to British Columbia, then south to Virginia, Tennessee, and Missouri.

The common name of false Solomon's-seal is based on the familiarity of the leaves to that plant. But they are not at all alike when the flowers appear. The lance-shaped alternate leaves are between three and six inches long, finely hairy underneath and are arranged along the two- to three-foot stems. The flowers are white or a greenish-white, slightly fragrant, blooming in a densely flowered terminal raceme. There are six stamens in each flower, giving a foamy look to the bloom. The fruit is a cluster of round, aromatic, pale red, speckled berries. Finally, if you compare the roots of the two species, Solomon's-plume has no scars on the rhizomes.

Solidago species

To plant this lovely native, start with a shady spot with decent soil, then add plenty of humus. When established, Solomon's-plume is fairly drought-resistant, but remember to add additional water when summers are dry. Otherwise the leaves of this plant look rather worn by the time fall approaches. Some gardeners advise having three or four plants in order to guarantee the formation of fruit. Many Amerindians used this plant for food, utilizing everything from the rhizomes to the fresh spring leaves to the berries, but all had to be cooked to make them palatable. Cooked rhizomes were also used medicinally as a poultice. Propagation is by seeds separated from the pulp and sown immediately or by division in spring or fall.

USDA Zones 4 to 10

Solidago species, a group of plants known as the goldenrods, have borne the brunt of bad press for centuries. Every autumn local TV stations warn against the hay fever season and blame the blooming goldenrods for the problem when the real culprit is ragweed pollen. Ragweed's tiny green flowers are missed by most observers, but goldenrod, with its bright golden-yellow blossoms is easily spotted, so goldenrod gets the blame. Goldenrod's genus is from the Latin *solido*, "to make whole," from its supposed healing qualities. Not only are goldenrods perfectly acceptable plants for the perennial bed or border, they are excellent as cut flowers and very attractive in late fall after the flowers have faded and gone to seed. And they naturalize in the wild garden. If taller plants are not wanted, cut them to about a foot high in early summer and they grow back shorter and bushier. Many of the larger goldenrods will move forward in the garden with wandering roots and once on

the march are difficult to control, so take care. Propagation of goldenrods is generally by division in spring or fall.

USDA Zones 3 to 9

Solidago canadensis, common or field goldenrod, is one of the plants often used by hybridizers; *Index Hortensis* alone lists thirty cultivars. Plants are found throughout the Southeast, even to northern Florida. Height can go up to ten feet or more (tall goldenrod, once called S. *altissima*, is now in this genus). Some selections include 'Golden Baby', a compact plant about two feet high; 'Golden Dwarf' with bright yellow flowers on foot-high stems; and 'Cloth of Gold', with golden-yellow blossoms on eighteen-inch stems.

Solidago odora, sweet goldenrod, is also called the anise-scented goldenrod, and when compared to the others in commerce, is a real old-fashioned lady in the garden. Small clusters of yellow flowers bloom on a slender wand-like stem, from two to four feet high. The dried leaves furnish a pleasant tea when steeped in hot water. This plant needs a well-drained, sandy soil and plenty of sun, but shade at noon.

Solidago rigida, stiff goldenrod, bears flat-topped golden-yellow flower clusters on top of perfectly upright stems and is especially suited to massing in the wild garden. Height varies from two to five feet. Provide partial shade or partial sun to full sun in soil ranging from dry to moist.

Solidago rugosa bears thin sprays of arching flowering stems at the top of sturdy, erect, two-to five-foot-high stems. The numerous, narrow, toothed leaves are rough-surfaced, with plants growing in clumps (the species name refers to the wrinkled stems). While the species is best for the wild garden there is a great cultivar called 'Fireworks', discovered in a parking lot mear Raleigh, North Carolina. It grows between three and four feet tall with golden-yellow flowers on arching stems, forming a plant that lives up to its name. Plant in full sun and it will not range out of the garden.

Solidago sempervirens, the seaside golden-rod, has fleshy, waxy leaves to protect it from salt spray, thus this stately plant is unexcelled for seaside gardens throughout the Southeast, even through most of Florida. The species means "evergreen." Individual flower heads are larger than the typical goldenrod. Height is from one to eight feet. Like most of the genus, it blooms in the fall.

Spigelia marilandica, the Indian pink, also boasts two other common names, pinkroot and wormgrass. It's one of those simply beautiful flowers that prompts everybody who sees it blooming to stop whatever he or she is saying and simply confront beauty! And it's interesting to note that the genus is named in honor of Adrian Spiegel (1578-1625), an Italian physician who, according to legend, was the first man to give instructions for preparing a herbarium. Linnaeus doled out the honors and, like many of his choices, named the species after Maryland, although the plant is not native to that state.

This perennial grows from about one to three feet tall with opposite leaves, narrowly or broadly lance-shaped, from two to five inches long. The flowers are borne in a one-sided cyme with the terminal flower opening first,

their shape being tubular. Flowers are up to two and a half inches long, scarlet red outside and greenish-yellow inside, the five pointed lobes of the tube showing the interior's chartreuse tints. With such an ostentatious color combination it's no surprise that hummingbirds dote on this flower. In fact, Indian pink is on the list of the top ten native plants that attract the ruby-throated hummingbird (*Archilochus colubris*), as listed in a survey done by the Hilton Pond Center for Piedmont Natural History in York, South Carolina, (www.rubythroat.org). The complete list is:

Bee-Balm (*Monarda didyma*)
Canada Lily (*Lilium canadense*)
Cardinal Flower (*Lobelia cardinalis*)
Indian Pink (*Spigelia marilandica*)
Red Buckeye (*Aesculus pavia*)
Red Columbine (*Aquilegia canadensis*)

Spigelia marilandica

Rosebay Rhododendron (*Rhododendron catawbiense*)

Spotted Jewelweed (*Impatiens capensis*)

Trumpet Creeper (*Campsis radicans*)

Trumpet Honeysuckle (*Lonicera sempervirens*)

In addition to being one for the birds, this plant also has an interesting medical history because the Amerindians used the yellow roots as an anthelmintic, a rather polite way of describing a medicine used to expel intestinal worms. As with many herbal remedies, the chemicals in this plant are highly toxic, perhaps fatal, if consumed in large doses. Once again it's Beauty and the Beast. Indian pinks want a fertile, well-drained soil in light shade to partial sun. If grown in full sun the soil must be evenly moist. Propagation is by seed and the plants often self-sow, or by division in early spring or early fall.

USDA Zones 5 to 9

Spiranthes cernua

Spiranthes cernua forma *odorata* 'Chadds Ford' is a native orchid of great beauty discovered by Dick Ryan, a citizen of Bear, Delaware, just as its habitat was about to fall victim to the great American rush to housing. Described by Barry Glick as being a rural crossroads back in the 1960s, the area where Ryan found this distinctive orchid is now overrun by tract homes. The Chadds Ford orchid is a fragrant member of the nodding ladies tresses, a lovely genus of orchids whose name is from the Greek *speira*, for "a coil" or "a spiral," and *anthos* or "flower," referring to the blossoms that twist up the flowering stalk exactly like a woman's hair bound into braids. The species means "waxy" and refers again to the flowers. Some members of the genus are called nodding ladies tresses because the individual flowers have a habit of nodding on the flower spike.

This downy perennial has three to six basal leaves from two to eight inches long, being a pleasant green and soft in texture. The flowering spike is usually between four and sixteen inches tall and the top is crowded with up to sixty fragrant, somewhat nodding, white flowers about a half-inch long.

'Chadds Ford' is a very fragrant form of the species, usually found in coastal regions of the southeastern states ranging from Virginia to Florida and west to Texas. Fragrance is one of this plant's distinctive qualities as its very strong perfume is redolent with vanilla or jasmine, depending on the nasal proclivities of the gardener. It was named in honor of Chadds Ford, a town in southeast Pennsylvania.

These orchids have thick roots, which are almost tuber-like, and in colder areas they are somewhat deciduous, as the leaves usually drop for the winter, returning in early spring. They are fall-bloomers and, in really warm places like Florida, can bloom in January. Provide a good, rich soil that is evenly moist. Propagate usually by the spreading stolons unless you wish an adventure, then seed may be the way to travel.

USDA Zones 4 to 10

Stokesia laevis

Stokesia laevis, Stokes' aster, sometimes called the cornflower aster, is a monotypic genus (it has only one species), known for its lovely flowers and its long period of bloom. While relatively rare in the wild, gardeners became fond of them up years ago and today most knowledgeable garden centers carry these flowers. The genus was named after the English physician and botanist, Jonathan Stokes, a friend of Linnaeus' son. Stokes' aster is native to the southeastern coastal plains from South Carolina to northern Florida, then west to Louisiana, where it's found in wetlands, including areas where pitcher plants abound. The seeds contain a high volume of an epoxy fatty acid known as vernolic acid and can be used in the manufacture of plastics, varnishes, and various super glues.

Plants grow between eight inches to almost two feet, having a wooly stem and a number of lanceolate basal leaves up to ten inches long with a few clasping, somewhat ruffled leaves on the stems. The fluffy blue to lavender flowers are from two to five inches across on well-branched stems. Arrangers of dried flowers value the thistly seedpods as well as the flowers. Pinching back the spent blossoms extends an already long period of bloom. Provide a well-drained, but moist garden loam in mostly full sun, and never add lime, as these plants dote on acidic soil. The soil should be dry through the winter. These plants are easily grown from seed and there's always considerable variation in color. Propagate cultivars by division in late winter or early spring, dividing the root clumps.

There are many cultivars on the market including 'Blue Moon' with deep blue flowers; 'Bluestone', a smaller plant with regular flowers; 'Mary Gregory' blooming with creamy yellow flowers; 'Rosea' bearing rosy-pink blossoms; 'Alba' is white; and 'Silver Moon' has larger silver-white blossoms.

USDA Zones 5 to 10 (needing protective mulch in a Zone 5 or 6 winter)

Stylophorum diphyllum, the celandine poppy, or sometimes the woodpoppy, is another

Stylophorum diphyllum

into five to seven oblong segments. True poppy that it is, the flowers have four yellow petals born in a terminal cluster of three or four flowers. The seedpods are egg-shaped, about an inch long and covered with silvery hairs. Occasionally, in a good year when rain is plentiful without flooding, some plants will provide a second bloom. If the earth is dry, the plants fade with the advance of summer heat, but in areas where moisture is available, the plants continue growing for a longer time.

The plant's acrid juice has a long history of use in treating diseases of the eye. Back in ancient Rome, Pliny reported that swallows discovered this. Provide a good, rich, humusy, evenly moist soil in partial shade. Propagation is by seed sown as soon as it's collected and division in spring and fall.

USDA Zones 4 to 8.

one of those native plants that many garden writers and dealers in wildflowers seem to overlook. Hundreds of these plants bloom every spring on a hillside near the side door of the botanical gardens at Asheville, turning the entire slope into a sea of golden-yellow. During the Middle Ages another European poppy, known as the greater celandine, was a major drug plant. It was called *Chelidonium* from the Greek *chelidon*, "a swallow" (the English being a corruption of the Greek), because it bloomed when swallows arrived and went to seed at their departure. The genus name is from the Greek *stylos*, or "style," and *phoros*, "bearing," alluding to the long style, one of the more distinctive characteristics of this plant. The species refers to the pair of stem leaves just below the flowers.

The plants have rhizomes, containing a saffron-colored juice, that give rise to several gray-green basal leaves and flowering stems with paired leaves, individual plants being about a foot high. The leaves are deeply lobed

Tephrosia virginiana, Virginia tephrosia, also has a number of other common names including goat's-rue, rabbit's-pea, and devil's-shoe-strings, not to mention catgut. Not only is this wildflower a host for the southern cloudy wing butterfly caterpiller (*Thorybes bathyllus*)—a medium-sized dark brown skipper with a fast, erratic flight—it's a minor source of rotenone, fairly organic insecticide, once used by the Amerindians to stun fish. The common names of this plant hint at its use in many recipes for witchcraft, including the long stringy roots supposedly used to lace up the devil's shoes (and "catgut," too). The genus is from the Greek word *tephros*, meaning "hoary" or "the color of ash," referring to the downy hairs that cover the plant, giving it a decidedly silvery aspect. Plants range from New York and New England west to Iowa, then south to Tennessee, Georgia, and most of the Southeast.

This is an erect perennial with a number of stems from twelve to almost thirty inches in height. The leaves are alternate and pinnately compound, each having from fifteen to twenty-five elliptical leaflets. Bi-colored, pea-like flowers bloom at the top of the stem, each about three-fourths-inch long with pale standards on top and pink to pale purple united petals (or keels) below. The fruits are whitish hairy pods, up to two inches long. Plants bloom from mid-May to August.

These plants are found naturally in the acidic soils of open woods and rocky glens and because of their long taproot (making them very drought-resistant), very difficult to transplant. They want full sun to partial shade and very well-drained soil, and have a penchant for sandy sites. Because of its tenacious roots, Amerindian women used a mixture containing this plant to wash their hair, hoping to prevent broken ends and strengthen the follicles. Athletes would use this same solution to strengthen their legs for various contests. Such decoctions were also used to treat urinary problems and as a vermifuge. Propagation is by seed but germination is sporadic so sow more than just a few.

USDA Zones 5 to 10

Thermopsis villosa [T. caroliniana], known as Aaron's rod in the Southeast and Carolina lupine in general, is (when in bloom) one of those spectacular plants that no garden should be without. The genus is Greek for "like a lupine," referring to the usual pea-like flowers found in most of the large-flowering ornamentals belonging to the great family of Fabaceae or the legumes. The common name of Aaron's rod is just another example of the biblical heritage ascribed to many wildflowers native to the Southeast. The tall stem, often over three feet high, begins its blooming with dozens of golden yellow flowers that open from bottom to top, over a few weeks eventually becoming a tall staff of furry, gray seedpods. This metamorphosis of a golden rod into an erect gray column was thought to resemble the transformation of Aaron's rod into a serpent, hence a horticultural reference to the Flight from Egypt.

Today it's a rainy day in early June but shining through the gloom I spy a large bouquet of Aaron's rod brought to us over a week ago by Holly Walker from her Spruce Pine garden. Every morning it continues to open new blossoms with their golden-yellow. Obviously, they make great cut flowers. The furry gray seedpods look like

Thermopsis villosa

small string beans and have been used for years in many craft projects. Plants closely resemble *Baptisia* except for the smaller pods. The trifoliate leaves are a fresh green and unlike *Baptisia*, do not turn black when touched by frost. It is native to much of the Southeast ranging from the Virginias, then south to northern Georgia.

When provided with a well-drained rich soil a clump of thermopsis can reach a height of five feet but usually logs in between three and four feet. While plants can adapt to full sun, this long-live perennial does best with a bit of shade, especially in the noonday sun. While native to the North Carolina mountains, *Thermopsis* does very well in the Piedmont and Coastal Plain. Seasoned gardeners suggest cutting back the stems about a month after flowering as a precaution against stem borers. Because plants resent root disturbance and mature with large root systems, they are difficult to transplant. Once sited they should be left done. Propagation is by fresh seed or division in early spring.

USDA Zones 3 to 9

Tiarella cordifolia

Tiarella cordifolia, the foam-flower, is an attractive plant both in and out of flower. It's a creeping perennial with maple-like leaves ranging throughout the country, both near and far. The genus name is Latin for "little tiara" in a salute to the fruits (Linneaus was known for such botanical fancies), tiaras being the headdress of the classical Persians. The species name refers to the heart-shaped leaves. The common name reflects the look of the foamy stamens. The range is from Nova Scotia south to Georgia. In appearance these are very delicate plants rarely more than a foot high. The underground rhizomes produce basal leaves only, broadly heart-shaped, from two to four inches

long, and in spring the flowers bloom in a raceme about four inches long on a leafless stalk up to fourteen inches high. The five petals are white with numerous yellow anthers, sometimes with a slight pinkish cast. There were medicinal uses for this plant including a tea that Amerindians used as a mouthwash and to treat eye discomforts.

Plant foam-flowers in partial shade using a soil that is evenly moist and high in organic matter. The moisture is necessary as the plants are not drought-tolerant. Using a few rocks at the site helps to maintain a cool root run. If the plant appreciates its site, there will soon be a colony of foam-flowers thanks to wandering rhizomes. Propagate foam-flower by seed sown in fall and by division in spring.

There is another Southern species, *Tiarella wherryi*, that ranges from Virginia and Tennessee to Georgia and Mississippi. The leaf blades are longer than they are broad and the petals are narrower. There is also a hybrid produced by crossing *Tiarella* with *Heuchera*, resulting in a bigeneric hybrid known as a *Heucherella*. It has characteristics intermediate between the two parents. Unfortunately, as a hybrid (and one created in Europe), it doesn't fit into this book.

USDA Zones 3 to 9

Tradescantia virginiana, the spiderwort, was on its way to English gardens in the mid-1600s, sent there by John Tradescant (hence the genus name), who was a subscriber to the Virginia Company (hence the species name), and the first gardener to grow this plant in cul-

Tradescantia virginiana

tivation. Spiderworts have flowers that last only a day, but are replaced by new blossoms over a long period of time. The hairs on the stamens have long been used in botany classes, because each stamen is composed of a line of single cells easily observed while still living, hence you see the flow of protoplasm in the individual cell. It is these hairs that give the plant the common name of spiderwort (*wort* being the old English word for plant).

Along with lilacs, ribbon grass (*Phalaris arundinacea* var. *picta*), and a number of shrub roses, spiderworts are often found in abandoned gardens. The three petals are usually shades of purple and blue, but today even rose, pink, and white cultivars are offered by the nursery trade. Narrow, sword-shaped, but floppy, leaves arise from succulent stems, and plants range between one and two feet in height. Although able to take full sun, spiderworts will adapt to partial shade in the Southeast and are not only handsome border plants, but very effective when planted against walls. After flowering is over, the leaves become lax and even more floppy, so shear them back almost to the ground for a second, but sparser, show of flowers. Propagation is by division.

Unless acquired from the wild or a bono fide wildflower nursery, the plants sold today are usually a series of hybrids (*Tradescantia* × *andersoniana*), produced with *T. virginiana* and a number of other wild species, and registered in 1954. Today there are more than thirty cultivars. Choices include 'Snow Cap', with pure white flowers on twenty-inch stems; 'Valor' bearing deep reddish purple flowers, also on twenty-inch stems; 'Pauline', having pink flowers on twelve-inch stems; and recently 'Concord Grape', a new cultivar growing about eighteen inches high, its dark bluish-green leaves in a lovely contrast to the beautiful purple flowers.

Tradescantia ohiensis has a whitish bloom on the smooth stems and leaves, and often reaches a height of four feet but is generally much shorter. The half-inch-long petals vary from shades of blue to rose. It's found from our northern range south to Florida and Texas. The cultivar 'Mrs. Loewer' has pale blue flowers above thin, grassy foliage with a blue sheen, the plants being about thirty inches high.

USDA Zones 3 to 9

Trillium grandiflorum, the great showy trillium, also known as the trinity-lily, is the most flagrantly beautiful of an amazing genus of native wildflowers. Today, we recognize some forty-eight species, the majority found in North America, with most species located east of the Rocky Mountains, ranging from the Great Lakes down to Florida. From North America the trilliums jump to Japan, China, Korea, the Himalayas, and Siberia, skipping Europe completely. It's part of the floral disjunction theory (see the entry for *Diphylleia cymosa*). The genus refers to the plant having three petals, three sepals, and three leaflets, named by Linnaeus from three North American samples that he examined. The species salutes the beautiful flower. The Asian species are generally more interesting than beautiful (except for the lovely and fragrant *Trillium kamtschaticum*).

No American woodland garden that grows native wildflowers can be without a few of these flowers. Remember that if the flowering stalk is picked, unless there is a very mature rhizome beneath the earthen floor, the plant often dies since its source of food (the foliage which collects and converts sunlight to energy) has been removed. There's a hillside in western North Carolina called Max Patch, and when it's in

Trillium grandiflorum

bloom with these great showy trilliums, there are few words in the English language to describe their beauty. These flowers are spring ephemerals, blooming in early spring and ripening for the next year's season as the leaves come out on the woodland trees above, then disappearing during summer's heat. But even with the heat there are trilliums quite at home in USDA Zone 9 of North Florida.

This is an erect perennial with three whorled, green leaves, broadly oval in shape, from three to five inches long. The flower is borne on a single stalk, from two to three inches above the leaves; its three-petaled white blossom has prominent yellow anthers. The petals change from white to pink with age. There is a rare double called 'Smith's Double'. When planting these wildflowers remember they need filtered sunlight (a network of overhead branches will do) and very good, evenly moist to only moderately dry soil, amended with humus. A few rocks buried beneath the rhizomes are always a good idea, as this keeps the root run on the cool side.

Propagation is by seed—the seeds generally distributed by ants attracted to chemicals in the seed coat—and by division when dormant. But be warned, to grow these beauties from seed takes about six years before they reach flowering size. Sow seeds immediately after collecting—if allowed to dry out they will take even longer to germinate.

Among the other beautiful members of this genus, look for sweet Betsy (*Trillium cuneatum*), with lovely mottled leaves and petals of a bronzy-maroon (USDA Zones 5 to 8); the yellow trillium (*T. luteum*), like sweet Betsy but with yellow petals; twisted trillium (*T. stamineum*), has flowers with twisted maroon petals—and an unpleasant odor (USDA Zones 5-8); the Southern red trillium (*T. sulcatum*), with petals of deep maroon; the painted trillium (*T. undulatum*), having petals streaked with a soft line of light red near the base; and *T. underwoodii*, from southern Alabama.

USDA Zones 4 to 9 (depending on the species)

Uvularia grandiflora, also known as bellwort, strawbell, or, the name I like best, great merrybells, is a member of the lily family and is a lovely wildflower for the shady garden. The scientific name was bestowed by Linnaeus and, in the words of Neltje Blanchan, "Hanging like a palate (*uvula*) from the roof of a mouth, according to the imaginative Linnaeus, the little bellwort droops, and so modestly hides behind the leaf its footstalk pierces that the eye often fails to find it when so many more showy blossoms arrest attention in the May woods. Slight fragrance helps to guide the keen bum-

blebee to the pale yellow bell." So the genus is named after the human uvula in the back of the throat and the species merely signifies that the flower is especially grand.

A mature clump of these plants in flower is a sight to be seen and luckily we have a fairly cool spring, so great merrybells does very well in our garden. This is a clump-forming perennial with prominent rhizomatous roots. The farther south you garden, the more important it is to find a cool place for its home.

The ovate-lanceolate leaves are a medium green, between five and six inches long and two to four inches wide, and, in the words of the botanist, perfoliate, or, they are wrapped around the stem. The two-inch-long pendant flowers are born in pairs or singly, tubular or bell-shaped, their twisted petals (really tepals) are yellow in color, sometimes with just a touch of green, blooming in mid- to late spring. When amending the site for growing these beauties,

Uvularia grandiflora

114

remember that air circulation and much shade, plus a good deal of humus in the soil, are necessary. The roots also dislike really acidic soil so marble-chip mulches are a great help in adjusting soil chemistry.

Uvularia perfoliata has forking stems up to twenty inches tall, and the main stem appears to go directly through each leaf, hence the species name. *U. sessile*, or wild-oats, is shorter, and has smaller, usually solitary, pale yellow flowers and, like others of the clan, eventually makes a nice patch of plants. The species name refers to the structure of the anthers. Both species want acidic soil. Propagation is by seed usually sown in the fall, but it takes three to four years for mature plants, or by division in spring or in fall.

USDA Zones 3 to 9

Verbena canadensis

Verbena canadensis, the rose verbena, belongs to the vervain family, and is part of a large genus with many members native to temperate and tropical America. This particular species is very showy and does very well in Southeastern gardens and rock gardens. The perennial species should not be confused with the weedy garden annual, *V. bonariensis* (the species referring to Buenos Aires, Argentina), introduced for garden use and now an escapee into the wild. The derivation of the genus is from ancient Rome and the name of a ceremonial crown made of laurel, olive, and myrtle, but the connection is obscure; vervain is from the Celtic word *fer*, for "away," and *faen*, for "stone," an allusion to a former use in the treatment of bladder stones. As to the species, in this case the plant was named centuries ago when Canada was accorded more landmass than today. Plants range from southern New England, west to Colorado, and south to Florida.

Rose verbena is a semievergreen, erect to clambering plant with a hairy stem and three-inch, toothed, opposite leaves, the stems topped with dense, terminal, flat-topped clusters of up to twenty flowers. The color is pinkish lavender and the tubular flowers have a flared end divided into five lobes. Blooming usually begins in late spring and continues into mid-fall.

The cultivar 'Homestead Purple' is a lesson in always looking down. Dr. Allan Armitage of the University of Georgia discovered this in a patch of weeds on the side of a Georgia country road. The plant bears large clusters of velvety purple flowers that bloom throughout the summer until frost stops activity. The mildew-resistant foliage is dark green above and gray-green below; except for really cold areas,

Verbena 'Homestead Purple'

Plants can reach a height of ten feet, so it's not exactly meant for setting next to a much shorter plant like a blue sage or a daisy. The leaves are alternate, about eight inches long, lanceolate and toothed, and they extend down the stem, forming a wing. The bright yellow flowers resemble large daisies with drooping (or reflexed) ray petals and a globular disk. Each flower is about three inches wide, and they can number in the hundreds, beginning to bloom in midsummer and on into late September and October.

Provide a good, well-drained garden soil because in nature these plants are found in moist thickets, open fields, and along the road-sides. Propagate by seed.

USDA Zones 5 to 9

the plants are evergreen. Both the species and its cultivar are effective ground covers that only ask for a good, well-drained garden soil, and a spot in full sun. Propagation is by seed, division, or stem cuttings.

USDA Zones 6 to 10

Verbisina alternifolia [*Actinomeris alternifolia*], wingstem, is usually described as a coarse perennial and I'd be the last person to suggest planting it in the formal border. But in the wild garden this is a fine native wildflower, especially for vibrant fall color. It's also visible growing along the interstates of the Southeast in late September. The genus name is thought to be the result of a printer's error, after Linneaus named it for *Forbesina*, or a misspelling of *Verbena*; either way, it stuck. The species refers to the alternate leaves. The natural distribution of wingstem ranges from New York west to Iowa, then south to Louisiana and the Florida Panhandle.

Vernonia species, the ironweeds, are mostly handsome plants of imposing stature and marvelous floral color; a color, by the way, that successfully eludes film cameras. Garden photographers have often noted that certain blues and purples found in nature turn to pink when the film is developed. As far as I know the cause is unknown. But, hey, wheels that always turned backward in movie film now turn in the right direction thanks to computers; perhaps digital cameras will finally present purple flowers in their correct shade. The genus is named in honor of William Vernon (d. 1711), an English botanist who collected in Maryland in the late 1600s.

One of the stories explaining the common name of ironweed reports the plants doing well in areas of old fires, especially with rusted metal nearby. Others report that the "iron" in ironweed refers to the tall and sturdy stems, while still others remark that pulling this plant up by the roots is nothing shore of battling a plant with a will of iron. Hardy from Maine to North Florida, various members of the genus grow from three to ten feet in height, crowned with lovely, deep-purple, aster-like flowers. They are spectacular fall-blooming plants perfect for the wild garden or even the back of a designed border. Ironweeds are also powerful butterfly magnets, with tiger swallowtails having a special preference for the flowers. These plants are usually found in moist or wet areas of fields, pastures, or abandoned land. Propagate ironweeds by seed or by division.

Vernonia altissima, or tall ironweed, often tops ten feet, with ten-inch-long toothed lanceolate leaves coming to a point. There are multiple flower heads with a few flowers in each, their color purple with yellow discs. Plants range from our northern borders south to Georgia and Louisiana. The species means "tallest."

Vernonia gigantea, is another tall ironweed, this time usually reaching a seven-foot height. Again the flowers are borne in loose clusters with from fifteen to thirty purple flowers in each. Again the range is from the northern borders down to Florida and Texas. The species means "giant."

Vernonia noveboracensis, or the New York ironweed, has a stout but smooth, downy stem bearing numerous lanceolate leaves, their edges toothed. There are from thirty to fifty flowers in a floral head. They range from the coast of Massachusetts down to Georgia, then west to Mississippi.

USDA Zones 5 to 9

Veronicastrum virginicum

Veronicastrum virginicum, or culver's root, is one of those wildflowers always at the back of my mind since Bebe Miles first introduced the plant to my Northern garden back in 1975. It wasn't until I was one of three tour guides on a 2002 *Carolina Gardener* trip to Scotland, and saw just what a bed of these beauties could be, that, upon returning home, I immediately brought them to my humble border. Culver's root was named after an early American physician who used the plant as a cathartic and emetic. The generic name comes from the genus *Veronica*; the suffix *astrum* indicates a resemblance to the speedwells or veronicas.

This is a beautiful perennial worthy of far more garden attention than it generally gets. Several long wands of tiny white flowers bloom on top of stems that range from three to five feet in height. The leaves vary in length from two to six inches, are finely toothed, and grow in whorls of three to six. The flowers have a tubular corolla, only three-tenths of an inch long, with two protuberant stamens. But in unity there is strength and the total effect of so many tiny flowers is one of great beauty.

While the plants will adapt to some shade, they do better with plenty of sun and in my garden are in sunlight from about 10:00 in the morning until 3:30 in the afternoon. Although older garden books talk about keeping this plant in scale, in Scottish gardens they are grown in large clumps, usually next to exotic plants like ligularias and various summer bulbs. Be sure to deadhead the plants in order to keep them blooming for most of the summer. Provide a good and rich soil, with plenty of moisture. Propagation is by seed and by division in spring or in fall.

USDA Zones 4 to 8

Viola pedata, the bird's-foot violet, is the only member of the violet family that appears in this book. Before the First World War, violets were the most popular flower a man could give his ladylove; in My Fair Lady Eliza Doolittle started out by selling the sweet-smelling Viola odorata in London's Covent Garden and look what that led to. But that means naught to me because the violets of America often run amuck, as suggested by Doretta Klaber, who wrote in Violets of the United States (New York: A. S. Barnes and Company, 1976), "With all the violets there are so many ifs and buts. You will look in vain in the book for many violets you may have come across in your wanderings. There will be different cutting or toothing of the leaves; there will be . . . many colors or shades of colors of the flowers, and sometimes of the leaves of a given species." And again in the words of

Mrs. Klaber: "This gorgeous violet is unmistakable." The scientific name of Viola comes from the Greek ion for "violet," the Latin viola, and the French violette. The species means "palmate."

The bird's-foot violet gets its common name from the resemblance of those palmate basal leaves to a bird's foot. The purple or lilac pansy-like flowers are often as large as one-and-a-half inches across, floating above the low tuft of finely cut foliage. Its natural range is from our northern borders, west to Kansas and south to Georgia and Texas. While the plants generally bloom in the spring, they often produce repeat blooms during the summer or fall.

In addition to being a most beautiful violet, this species also has a fondness for sun. It also wants a more acidic soil than most of its cousins, and unless you have the proper soil, you should prepare a special place for this beauty. First make a slightly raised bed using rocks, not railroad ties or bricks, for your edging. Then add sharp sand or builder's sand along with sphagnum peat, say one- to two-thirds, into your existing soil and mulch the crowns with pine needles after planting.

Unlike other violets, the bird's-foot will not produce cleistogamous seeds (those pesky seeds formed underground in closed flowers that make many violets so invasive), so if you want them to spread, don't pick the flowers. Propagation is by seed.

USDA Zones 4 to 9

Wisteria frutescens, the American wisteria, is admittedly a vine but a beautiful vine and when compared to its thug cousins from the Orient, is one great addition to any Southeastern garden. Want to witness a vine that can

Wisteria frutescens

will adapt to most soils but prefer a soil rich in organic matter and moist but well-drained. Once established, American wisterias are fairly drought-resistant. Also, like most wild plants, fertilizer is not needed. Unless you want to grow some from seed, remove the pods because that drain on the system is not needed.

As to deportment, try to guide the vines in the direction you wish them to go, using nails or lead hook attachments to encourage them up stone walls. When autumn appears, you can easily see the direction of the vines and they are easily moved to where you want them to go. In my garden, they clamber over a large weeping juniper (seven feet tall), then amble through various hydrangea bushes. Propagation is by seed, or just purchase container-grown plants and set them out in spring or fall.

USDA 6 to 9, possibly 10

twist a metal post or strangle a tree to death? Then treat yourself to the dangerous beauty of the imports. But if you want a vine that can actually be moved from support to support, then buy American. As a genus, *Wisteria* was named in honor of Caspar Wistar (1761-1818), Professor of Anatomy at the University of Pennsylvania. The species means this vine becomes shrubby in appearance.

Our American wisteria is a woody, deciduous vine, high- or low-climbing depending on its position, with alternate, pinnately compound leaves, and usually six leaflet pairs. The leaflets are dark green above and light green below. The many flowers bloom in bunches, or more accurately, compact racemes, averaging about six inches in length, the colors being purple and white. These vines bloom at a younger age than the Asian species and later in the season, only budding after the leaves have unfurled. Plants

Xerophyllum asphodeloides, called bear grass, turkey-beard, or mountain asphodel, is a fantastic plant that looks for all the world like a beautiful and incredibly healthy mountain grass until it sends up its many-flowered stem. The genus name is from the Greek *xeros*, or "arid," and *phyllon*, for "leaf," referring to the dry leaves found on this plant. The species name reflects the resemblance of the blossoms to the plant asphodel. There is another species, *X. tenax*, known as the Indian basket grass, native to the West Coast from central California and north.

These spectacular plants range from our northern borders to the mountainous woods of Virginia, then south Georgia and Tennessee. Stems are up to four feet tall and topped with light green, grass-like leaves that form dense tufts of growth, about six inches long at the top

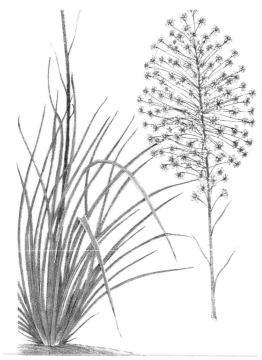

Xerophyllum asphodeloides

generic name is from the Greek *xyris*, a plant with two-edged leaves, that name coming from the Greek *xyron*, or "razor." The species name is Greek for "dwelling in sand."

Plants have fine-textured leaves of gray or bluish-green, very narrow, up to sixteen inches long. When in flower, spirally twisted stems (or scapes) grow a little over two feet high topped with scale-like bracts, not unlike tiny pine cones, that give rise to half-inch-wide, three-petaled flowers. While not exactly show-stoppers, yellow-eyed are grasses a delight growing and naturalizing at the edges of bogs or small pools.

Xyris fimbriata, another yellow-eyed grass, is a larger species with leaves up to four feet high and yellow flowers (the bracts are fringed, hence the species name, from the Latin *fimbriae*, meaning "fringe"). This, too, is a plant for naturalizing in low, wet, but sandy sites. Propagation for *Xyris* species is by seed or by division.

USDA Zones 6 to 10

of the mound and over six inches long at the base. They grow in the mountains around Asheville, especially on mountain summits, where the drainage is close to perfect, and at the edge of bogs. I've found them growing in the mountains where the plants are buffeted by weather, in full sun, or even partial shade. Propagation is by division or by seed.

USDA Zones 5 to 9

Xyris arenicola, or yellow-eyed grass, is one of several species of *Xyris* in North America. These plants are tufted herbs with decidedly rush-like basal leaves, and they are usually taken for a rush or a grass until they bloom. The

Yucca filamentosa, the common yucca or Adam's needle, is an American native plant with a great deal of history and many uses in the garden. The most popular name for this species is biblical, referring to Adam being the first (or second) needle-smith, because the leaves come to a sharp point and the edges throw off numerous fine white hairs that are the thickness of buttonhole thread. *Yucca* is based on the Spanish *yucca*, a word for manioc (*Manihot esculenta*), a major source for the bitter cassava, the name of which is based on a Taino Indian word for this plant. The species name refers to the loose fibers on the leaf margins.

Yucca filamentosa

in dry, sandy, or rocky habitats, on banks overlooking back-country roads and at the edges of open woods. Yuccas have naturalized far outside their original range. Because a well-grown plant will often be over three feet in diameter, these are not for the small garden. But the plant form plus the interesting seedpods make yuccas valuable additions to a landscape that has the space to hold them. Use these plants with plenty of rocks or in groups of three or more. Gravel mulch is more in keeping with the look of the plant than leaf mulch or peat moss (always a no-no because it's either too wet or too dry). Once established, yuccas will perform every year regardless of how little rain might fall because they have a very deep taproot. Propagation is by seed or by root cuttings. Offsets from the main plant, with some root adhering, can also be cut off and propagated.

There are many cultivars, including 'Color Guard', thirty inches tall and thirty inches wide with clumps of green-striped leaves and a wide band of yellow that turns a creamy-gold in midsummer; 'Variegata' bears eighteen-inch, dark green leaves edged with creamy white; and 'Golden Sword' grows about thirty inches tall and two feet wide, with dark green leaves with a bright yellow center.

USDA Zones 5 to 10

Yucca aloifolia, or Spanish bayonet, is a native yucca that eventually forms a trunk as the lower leaves die off. The dark green foliage is stiff and pointed, up to two and a half feet long, and two inches wide, with toothed margins. The species name alludes to the resemblance of the leaves to those of the American aloe. Eventually plants can reach a height of eighteen feet with a five-foot spread. Summer-blooming flowers are fragrant and

Yuccas appear to be related to grasses until midsummer, when a strong flower stem appears, shooting up higher than the surrounding leaves—often to six feet of more—and bearing numerous cream-colored, bell-like pendant flowers. Most gardeners are familiar with these imposing plants, but few realize that the tall spires of summer-blooming, bell-shaped flowers are pollinated in their native homes by a night-flying species of moth. While not specifically night-blooming plants since the flowers are also open during the day, yucca flowers exhibit nyctinasty, meaning they are nyctitropic—in other words the flowers move at night.

Adam's needle is native to the Southeast from North Carolina to Florida and west to Tennessee and Mississippi. In nature it grows

Yucca aloifolia

night blooming. Provide sun or partial shade, and average soil with good drainage—sandy loam is best. This plant works at the seashore and in city gardens. The only maintenance is removing dead leaves.

USDA Zones 8 and 9

Yucca gloriosa 'Variegata' the variegated soapwort, originally came from the JC Raulston Arboretum in Raleigh, where the two- to three-foot-wide clumps reached a four-foot height in ten years. The blue-green leaves are bordered with a margin that begins as a golden yellow, then with the advance of summer's heat changes to a rich creamy white.

USDA Zones 7 to 10

Zigadenus leimanthoides, the death camus, sometimes called the pinebarren or coastal death camas, is one of eighteen plant species (some quite beautiful) belonging to an interesting but dangerous group. The entire plant is poisonous, especially the bulb. The derivation of the generic name is not very frightening because it's adapted from the Greek *zygos*, "a yoke," and *aden*, "a gland," referring to the small yellow gland located at the base of each flower, sometimes in pairs. The species translates to "smooth flowering," but I haven't the foggiest dea what the logic to that is. According to Schmutz and Hamilton, authors of *Plants That Poison* (Northland Press, Flagstaff, Ariz., 1988), "Flour made from the bulbs of death camas produced violent intestinal symptoms in the expeditionary forces of Lewis and Clark. Later, pioneers were killed by eating the bulbs which were mistaken for the edible camas and wild onion or garlic."

As to why I would include such a plant in the listing for gardens in the Southeast, it's a fairly common woodland plant, and really quite beautiful in the garden when in bloom. In nature they are found in the Coastal Plain, west to Virginia to West Virginia, and south to Alabama and Georgia. The flowers are stalked, pale white to a greenish white, with six petals (really tepals) that have the aforementioned small yellow gland at their base. The linear leaves arise from a bulb and vary in length from eight to twenty inches in length, measuring about a half-inch at their widest spot. They bloom in June or July. Death camus does best in well-drained, sandy soil, in partial shade. Propagate by seed.

USDA Zones 5 to 9

FERNS

Back in 1853, Henry Thoreau wrote: "—the ferns of various species and in various stages, some now in their most perfect and beautiful condition, completely unfolded, tender and delicate, but perfect in all their details, far more than any lace work—the most elaborate leaf we have." He knew whereof he wrote. In the geologic timetable, ferns are very old and were in existence long before the more sophisticated annuals, perennials, grasses, shrubs, and trees appeared upon the earth.

Ferns grow from crowns or creeping rootstocks, more properly called rhizomes. Usually covered with scales or hairs, these rhizomes are perennial (although *Annogramma leptophylla,* a little fern discovered about a hundred years ago on the Channel Islands, is an annual). The stalk or stipe (preferred to the word "stem," which is usually used for flowering plants) supports the leaf or leaflets (pinnae) and is often flat or concave in front, rounded in back, and covered with hairs or scales, especially when stalks are young. The section on the stalk where the leaflets emerge is called the "rachis."

A lady fern unfurls its fiddlehead in a greeting to spring.

Fern leaves are called fronds or blades. The species are differentiated by the character of the leaves, the shapes of which vary from simple to compound, with many divisions. Some ferns have two kinds of leaves: Sterile leaves only function for photosynthesis while the fertile leaves bear the spores and often do both. The word "fiddlehead" refers to the young, unfurling leaves of the true ferns. In the spring the new leaves are tightly coiled and look like the head of a violin or the top of a bishop's crosier. Many fiddleheads are covered with dense woolly scales for added protection against late spring freezes.

Most ferns prefer well-drained soil that contains plenty of organic matter. That's why so many can live in the woods, underneath the canopy of tall trees, thriving in the rich soil provided by many years of falling leaves. If you are gardening in heavy clay soil, in order to improve drainage, mix a two-inch layer of composted pine bark or other organic material into the top ten inches of dirt before planting. Bird gravel or poultry grit (crushed granite) also works well to improve drainage and adds some mineral content to organic material.

Sandy soils usually drain too quickly for ferns so always work in at least a two-inch layer of organic material before planting because it helps the sand to retain moisture. Finally, if making a fern bed, don't do it one hole at a time but prepare the entire area. This prevents water from standing in the holes and rotting the rhizomes. If drainage is a problem, ferns also do beautifully in raised beds that provide great drainage. Except for a few species, ferns need good, moist soil in partial shade. Always plan on watering if the rains don't do their job.

Most of the ferns described in the pages that follow prefer acidic soils with a pH that ranges from 4 to 7. The maidenhairs and the spleenworts prefer a more alkaline soil with a pH of 7 to 8. You can mix in horticultural limestone or crushed oyster shells to make the soil sweeter.

Reproduction of Ferns

Once you know about their reproductive habits, it's sometimes amazing there are ferns at all. In the summertime, tiny greenish and usually rounded specks appear on the undersides of fern leaves, and gardeners often fear that the ferns are diseased or infested with bugs. But these specks soon turn into dark brown spots called sori, from the Greek word for "heaps." These sori, or fruit dots, are tiny masses of spore cases, or sporangia, which contain the fern's spores.

The spores are like seeds, but the life cycle of a fern is more complex than that of flowering plants. When a spore finds a warm, damp place, it develops into a prothallus, as structure that begins life as one cell but soon grows into a heart-shaped, flat structure about one-quarter of an inch wide, with tiny roots on its lower surface.

Soon both egg-containing organs, called archegonia, and sperm-producing organs, called antheridia, appear on the underside of the prothallus. When mature, the antheridia release sperm that swim though the tiniest bit of moisture to the archegonia, fertilizing the eggs inside. When that happens, a true fern begins to grow. Imagine all of this activity in the fern bed. As a gardener, you can join various fern societies, trade spores, and raise your own ferns—a great way to expand fern collections without a large expenditure of money.

Adiantum pedatum, the Northern maidenhair fern, is one of the most beautiful of the ferns that are so at home in Southern gardens. The common name is open to debate as some think it refers to the slender and shiny black leaf stalks while others attribute it to the fine fibrous roots. The genus name is from the Greek *adiantos*, meaning "not to wet" or "to keep dry," for when it rains, the droplets run across the fronds just like beads of mercury and the leaves remain dry. The species means "foot-like" referring to the bird-foot branching of the fronds. The Southern maidenhair is A. *capillus-veneris*, sometimes known as Venus's-hair or dudder grass. The species name refers to the first common name. Make no mistake about it: Maidenhairs are absolutely the most beautiful of ferns—unfortunately they are generally deciduous, going dormant in winter.

Maidenhairs grow in clumps, the blades being light green in color; the thin black stalks make the fronds seem to hover over the ground without any visible means of support, just moving hither, thither, and yon in the gentlest of breezes. The fronds form a horseshoe shape. The height is usually about eighteen inches but a mature clump can easily reach a height of two feet. Look at the underside of the outer edges of individual leaf segments to see the thin line of sporangia.

Maidenhairs will not tolerate sun or exceedingly dry conditions, especially during the hottest part of the summer; if rains are lacking, make sure you water at least twice a week. They also need a rich organic soil and if your soil is very acid, add some lime during your prep work. Mine grow in very good soil, at the edge of our upper garden steps, their area set off with a line of great looking stones, the stones keeping the soil on the sweet side. A summer mulch of aged compost also helps. Prune any brown fronds. Remember, these ferns are great additions to summer bouquets and look great in hanging baskets where the fronds can hang over the edge. Propagation is by growing spores or by division.

The Northern maidenhair is difficult to grow south of mid-Georgia and west.

USDA Zones 3 to 8

Where temperatures are warmer, it's best to grow the Southern maidenhair.

USDA Zones 7 to 10

***

Asplenium platyneuron, the ebony spleenwort, is an evergreen fern always found in my garden, usually growing as a small outcrop from stone steps or walls. Apparently, it's fond of the lime present in the stones themselves or in the mortar. The genus is taken from the Greek *a*, "without," and *splenium*, for "spleen," referring to the old belief in the Doctrine of Signatures. That science taught that a plant seeming to

Adiantum pedatum

have structures resembling parts of the human body, was thought to be a cure for diseases afflicting that part. The sori on the underside of ebony spleenwort leaves do resemble the shape of the human spleen, hence it once was an important herb of healing. *Wort*, by-the-by, is an old English word for "plant." The species is from the Greek *platys*, for "wide or broad," and *neuron* for "tendon or nerve."

Plant height is between eight and twenty inches. The slender, sterile fronds are usually arching and light green in color and lie close to the ground, while the fertile fronds stand upright, are dark green in color, and are her-ringbone or ladder-like in aspect, the fronds tapering at both ends. The midrib is a reddish brown. The sori are elongated capsules.

It should be noted that fern botanists point out there is a great degree of variability seen in this species. Its range extends down to northern peninsular Florida where it grows with a num-ber of tropical ferns.

Ebony spleenwort is often confused with the black-stem spleenwort (*A. resiliens*). But the pinnae, or leaflets, of the ebony spleenwort are alternate and the stalk is reddish brown while the pinnae of the black-stemmed spleenwort are opposite and the stalk is a shiny black. Sometimes it's also confused with the maiden-hair spleenwort (*A. trichomanes*), but the leaflets of the maidenhair spleenwort are rounder. However, the various species will cross.

I've never had to plant one of these ferns as they continually volunteer around the garden, but the spots they choose are always in partial shade and have perfect drainage. They are durable in the garden and quite tolerant of drought. Propagate by spores or division of the rhizomes.

USDA Zones 3 to 9

Athyrium filix-femina, the lady fern, gets its common name from the delicate look of the fronds. It's a garden fern of long standing and Sir Walter Scott points out in *Waverly* "...that where the morning dew lies longest, There the Lady Fern grows stongest." The genus is from the Greek *athyro*, "to sport," referring to the many shapes of the sori in this genus. The species name of *filix-femina* hearkens back to the Greeks and Romans who, while very sophisti-cated about animal sex, were completely at sea when it came to plants. If two plants were simi-lar, the larger was male and the smaller was female. *Filix* is from the Latin for "fern," so, being a smallish fern, lady fern was considered female.

This deciduous fern grows up to three feet tall with very feathery and erect lance-shaped fronds, the fronds growing from a circular clus-ter. Because of the finely cut leaves this is a very

Athyrium filix-femina

showy plant. Frond color ranges from a yellow-to a medium-green and the plants continue to produce new fronds during the summer. The stipes or blade stalks are green or red. The sori are hook-shaped or elongated.

Lady fern is no weakling when it comes to growth and stature, and will soon form a dense clump. But the stalks are easily broken, so protect plants from the wind and from stray animals. Plants prefer shade but will adapt to partial sun if given adequate moisture. Propagate with spores or by division.

The cultivar 'Frizelliae' or tatting fern, grows about eighteen inches tall, has narrow inch-wide fronds, and the final leaflets are reduced to bead-like balls.

Athyrium filix-femina* var. *asplenioides is the Southern lady fern, growing up to three feet tall. The blades are ovate-lanceolate in shape, being broadest at their base. These ferns like low to high light, moist to wet soil, and are easy to grow.

USDA Zones 3 to 8

Dennstaedtia punctilobula

In her 1899 book, *How to Know the Ferns*, Frances Theodora Parsons writes that this fern often grows "along roadsides [forming] great masses of feathery foliage, tempting the weary pedestrian or bicycler (way ahead of her time) to fling himself [or herself] upon a couch sufficiently soft and luxurious in appearance to satisfy a Sybarite."

These delicate and fragrant deciduous ferns have slender, creeping, branching, and hairy rhizomes topped with deciduous, compound fronds that tend to be ragged by late summer. Stalks are about seven inches long, dark at the base, with scattered hairs. The blades are often sixteen inches tall, yellow-green, lance shaped, cut into about twenty pairs of leaflets. The sori are very small, and found at leaflet margins.

Waning sunlight and cooler nights apparently prime the hay-scented fern for the coming demise of its upper parts. In the mountains around Asheville, as early as late September,

Dennstaedtia punctilobula, the hay-scented fern, is considered by many gardeners to be invasive—and if you want to cover bare ground without wasting too much time, yes, it's invasive. But unlike many other garden thugs, if you want to rid yourself of this beauty, simply bend over and snatch it up. Older books call it *Dicksonia*, named for James Dickson, a British nurseryman and botanist. But the genus is now *Dennstaedtia*, named for August Wilhelm Dennstedt, a German botanist of the early nineteenth century. The species name refers to the blades being dotted with minute glands.

the fronds begin their color decline from light green to light tan, often to pure white, as the season marches on to winter.

The fragrance is attributed to the chemical coumarin, which is contained in the glandular hairs that sprout from the blades. Coumarin, a white crystalline substance with a vanilla-like odor is found in many plants and back in seventeenth century Paris, fruit vendors would wrap wild strawberries in hay-scented fern for their trip to the market. Harris-Teeter, pay attention! Light shade and permeable soil are all this beauty needs.

USDA Zones 3 to 8

Dryopteris marginalis, the marginal woodfern, has other common names including the evergreen woodfern and the leather woodfern. It's an evergreen fern of rich woodlands and rock slopes that, once established, is a garden

Dryopteris marginalis

winner. The genus is from the Greek *drus*, for "oak" and *pteris*, for "fern," translating as the fern of oak woods. The species name refers to the spores that cluster along the edges of the fertile leaflets.

Marginal woodfern is common throughout the woods at most altitudes and has a fondness for rocky slopes and ravines, especially when the soil is rich with humus, having little care whether the chemistry errs to acid or alkaline.

The fronds are from one to two feet tall, with a stout, ungrooved stalk of a brownish-green that is darker towards the base where stems are covered with dense, light-brown scales. The fronds are a bluish to a dull olive green and arch out from their crown. The blade is lance-shaped and the leaflets are deeply cut. The crown is densely covered with light brown scales. It's a welcome addition to any woodland garden.

This fern prefers a moist, well-drained, humus-rich soil in partial to full shade. It is a non-spreader. Propagate by spores or by division of clumps.

USDA Zones 4 to 9

Matteuccia struthiopteris, the ostrich fern, is also known as the shuttlecock fern, both common names referring to the shape of the blades. This is a circumpolar fern, native to both America and Europe, but this commonality is in no way a reflection on its beauty. The edible fiddlehead is the state vegetable of Vermont. The genus was named in honor of Carlo Matteucci (1800-1868), an Italian physicist. The species name is from the Greek *stroutheias*, "of an ostrich," and *pteris*, "the fern."

Technically, it's not a fern of the Southeast, since one thing this beauty dislikes is heat in

Matteuccia struthiopteris

any form, but I include it here for those lucky enough to garden where summer is a reasonable season and not one of stress.

The large, leathery blades of this deciduous fern grow between three and five feet tall, forming a beautiful and symmetrical, vase-like cluster actually resembling an arrangement of green ostrich feathers. The leaf stalk is black, about a foot long, and the primary leaflets are deeply cut with thirty or more pairs ranging up the stalk. In midsummer, the sterile stalks rise from the center of the clump and are shorter, less than a foot long, and dark brown and green in color. The roots are black and wiry.

In nature this fern grows along stream banks and riversides where moisture is plentiful and there is lots of sun. For best garden growth provide a cool growing season and constant moisture. Propagation is by spores and by division along the edge of the clump.

USDA Zones 3 to 7

Onoclea sensibilis, the sensitive or bead fern, is grown both for its leaves, which are decidedly un-fernlike, and for its spore-bearing fertile spikes, which look like beaded feathers and are often gathered by the florist trade for use in dried arrangements. This is a one-species genus, first found in Virginia and named in 1753. The genus is from the Greek *onos*, "a vessel," and *kleio*, "to close," referring to the tightly rolled fertile frond leaflets.

These ferns are called sensitive because the blades quickly die back when touched by the first frosts of autumn (or in extreme drought). But for most of the garden year, they are a good contrast to the typically feathery look of other types of ferns. They are also dimorphic, meaning "two forms" because the juvenile form is entirely different from the mature form.

Un-fernlike, prominently veined leaves, about two feet tall, are leathery, of a light grass-green, cut into usually twelve, nearly opposite pairs of leaflets. The spore cases are contained within small, hard, beadlike divisions on fertile leaflets that turn dark brown with maturity and usually last throughout the winter.

These ferns will often stand up to Southern sun with impunity, as long as their rhizomes are in damp or partially wet soil. They are especially fine along banks or at the edges of wooded areas. Sensitive ferns have a tendency to be invasive so be sure and plant them where they remain under your control.

USDA Zones 3 to 9

Osmunda cinnamomea, the cinnamon fern, is generally considered a coarse and common fern, especially because the rootstock resembles the horsehair stuffing from an antique sofa. But most ferns in this genus pro-

Osmunda cinnamomea

three feet high, lance shaped, and in spring covered with scattered balls of wool. The leaflets are pointed, deeply cut, and arranged in twenty or more nearly opposite pairs. The golden, club-like fertile leaves of late spring and the very large fiddleheads covered with silver hairs, easily identify this fern. The sori contain spores that are rich with chlorophyll and must germinate quickly or die. They are held in green spore cases that turn a cinnamon brown on the fertile leaves.

This is a great fern for naturalizing in the wild garden, especially in a damp and shady spot. Small specimens transplant with ease but larger ferns take a great deal of effort to move. They prefer damp or wet locations and are especially fond of growing in swamps, where they impart a tropical look to the landscape. If their feet are wet they will adapt to sunlight but always look better with partial shade; they will withstand partial drought conditions when in shade. Propagate by spores or division of the outer edge.

USDA Zones 3 to 9

Osmunda regalis, the royal fern, is another deciduous American fern of imposing stature that from a distance is decidedly ferny, but up close looks more like a mini-shrub. Reaching a height of over six feet, its translucent pale green fronds sparkle in the sunlight, the foliage becoming a brighter green when growing in partial shade. The fertile sections are at the tips of certain fronds, looking like the plumes atop royal hats.

This is a fern of the damp usually found growing in wetlands or along slow-moving streams, and even bogs where it will survive with water just below the expanding crown of black and wiry roots.

USDA Zones 4 to 11

duce a tough and viable growing medium for orchids, providing a good root holdfast and needed nutrients as they decay. The genus is named after Osmunder, the Saxon name of Thor. The original specimens used to identify this plant came from Maryland in 1753. The species is in honor of the club-like fertile leaves that do look like a cinnamon treat.

The stalks are stout, round, smooth, and green, with cinnamon-colored wool that clings throughout the season. The leaves are about

Osmunda regalis

Polypodium virginianum, American wall or rock fern, grows in a mat-like arrangement, often following the contours of rocks, walls, and earth, especially where the rocks are covered with thin sections of soil. The French Canadians call the common polypody *tripe de roche* ("tripe of rocks," not to be confused with some species of lichens that grow in the same rock-hugging manner) referring to the rich and velvety growth that bounds over rocks and boulders. The genus name of *Polypodium* means "many feet" and refers to the traces left behind by the stalk stumps of old rhizomes. For years this fern was called *P. vulgare*, the species name (meaning "common") saluting its European counterpart, but now it is recognized as a distinct species and salutes Virginia.

The stalks are about a third the length of a leaf, and dull green, while the leaves are about a foot long, oblong or triangular in shape, leathery in texture, and deep green on either side but often a shining golden color above. The blades are cut into ten to twenty pairs of leaflets. The sori are large, round, reddish-brown, and usually arranged in two rows but often scattered.

The Druids held the oak in high esteem and believed that anything that grew on an oak, like these rock ferns, would inherit the oak's magic. The Amerindians used the rhizomes to make a root tea for the treatment of hives and sore throats. Those same roots contain the sugars fructose, glucose, and sucrose, plus a wintergreen flavoring that produces a sweetish taste that quickly becomes nauseating.

Seemingly impervious to dry summers, these ferns get much of their moisture requirements from early morning dews. They delight in sparse but well-drained soil, and are great ground covers over rocks, fallen tree trunks, and are easily transplanted as long as soil conditions remain the same as their original site.

USDA Zones 4 to 7

Polypodium polypodioides, the resurrection fern, is so called because during extended periods of dry weather the leaves shrink and curl up, but after a rainstorm they snap back to their pre-dry condition. This small evergreen fern of the Southeast grows like ivy on tree trunks, both alive and dead, and rambles about on rocks and ridges, even along thin ground. This fern not only has a predilection for old live oaks (*Quercus virginiana*), but often grows alongside Spanish moss (*Tillandsia usneoides*).

The leathery leaves are between four and six inches long, the individual leaflets uncut, blunt-tipped, deep green, and smooth above, gray-green and densely scaly beneath. The creeping rootstocks can find holdfasts in the most unlikely places. Resurrection fern occurs in hardwood forests from Delaware, south to Texas and Florida, and down into tropical America.

Provide full sun to partial shade and, unless you want the dormant phase, constant moisture at the roots. A garden friend of mine actually cut a crevice in a larger boulder with a cold chisel, and planted this fern, using damp bits of organic matter including some shredded oak leaves. Now half the rock is covered. Propagate by spores or division of the rhizomes.

USDA Zones 6 to 11

Polystichum acrostichoides, the Christmas fern, stays green for the holidays and cut fronds make excellent decorations. It's the sterile leaves that are evergreen—those without sori—while the fertile leaves wither after spores ripen. It's a welcome sight in the winter woodland garden where its leaflets stand out, often against a background of a light snow. The common name Christmas fern not only refers to the evergreen habit, but to the resemblance of the leaflets to Christmas stockings. The genus name is from *poly*, for "many," and *stichos*, for "row," referring to the spore cases appearing in several rows on the undersides of the leaflets.

Upright, leathery leaves grow in clusters from a central rootstock and are often found in colonies where soil conditions are right. The total length of the evergreen blades is between two and three feet, with the individual leaflets looking much like the other common name of dagger fern.

In *Ferns of the Southeast*, the classic fern book for the South, author John Kunkel Small writes: "The Christmas fern is a northern type, but curiously enough, the plants growing at the Gulf of Mexico and those growing in Canada are identical in habit and in the evergreen leaves. The rigors of the ice-age may have been the chief agent in pushing the ancestors of [this fern] from the more northern regions to beyond the shores of the Gulf of Mexico. In Florida it still inhabits as far south as Hernando County. Being a real cold climate fern we are not surprised to find plants in the Blue Ridge up to at least 5,000 feet altitude."

While Christmas ferns prefer a moist soil in light to almost full shade, they can stand up to some drought; but in dry places, more so than other locations, keep them out of the sun. These ferns are excellent for the rock garden, along the edges of pathways, and in the shady part of the garden proper. Propagate by spores and by division.

USDA Zones 3 to 9

Polystichum acrostichoides

GRASSES AND SEDGES

When confronted with cutting the lawn or bush-hogging a field full of weedy grasses, it's easy to forget that ornamental grasses are annuals and perennials that should be grown in gardens not only for their leaves but also for their blossoms.

While most of the grasses described below can be grown from seed—and sometimes that's the only way to find a rare or unusual grass—it's often faster (sometimes by more than two or three years) to buy established plants from nursery centers or mail-order suppliers. I've also included more than a fair share of sedges, as these are not only attractive plants but many of the first-rate species come from North America.

In most of the South only two major chores are connected with growing and maintaining grasses: dividing a mature clump when it gets too big for the site and cutting back last year's growth to make way for the new. In areas with mild winters and not too much ice or snow, the dead tops of perennial grasses can last a long time. So it's up to the gardener to decide when he or she is really getting tired of the tattered look of the leaves and that the time has come for shearing. Remember, get the job done before the new growth is so high that it will be clipped in the process. Usually just a sharp pair of secateurs or pruners will do, but for really tough grass clumps, use an electric hedge trimmer.

In early spring, after you have finished cutting back the old growth, you can side-dress the clump with a 12-6-6 fertilizer, erring on the side of less-is-more. Mulching helps, too, especially in conserving water, keeping roots cool, and discouraging weeds.

The plantain-leafed sedge is a great specimen plant and a marvelous groundcover.

Ammophila breviligulata

Ammophila breviligulata, American beach grass, is known by every beach-walker from the dunes of Pawley's Island to the ocean-sides of Florida. It's a rhizomatous, sod-forming perennial that is a Godsend to beaches under the threat of erosion from either wind or wave. The scientific name is derived from the Greek *ammos*, for "sand," and *philos*, for "loving," and that's exactly what this grass delights in; the species name refers to an anatomical detail of no interest to gardeners.

The waving blades grow about forty inches tall and in late summer produce sandy-yellow cylindrical flower clusters borne on tall stems. While not one of the most attractive native ornamental grasses, it has such great value for protecting the environment that I include it here. A cultivar called 'Hatteras' (for the cape of the same name) is best for Southern beaches.

Propagation is by seed or division, but plant in early spring or wait for the fall so the plants have a chance to acclimate before the sand heats up in the summer.

USDA Zones 6 to 10

Andropogon gerardii, big bluestem or turkey-foot grass, is one of America's great native grasses, its robust growth making it a great foil for a bright blue summer sky. At one time big bluestem was the most important constituent of the wild hay output of the prairie states. But continual development and poor land management have taken their toll. The scientific name is derived from the Greek *aner*, or "man," and *pogon* for "beard," referring to the white stalks of the individual spikelets. The inflorescence consists of three (or multiples of three) stalks that resemble a turkey's foot. The species, *gerardii*, refers to the French botanist, Louis Gerard (1733-1819), who discovered the plant.

This is a fine-textured grass, with blue-green blades, reaching a height of six feet (sometimes up to nine feet) that, once established, is so deep-rooted it becomes drought tolerant, thriving in both heavy and sandy soil. The flowers appear in late summer through

Andropogon gerardii

September. The blades turn a beautiful shade of light reddish-brown after the approach of frost and persist through the winter.

Turkey-foot is a warm-season species and has great virtue when planted as a natural hedge of grass set along the edge of a woodland area, or massed in the wild garden (it and its seeds are important foods for birds and other animals). It's native to all the states of the Southeast.

To get a great stand of this grass provide a moist, fertile soil in full sun or partial shade. Have patience if growing plants from seed: During the first year most of the plant's energy is spent sending down roots that eventually reach a ten-foot depth (that's why this grass is impervious to prairie fires). Propagate by seed or division.

Carex grayi

Carex species, the ubiquitous sedges, are usually thought of as grasses but they're older, more primitive plants. Some are small, some large, some unattractive, and some should be in every garden. *Carex* is the Latin word for "sedge" though another source claims that *Carex* is from the Greek *keiro*, "to cut," referring to the minutely toothed leave margins often capable of cutting a finger or a hand. The word "sedge" is from the Anglo-Saxon *secg*, meaning a small sword or dagger, this time referring to the narrow, pointed leaves found on these plants.

Carex flaccosperma, the blue wood sedge, is a great native ground cover found from southern Virginia down to Florida and west to Texas, where its natural habitats are wet woods and swamps. This sedge is a slow creeper, mixing well with ferns and native wildflowers in a wooded garden. The clumps are about ten inches tall with bluish, quilted, half-inch-wide leaves.

Rob Gardner, curator at The North Carolina Botanical Garden in Chapel Hill, writes: "This attractive evergreen southeastern native is very suitable for woodland conditions, as its color and vigor seem to suffer when planted in the full sun."

Gardner likes to see this plant set out at the edge of a stream or pool, next to rocks, or even beside a ditch. He also notes that the blue wood sedge has a small quirk connected to the flowering and fruiting phase: The plants have a tendency to lean on and co-mingle with their neighbors in "unexpected and charming ways." It prefers light shade and damp soil. Propagate by seed and division.

USDA Zones 5 to 8

Carex grayi, Gray's sedge, produces a handsome clump of light green leaves with a papery texture that stays green well into the fall. The species was named in honor of America's great

Carex muskingumensis

Plants grow about twenty inches tall with eight-inch, grass-like, light green leaves that turn yellow with frost. They spread by rhizomes and make excellent ground covers. These sedges are easily grown in good moist soil (although they will adapt to an average soil, too), and in partial shade as you journey down into the South. They do well in shallow water (three to four inches), but if moved to a dryer spot must never be allowed to dry out. Cut them down to the ground over winter.

At this time there are at least three cultivars: 'Little Midge' is smaller than the species, never topping ten inches, with palm-like, bright green leaves; 'Oehme' was a 1994 introduction by Tony Avent from a sport originally found in Wolfgang Oehme's garden, with leaves having a clear yellow border, the stripes appearing soon after leaves unfold; and 'Wachtposten' (meaning "sentry tower"), a cultivar that can reach three feet with light green leaves radiating from the stems like fans. Propagate by seed or division.

USDA Zones 5 to 9

botanist, Asa Gray. Clumps can reach a height of three feet but usually measure in at two to two and a half. The grass-like leaves are up to a half-inch wide. While adaptable to most soils and locations, this sedge does appreciate moist soil and good sun, with only a bit of dappled shade. The flowers of midsummer give rise to fruiting bodies that look for all the world like a miniature model of the glass and wrought-iron hanging lights found in hallways of Spanish stucco houses in the 1920s. These fruits are attractive in both fresh and dried arrangements and remain on the plant in winter. When in the wild, look for plants along streams and brooks flowing through open woods. Propagation is by seed or division.

USDA Zones 6 to 8

Carex muskingumensis, the palm-leaved sedge, gets its name from the plant's resemblance to miniature palm trees—curious when you realize these carexes are American natives from the low woods and wet meadows of Michigan, Ohio, and Kentucky. The species name is in honor of Ohio's Muskingum River.

Carex plantaginea, the plantain-leaved sedge or seersucker sedge, should be one of the pop-plants in the nursery trade but for some reason this species has yet to catch on. Still, every year a few more nurseries jump on board to promote this truly charming sedge that thrives in rich, moist woodland soil. It is found in most of eastern North America, ranging from our northern borders south to the Carolinas, northern Georgia, then west to Kentucky. The species name refers to a slight resemblance to that common lawn weed, the plantain or white-man's foot (*Plantago major*)—and all comparisons end there.

This sedge forms evergreen clumps with broad, almost hosta-like foliage of a soft green color, pleated like seersucker cloth. The leaves are about an inch wide and can reach a two-foot length, with purple sheaths at the base, blooming in spring with purple-striped flower spikes. The plants make great ground covers and desirable specimen plants, easy and dependable even in dry shade. Seersucker sedges are especially suited for lining a woodland path, for planting by water gardens or the edges of pools, and along streams in shady locations.

When buying this sedge, use a nursery that doesn't collect in the wild, as it's on the endangered species list for many states. Propagate by seed or division.

USDA Zones 5 to 8

Carex platyphylla, the silver sedge, is another native sedge of great beauty, featuring unusually wide leaves—sometimes up to an inch—with a lovely blue color. The species name is Greek for "having wide leaves." As a slow-spreading ground cover, with its eight- to twelve-inch height, it makes a valuable addition for mixing into a woodland garden or even growing in a container. Provide well-drained soil in partial shade. The species is native to much of the eastern part of the country, and like the plantain-leaved sedge, it's on the endangered species list for several states. Propagate by seed or division.

USDA Zones 4 to 8

Chasmanthium latifolium [***Uniola latifolia***], upland sea oats, river oats, or wild oats, is one of our most beautiful native grasses, long admired in the trade and at home in many Southern gardens. It is a rather tall and graceful perennial, with flat leaf blades and open panicles of compressed, flat spikelets that resemble oats, hence the common name. Even that English doyen of the garden, William Robinson, said of river oats: "[It's] a handsome perennial grass . . . [and] a clump, placed in rich garden soil, gathers strength from year to year, and when well established is a beautiful object." The genus name is attributed to an ancient Latin name of a plant and the species means "broad-leaved."

In moist soil plant height is often up to five feet, but only three to four feet on dry sties. While the foliage is valuable in the winter garden and arrangements because it turns from light green to a polished bronze at maturity, the panicles are truly fine because they retain the color they had when picked. These same seedheads do not absorb artificial colors so are, luckily, usually offered as nature provides, not dyed in unnatural shades of fuchsia or violet.

Grow river oats in pots, in the perennial border as a specimen plant, along a woodland walkway, at streamside, or wherever a particularly decorative plant would be welcome. The

Chasmanthium latifolium

plants will seed about but it's a very easy chore to pick out unwanted seedlings or pot them up for a friend.

Luckily for the gardener, these grasses do beautifully in shade; while they prefer a well-drained but evenly moist soil with added humus, they are also drought tolerant. Cut back in spring before the new growth appears. Propagate by seed or division.

USDA Zones 5 to 9

Cymophyllus fraseri, Fraser's sedge, was named in honor of John Fraser (1750-1811), the famous Scottish botanist. It once belonged to the Carex Clan but moved to its own genus because of botanical differences. It's native to the southern Appalachian Mountains and is also known as the lily-leaf sedge. The genus refers to the Greek word *cyma* or "wave," and *phylon* or "leaf," from the minutely undulate margins.

Cymophyllus fraseri

Here is a perennial sedge with beautiful strap-like basal leaves and plants that grow larger in circumference with age. They bloom in very early spring with white spikes of flowers on stalks up to two feet high. In John Cram's next-door garden, a mature clump of this pant has been blooming in late March for decades, surrounded by emerging whippoorwill flowers (*Trillium cuneatum*) and burgeoning ferns. As the trilliums fade, Fraser's sedge then demands your complete attention.

A bit fussy about location, Fraser's sedge deserves all the help you can provide, beginning with a soil rich in humus and adequate moisture. The plant resents growing in water but the roots will reach for it, so a great place for this sedge is along the low banks of a stream or beside a pond. My long-time garden friend Bebe Miles suggests that if it doesn't rain or the surrounding terrain is not damp enough, be prepared to water this plant to guarantee survival. Propagation is by division but it is a long, slow process.

USDA Zones 7 and 8

Hystrix patula, or bottlebrush grass, is so aptly named that one wonders why some plants get great common names and others spend their existence suffering from a name signifying an acute lack of imagination. This species is a most attractive grass of the Southeast woodlands, named for the blooming, awned spikelets lined up and down the stem, looking exactly like a laboratory bottlebrush waiting to clean a test tube. In Greek, *hystrix* means "hedgehog" (the European porcupine), referring to the resemblance of the seedhead bristles to their quills. The species name means the seedheads are spread apart.

Hystrix patula

This native grass is one of four species, with the others found in California, New Zealand, and the Himalayas. In the United States, look for the plant in dry or moist woods from our northern borders down to Georgia, then west to Oklahoma.

Plant height is from two to three feet with an eighteen-inch spread. The spikelets open green but quickly change to tan and last throughout the summer into fall. With the arrival of autumn winds and rains, the seedheads shatter.

Provide a good, dry or slightly wet, well-drained soil, in open shade. In Asheville it is often found at the edge of the woods, well within city limits, and every year adds a bit of class to the wooded hillside just above the Antique Tobacco Warehouse. Propagate by seed or division.

USDA Zones 5 to 9

***

Muhlenbergia species, is a genus collectively (but improperly) known as deer grass, including a widely varying group of great-looking ornamental grasses, generally from Mexico and the southeastern United States. They are called muhly for short. The genus was named in homage to G.H.E. Muhlenberg (1753-1815), the third son of a Lutheran minister and a self-taught botanist, called by his contemporaries the American Linnaeus; he personally named about 150 plant species.

The muhly grasses represent about 125 species and many should be stars on the grass horizon but, so far, are getting short shrift from many nurseries. Thanks to a number of native plant societies, they are slowly getting the attention they deserve. Muhly grasses are tough, love the heat, and if not adaptable to a particular climate, respond well when grown as annuals.

Muhlenbergia capillaris [M. filipes], the hairy awn muhly (the species designation means "hair-like or delicate," referring to the flowers), was described by Hitchcock as a tufted perennial bearing purple panicles in a color best described by imagining a purple haze on the horizon, with the Sons of the Pioneers humming in the background. Until blooming in mid- to late August, the plant is a nondescript clump of blades, about thirty by thirty inches), but when the bloom-tipped culms are adorned with a top-dressing of cloud-like wisps

Muhlenbergia capillaris

tured it in his North Carolina State University Arboretum Plant Distribution, a collection of plants given to North Carolina nurserymen as a way of spreading the world's plant wealth around. It's a clump-forming grass (no aggressive runners) with coarse bamboo-like stems that emerge from the ground to a height of five feet, and arch out from five to seven feet, like a graceful fountain of finely divided, almost gossamer-like pale green foliage. And if you can't provide the necessary heat for winter survival, then be sure to find a great container and grow this plant for the glories of the summer in your area. Propagate by seed or division.

USDA Zones 8 to 10

Muhlenbergia emersleyi, or bull grass, is a native grass found in rocky woods and ravines from Texas to Arizona and Mexico. The plants

of reddish-purple, you will be in awe. This grass is a native of the moist pine barrens near the Atlantic coast of North and South Carolina, Florida, Georgia, and parts of Mississippi and Texas. Provide full sun to partial shade. In late winter or early spring cut the blades almost to the ground to remove the browned leaves and spent flowers. Propagate by seed or division.

USDA Zones 7 to 10

Muhlenbergia dumosa, a muhly grass described by America's grass maven, A.S. Hitchcock, is found growing in the canyons and valley flats of southern Arizona to Jalisco, Mexico. The species name means "of bushy habit." My first introduction to this grass was back in 1994 when JC Raulston (of the great arboretum in Raleigh, North Carolina), fea-

Muhlenbergia dumosa

boast clumps of graceful evergreen leaves that vary between an eighth and a quarter-inch width and a two-foot length. Reddish flower plumes appear in the fall and easily top four feet. Look for the cultivar 'El Toro' collected in southeastern Arizona, where it's found in dense colonies. This blue-green grass is smaller and more compact than deer grass (M. *rigens*), growing up to three feet tall and about three feet in width. Dark purple flower spikes appear in late summer. This is a very drought tolerant grass, doing well in full sun or partial shade.

USDA Zones 6 to 10

Muhlenbergia lindheimeri, or Lindheimer's muhly, is at home in Texas and northern Mexico where it grows on rocky slopes, often in calcareous soils, and along the edges of creeks and on open plains. It is a clumping grass with blue foliage, about eighteen inches tall, and pale gray floral spikes on two- to two-and-a-half-foot culms. In cross-section the leaves are v-shaped. 'Autumn Glow' is a lower growing plant up to two feet in height and up to four feet in diameter. Dense, fluffy tufts of plumes give an appearance of a dwarf version of pampas grass. Taking a cue from its home grounds, provide this grass with moist, well-drained, fertile soil in full sun. It will grow in clay soil, provided the clay is amended with organic material.

USDA Zones 7 to 9

Muhlenbergia pubescens, or the Mexican muhly, originates in central Mexico growing on rocky cliffs and high on canyon walls. The species name refers to the down-like covering on the leaves. Like most muhlys, this grass is a clumper that produces blue-green blades, up to three-eighths of an inch wide and usually about a foot long. The downy leaves evidence a weeping

Muhlenbergia lindheimeri

habit with pale lilac-colored flowers that bloom in September and stand about three feet above the ground. The foliage turns a reddish-purple when frosts threaten. Provide well-drained, fertile soil, and full sun. If you have clay soil it must be amended with plenty of humus and, if necessary, drain tiles underneath the garden to guarantee perfect drainage. Propagate by seed in spring or division in the fall.

USDA Zones 9 and 10

Panicum species, the panic grasses, include proso millet (*Panicum miliaceum*), a grain that is often grown for food and forage. The common

Panicum virgatum

The species name is the Latin word for "bitter." Provide a dry, well-drained soil.

Zones 3 to 9

Panicum clandestinum [*Dichanthelium clandestinum*]

Panicum clandestinum [*Dichanthelium clandestinum*], or deer-tongue grass, was named by Linnaeus in 1753. This grass comes into its own when the light touch of frost enters the garden. Deer-tongue is a native found growing throughout most of the Southeast with the possible exception of Florida. It is a clumping, warm-season grass bearing short but wide, bright green, bamboo-like leaves about seven inches long on culms usually up to thirty inches high. The species name is a nod to the creeping rhizomes just beneath the soil's surface.

name of panic grass has nothing to do with sounding an alarm. Rather it's from the Middle English word *panik*, from the Middle French or Latin, in turn from the Latin *panicum*, referring to the *panus* or stalk that connects the panicle to the stem.

Panicum amarum 'Dewey Blue'

Panicum amarum 'Dewey Blue' is a new variation on the common beach grass called bitter panic grass and found growing along the coast from Connecticut to eastern Texas, even down to Cuba. This cultivar reaches a three-foot height and although initially a clumper, it does spread with creeping rhizomes, hence its value for erosion control. The leaves are distinctly blue and plants grow about three feet tall. Airy flowers appear in the fall, and with the arrival of frost turn a light beige color. Thanks to its ability to withstand salt spray, this is a great grass to plant along ocean property.

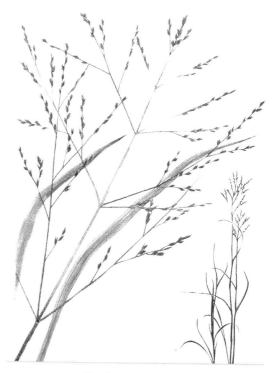

Panicum virgatum

Except in very poor soil, it's an aggressive spreader as witnessed by the warnings put out by the State of Hawaii: "In the past, often used for soil stabilization [but] not recommended due to its invasive nature [and] a problem in Hawaii, La Réunion, Australia, New Zealand, and South Africa." But when kept in bounds, its autumn foliage is most beautiful, the leaves tinted with subtle hints of red and golden-brown. Propagate by seed or division.

Zones 4 to 9

Panicum virgatum, or switch grass, is one of the most valuable native grasses of the American prairies. The species name refers to the long and slender culms. It's actually found growing in those prairies and also around sites in open woods and brackish marshes from Nova Scotia and Ontario, Maine to North Dakota, and south to Florida, Nevada, and Arizona.

While the original species is not really suited for the more formal garden, it's a natural for mass plantings or when used as a low screen to block an unwanted view. The open panicles are especially attractive when viewed against a dark background. The quarter- to half-inch-wide leaves are up to two feet long and clothe stiff culms; plants can be up to seven feet high. The blooming panicles rise about two feet above the foliage and begin to flower in July with airy spikelets, beginning with pink and red tints but fading to tan. They make great additions to dried bouquets. This grass is simply magnificent in the fall after a touch of frost.

Cultivars include 'Hänse Herms', or red switch grass, which is shorter that the species, reaching a height of about three feet, or a bit more, with purple-red highlights beginning to appear in midsummer; 'Heavy Metal', which has stiff metallic blue leaves growing in a tight clump, reaching a height of about three and a

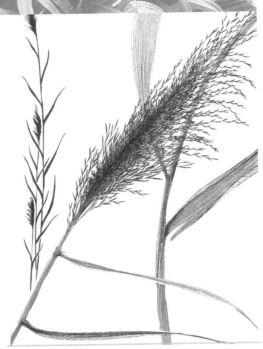

Phragmites australis

half feet; and 'Northwind' which has five feet of upright foliage, with over a two-foot spread, and is tolerant of many soil conditions ranging from downright dry to boggy.

Switch grass will withstand poor drainage and flooding, growing with wet feet for weeks without visible discomfort, so it makes a great erosion control for banks prone to seasonal flooding; it also tolerates salt spray. It withstands some light shade but begins to bend if there's too much. Propagate by seed and by division in spring.

Zones 5 to 9

Phragmites australis, or common reed grass, is present in European fossil evidence as one of the oldest grasses known. It grows on all the continents of the world and has different uses in different cultures. In England, it has been used to thatch roofs and to make fences and even some types of furniture. In our American West, Native Americans used this most adaptable plant to make lattices for adobe huts, rugs and mats, shafts for arrows, and even portable nets. While often too large and demanding for the ordinary garden, it makes a visual statement all year-round and reed grass will do very well in a damp and poorly drained site that supports little else. It grows in highway ditches throughout the eastern part of America and, finally, has the distinction of holding much of the New Jersey marshlands together. The genus is the Latin word for "reed" and the species means "from the south." This grass is known as a pioneer plant and, like cattails, it fills in shallow ponds until they eventually become dry land.

Common reed grass bears bluish-green leaves, up to an inch wide and a foot long, emerging from stout culms. A healthy grass can reach a height of eighteen feet, but usually measures about twelve. The attractive blooming plumes rise two feet above the foliage, and a field of this grass in bloom is a stunning sight indeed. The spikelets emerge as a purplish red but slowly change to a medium tan in the fall.

This grass is best in areas where the reclamation of land is of primary import and there is plenty of room for spread. If in the home setting, it must be contained, using drainage tiles or a similar barrier. If bordered by a lawn, the mower should do the trick.

Phragmites australis 'Variegatus' is a

much shorter grass, usually reaching eight feet. The leaves are striped with bright yellow. It looks great reflected in a small pond but is probably best grown in a pot.

USDA Zones 5 to 9

Uniola paniculata, sea oats or spike grass, is

probably the most conspicuous plant growing on the sand dunes of Southeastern beaches, but in no way does this commonness diminish the beauty and the value of this grass. The genus *Uniola* is an ancient Greek name for a type of this grass and the species refers to the branched panicles of the blooms.

Sea oats is tolerant of salt spray and saline soils. Name the sand dune and hopefully this grass will be there. It's protected in Florida and Georgia, among other species, not because it is rare but because it is one of the most valuable plants for stabilizing sand dunes. While unlawful to pick even the flowers or seedheads, you can still buy plants from native plant nurseries that have permits to propagate this grass. Also, gardeners can contact their local Extension agents for sources. Sea oats grows on sand dunes along the Atlantic coast from Virginia to Florida and around the Gulf to eastern Mexico.

The blades are up to two feet long and about an inch wide; in the heat of summer six-foot-high, aboveground stems (called culms) are topped with gracefully drooping clusters of flat, yellowish seed heads called spikelets, their appearance looking a great deal like oats. The underground rhizomes tunnel through the sand, making a network of stems that hold the sand together. The mature seedheads are very decorative.

Soil must be well drained and a spot in full sun is necessary, although plants will adapt to a bit of shade. Remember, because of its primary use, this grass can be invasive, so if worried about its spreading beyond the garden, dig a trench about a foot from the plants, then bury a plastic barrier to thwart the roots. Propagation is by seed or division.

USDA Zones 6 to 10

WATER AND BOG PLANTS

The wonder of a water garden is that anybody with room for a bunch of marigolds or a large pot of ivy can make a space to install a plastic washtub or preformed plastic pool to hold a water lily, or half a wine keg (lined with plastic) to grow a few small aquatics.

"Water in a landscape is a mirror to a room, the feature that doubles and enhances all its charms" wrote Neltje Blanchan in *The American Flower Garden*, published in 1909. "Whoever may possess a lake, a pond, or a pool to catch the sunbeams, duplicate the trees and flowers on its bank, reflect the moon, and multiply the stars, surely will."

The plants described in this chapter usually inhabit moist spots whether in swamps, bogs, or wet meadows, along streams, or on the edges of ponds and lakes. Some, like the water lilies, grow right in the water. Others, if given a reasonable amount of moisture in the soil and plenty of spongy humus—not to mention good mulch—can be grown quite a distance from the water's edge

A serene water garden with native arrowheads at left and the twisting stems of an exotic corkscrew rush at right.

145

Acorus calamus

Acorus calamus, the sweet flag or myrtle flag, is native throughout both the Northeast and the Southeast, extending from Canada south to Louisiana and even west to Kansas. It's another one of those plants found in both Europe and America. The scientific name is derived from the Greek *akoras*, the classic name for the plant, in turn derived from the word *lakamos*, or "reed." The species name refers to the drug calamas of which this plant is the source.

Although this plant is often thought to be a grass at first glance, it's really a member of the arum or philodendron family. Its popular name comes from the pleasant scent emitted by all parts of the plant when crushed by the fingers; if eaten, it yields a pungent, bitter taste. In early Greece, the European counterpart produced a chemical used for treating eye diseases and sailors would chew the root to relieve flat-

ulence. It was also widely used in Wildroot Creme Oil.

The leaves are stiff, erect, sword-shaped and often reach a height of six feet. When in bloom, they produce yellow-green spathes that arise in the midsection of a leaf, and jut out at about a 90-degree angle. The spathe tapers toward the end and the minute flowers are arranged around this spike with mathematical precision.

Acorus calamus 'Variegatus' bears leaves that are variegated with longitudinal, alternating stripes of green and yellow. In this cultivar the foliage is usually about four feet tall. Like the species, it grows well in containers and tubs.

Sweet flag is a valuable addition as a ground cover in both the bog and water garden, and as long as there is water available and some shade is offered in the Deep South, these plants will prosper. Propagation is by dividing the large roots in spring or fall.

USDA Zones 3 to 9

Caltha palustris, the marsh marigold, is also called American cowslip and meadow-gowan, *gowan* being an old Scottish word for a flower. Cowslip, of course, means exactly what you think it means: A place where your foot just might meet an offering from a passing bovine. The genus name *Caltha* is from an old name for the true marigold, a member of the daisy family, though marsh marigold is in the buttercup family. The species, *palustris*, is a Latin word referring to bogs and marshes. In England this flower is also called crazy-berry, bulldogs, and monkey-bells.

In nature, look for these plants to bloom in early spring, in bogs, wet meadows, and swamps—it is even at home growing on a partially submerged log—throughout the

Caltha palustris

There has been some discussion as to whether some forms are new species or merely varieties. But for now, let's stick with what we know. Cultivars include 'Flore Pleno' with larger and more numerous blossoms. Occasionally you can find a white-flowered variety and a double form. 'Plena' has small double blooms like fairy pompoms. Propagation is by seed sown immediately after ripening or by division in spring or fall.

USDA Zones 3 to 10

Southeast down to South Carolina, Tennessee, and west to Iowa.

The plants are as crisp as celery, with branched, hollow stems topped with loose clusters of five bright yellow, petal-like sepals (there are no petals). Numerous stamens stand at the center. Heart-shaped leaves are borne on succulent stems from one to two feet high.

A yellow dye is extracted from the petals and young cowslip leaves are often cooked as greens—old-timers, especially in New England, claim they are as good as spinach. Finally, flower buds are used as a substitute for capers. But never eat this plant raw since the leaves contain an irritant called protoanemonin that causes inflammation of the mouth and throat.

Bebe Miles advised planting cowslips where your biggest downspout carries the water from the roof. Add plenty of humus and mulch plants well. If you experience a summer drought, this plant will need extra water. Here in the South, cowslips want shaded full sun in spring, then as the weather gets hotter, more shade and always plenty of water.

Equisetum hyemale, the common horsetail, is sometimes grouped with grasses because it does resemble an ornamental grass upon first sight. This plant is a direct descendent of a genus that grew on earth millions of years ago during the Carboniferous Period. The vast American coalfields were formed as mounds of

Equisetum hyemale

this (and other vegetation) sank ever deeper into the mire and through chemical action became great veins of coal. Today horsetails have diminished in size, the largest rarely topping six feet and the smallest on par with a shredded Brillo® pad. The scientific name is from the Latin, *equus*, or "horse," and *seta*, "bristle," referring the plant's resemblance to a horse's tail, especially since many of the species produce stems covered with whorled branchlets. The species name of *hyemale* means "like winter," pointing out the absence of leaves on the stems. They grow along streams, lakes, ditches, the sides of roads, and railroad beds, as they are truly easy-going in their cultural demands.

Evergreen shoots grow from a perennial rhizome and have such high silica content that they were used to clean and polish pots and pans in pioneer days. The cone-like caps that top the ringed stems produce spores, not seeds, and follow a complicated reproductive cycle like the ferns. The tiny pennants that circle the rings, which in turn section off the stems, are primitive, scale-like leaves, so the major part of photosynthesis occurs in the stem.

Plant height for most is two to three feet. Provide wet and fertile soil in full sun; it will also do well in pots either in a saucer of water or plunged into a pond. It will run rampant in a garden setting, so be sure it is held back by a barrier. Propagation is by division.

USDA Zones 3 to 9

Lobelia cardinalis, the cardinal flower, would seem to be a strange choice for a section on water-loving plants, but this beauty is just that: a flower that loves to have its roots bathed in the wet. Other common names include Indian-pink, and red-birds. The genus is named

Lobelia cardinalis

in honor of Matthias de L'Obel (1538-1616), botanist and physician to James I.

Leaves of cardinal flower are oblong to lance-shaped, slightly toothed, and mostly sessile—a botanical way of saying they lack a stalk. The flowers are a rich vermilion, rarely rose, and more rarely white. The numerous blooms are about one and a half inches long, growing in terminal racemes on stems often to four feet in height. The lower lip of each flower is divided into three spreading lobes while the upper lip is two-lobed. Their color is so intense they were named not for our Southern bird, the cardinal, but for the color worn by the seventy ecclesiastical princes of the Roman Church. Cardinal flower ranges from southern Canada, south to Florida, then west to Texas. Remember, too, that this plant can be deadly. It contains at least fourteen alkaloids similar to those found in nicotine, and can cause vomiting, sweating, pain, and death.

For years I've watched gardeners buy the plants at nurseries then plant them in average garden soil, where they survive but never really achieve the punch that they should. But during those same years when walking in the woods along the banks of streams, I found their growth to be imposing and the number of flowers on each stalk numbering fifty—or more.

Then one afternoon in the Brooklyn Botanic Garden, I saw a wondrous collection of the plants in full bloom. "There's a good reason for its success and that's water," the gardener said. "This area is a bog area since I trenched it down about a foot or more and lined it with plastic sheeting, then I added this rock."

He pointed to a rock, about three feet high, but it was a special rock from a Penjing exhibit shown back in the 1970s. He ran copper tubing underground and through a cleft in the rock, filing the cleft with cement to match the stone's color. The water trickles down to provide refreshment for moisture-loving herbs, including the cardinal flower. With such care they bloom from midsummer to frost.

In your garden, use plenty of organic material and mulch well to keep plants cool and moist, and be sure to water if rains are sparse. Or create a little stream to run through the garden and plant these lobelias along the edge. Remember cardinal flowers need moist soil. They can even tolerate flooding but never drought. If you must grow them in normal garden soil be prepared to continually water the plants.

Although neat gardeners like to remove the spent stalks, always leave at least one to set seed. And also remember that in the South they want partial shade. In colder parts of the South, winterkill is serious where there isn't enough moisture in the soil; a good mulch also helps, but don't cover the crown.

Today there are many new cultivars, ranging from pure white to fuchsia and even a shade of lavender. 'Alba' has white flowers, 'Twilight Zone' bears pink flowers, and a few hybrids include 'Russian Princess' with purple leaves and 'Queen Victoria' with reddish leaves.

USDA Zones 3 to 10

Lobelia siphilitica, the great blue lobelia, bears dense spikes of small blue flowers on stout stems up to three feet high. The basal foliage is evergreen in most of the South. The species name refers to an old medicinal use for curing syphilis, which didn't work. And like its cardinal red counterpart, this plant, too, is dangerous to ingest. Plant this lobelia in a moist soil in light shade. It can be cut back to keep plants from being too rangy. Here again, while walking the old Bent Creek Road, there was a rocky outcrop that dripped water year-round. Yellow root (*Xanthorhiza simplicissima*) clung to the rock's surface and below was a grand mix of native sedges, the common rush (*Juncus effusus*), and a great stand of blue lobelias. Propagation is by seed, by offsets, and by stem cuttings for both members of the *Lobelia* genus.

USDA Zones 3 to 10

Nelumbo lutea, or **N. pentapetala** as it is called in older books, is the American lotus, also known as the yellow lotus, water chinquapin, pond nuts, or nelumbium. Plants live in ponds, both shallow and deep, in addition to slow-moving streams. This is a true lotus that's native to North America (the other species in the genus is native to Asia), and has all the exotic characteristics of an incredibly showy tropical plant. The

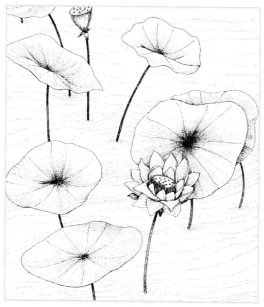

Nelumbo lutea

veins on their undersides. Lotus leaves are fascinating, not only for their tropical beauty but also for the way water hitting the surface forms round droplets that follow the force of gravity across the leaf surface like blobs of mercury. The flowers are about ten inches across and stand above the leaves. Eventually, very attractive flat-topped seedpods form and look for all the world like brown showerheads and are often used in dried flower arrangements.

The cultivar 'Flavescens' has smaller, but more numerous flowers standing above leaves that each sport a red spot in the center. 'Mrs. Perry D. Slocum' has larger flowers that open pink but change to yellow as they mature.

Because this aquatic does well in shallow water, it even adapts to living in a small garden pool, but the water should be at least two feet deep. For that environment, it's best to grow the roots in a container providing three to four inches of water above the top of the pot. A claylike soil is best and be sure to mix in some bulb fertilizer or well-rotted (or composted) cow or sheep manure.

The large, spongy tuberous rootstocks (actually rhizomes) resemble bananas. When planting lotus roots you must be careful to handle with care since the very brittle growing points of the tubers break easily. It's a good idea to lift and separate the roots of container-grown plants every two or three seasons. If planted directly in the soil, remember to surround them with a chicken-wire basket so the tubers are protected from roving animals like muskrats. These plants also need full sun, even in the South.

The Amerindians used the native lotus as an important food source: The tuberous rhizomes were cooked like sweet potatoes and young leaves were used like spinach. Immature seeds were eaten raw while mature seeds were roasted like nuts or milled into flour.

genus name *Nelumbo* is taken from the Cingalese name for the East Indian lotus. The species name means the petals are yellow.

The American lotus produces the largest flower of any native in this country, followed by the bloom of *Magnolia grandiflora*. Once included in the family of water lilies, this lotus now has its own family Nelumbonaceae. It's found throughout the entire Southeast and is hardy as long as the rootstocks do not freeze.

American lotus is a perennial water plant of great beauty. The large pale-yellow flowers are usually held above the water on graceful stems, surrounded by plate-sized leaves as much as two feet across. The leaf petiole attaches to the leaf's underside at the center; in deep water, the leaves lie on the water's surface but in shallower spots stand above the water, their reflections making scenes of great beauty. The bluish-green, satiny leaves have prominent

Propagate by seed. First scratch the seed coat with a metal file, then wrap in a ball of clay and drop in a tub of shallow water. Or, you can file through the shell, then soak in tepid water for two days. Then sow the seed in sand kept warm and wet until the seeds sprout. Plant seedlings in small boxes and submerge on the edge of a sunny pool until the plants are larger and ready for deep water. Save plant division for the fall.

USDA Zones 6 to 10

Nuphar luteum, the spatterdock—sometimes called cow-lily, yellow pond lily, or brandy bottle—is not as beautiful as the American lotus, but is interesting all the same. The generic name is from *naufar*, the Arabic name for a water lily. The species name refers to the yellow flowers. Today there are at least six species of spatterdock, but *N. luteum* is the best

Nuphar luteum

for water gardens. Spatterdocks are found in waterways throughout the Southeast.

Flowers of spatterdock have a ring of small greenish sepals that in turn surround five or six thick, concave sepals that make up the flower, resembling a golden globe. Inside, numerous golden to purplish stamens surround the ovary. The true petals are much smaller and ten to twenty are mixed in among the stamens. They flower from late May into October. Spatterdock flowers are a lesson in natural history, as a large and varied insect population wanders about inside the sepals, eating the nectar and the pollen grains. The Amerindians used spatterdock as part of their medicine chest, mixing dried leaves with bear grease to make ointments for treating insect bites and infections. Like the lotus, seeds were also gathered and eaten.

The thick leaves are round or heart-shaped, about a foot across, and rise up on long stout stalks, going down to the heart of the plant in the mud below. They are stout enough to support bullfrogs that often sit amidst the spatterdocks for evening vocalizing. Usually the leaves float on the water but in some cases, when water levels drop, they can stand above the mud until proper levels return. The fruits are pods and contain many seeds. Like the lotus and water lilies, the thick rhizomatous roots are full of spongy tissue that helps with the exchange of gasses, necessary to the survival of all plants.

Spatterdocks are vigorous spreaders, using their large creeping roots to form extensive colonies; thus they are too robust for a small, decorative water garden. But in an outdoor pond, their long blooming period and attractive leaves, not to mention the frogs living among the leaves and the fresh-water sponges that use the leaf stalks as anchoring spots, make them a valuable addition to your plant list. Set the rhizomes into the muddy pond bottom, anchor with some rocks, and forget about them. Propagate by seed as with the American lotus or divide the roots in spring, being sure to replant pieces with growing tips.

USDA Zones 5 to 10

* *

Nymphaea odorata, the fragrant water lily, or alligator bonnet as it is sometimes called in the Deep South, is a lovely water-growing perennial. The genus is taken from the Greek word *nymphe* for "a water nymph," referring to both the beauty and the habit of the flower. The species name salutes the fragrance. This species is found throughout the United States and, amazingly, south to Puerto Rico and north to Alaska. Water garden experts classify this water lily as a miniature, so plants can be grown even in a six-inch flowerpot submerged in a small pool.

Sharp-pointed petals of white or pink form fragrant double flowers two to four inches across, the outer sepals are red or purplish on their nether side. The flowers open in the morning for three or four successive days. Rounded leaves are two to ten inches across and have one slit from edge to center. They sit slightly above the water. *Nymphaea tuberosa*, sometimes mentioned in catalogs, is the northern species of this water lily but it has no fragrance. It extends southward to Arkansas.

Again, Amerindians gathered this plant for a number of uses: Roots were used as a poultice for infections and even tumors, as a mouthwash for infected gums, and were ingested for stomach and intestinal complaints. Leaves served as cooling compresses. Rhizomes were cooked for food or milled into flour. It is also useful for wildlife, including fish, animals, and birds.

Nymphaea odorata

Mix a handful of bulb food or water lily fertilizer with some garden soil (clay soil is perfect), saturate with water, then plant the root so it's covered to the crown. Finish with a layer of bird gravel or pea gravel over the dirt to prevent the water riling up the soil—or fish from poking around—thus keeping the water clean. Gently lower the pot into the pond water, propping the pot with a concrete block or another pot so the depth is correct. A mature fragrant water lily needs at least a foot of water above the pot so leaves can float on the surface above. When starting a plant you might find it's best to put a rock under the pot so it's a few inches below the water level until active growth begins. If the pool is deep enough, you can winter over the pots, roots and all, beneath the ice line. With a shallow pool, store the containers in a cool spot where 40-degree temperatures are maintained.

Warning: Some native plants aren't perfect. When planted in an open area, especially a large pond or small lake, this species of water lily will grow in dense patches, eventually crowding out other native plants and possibly contributing to stagnant water below the mats of floating leaves, creating areas where oxygen is diminished. Propagation is by seed or growing the fleshy fruits that form under water. Tuberous roots can be divided in early spring.

USDA Zones 4 to 10

Nymphaea elegans, the blue water lily, is found in the swamps of southern Florida, southern Louisiana, and southern Texas, but I was unable to find documentation of its being in the trade or whether it is suitable for gardens.

Nymphaea mexicana, the yellow water lily, sun-lotus, or banana water lily, is our only native water lily with yellow petals. It's a native of Florida, South Carolina, and Mexico. Back in the 1700s, Audubon used the plant in one of his bird paintings and people immediately thought this lovely flower to be artistic imagination. That is, until plants were rediscovered at the beginning of the 1900s. Like fragrant water lilies, the rounded leaves float on the water's surface and frame the flowers, which open for several days, closing in late afternoon and at night. Compared to most water lilies, the leaves are short-lived, lasting about six weeks before turning yellow, but are quickly replaced by new leaves.

USDA Zones 4 to 11

Orontium aquaticum, the golden club, or sometimes called never-wet, is the sole aquatic perennial species of a genus belonging to the family Araceae, or arum family, thus sharing kinship with the Jack-in-the-pulpit. It's been in the trade for some time and was actually cataloged back in 1775. The genus name is from an ancient Greek name for a water plant said to grow in the Syrian river Orontes.

The bluish-green, velvety, elliptical leaves are up to a foot long and between two and four inches in width, emerging from the water on stalks. The leaves are glaucus (having a powdery coating) and water-repellent. The common name refers to the flower stalk, a white spadix arising from the plant's crown that carries many tiny yellow flowers surrounding the top four inches. Small blue-green berries follow in summer.

Like the houseplant dumb cane (*Dieffenbachia* species), golden club sap contains

Orontium aquaticum

calcium oxalate crystals. These crystals can cause burning and swelling of the lips and mouth, sometimes resulting in vomiting and diarrhea—not to mention skin irritation. That said, golden club is sometimes used as a spring green and the nut-like seeds are said to be relished by some.

This plant is a native of most of the Southeast, growing naturally in shallow ponds, lakeshores, backwoods ditches, bogs, and swamps, from Pennsylvania south to Florida, then west to Louisiana. At the botanical gardens in Asheville, golden club grows at the edge of a small pool of trickling water, shaded from the hot sun by rocks and ferns that sit above its grotto site. While plants do best in bright light they will tolerate semi-shade. The roots must be wet at all times but if standing water is not available, continually moist soil will do. Propagate by seed (seed must be under water at all times) or by spring division of the rootstock.

USDA Zones 6 to 11

Peltandra virginica, the arrow arum, is a little-known aquatic perennial with great leaves and interesting flowers. One glance at the flower spike and it's clear this is another member of the Araceae, or arum family. The genus is from the Latin *pelte*, meaning "small shield," and *aner*, the Greek for "man," referring to the shape of the stamen. The species name means that the plant was first described in Virginia.

Arrow arum is a plant of swamps and marshes where its leaves are often mistaken for the more common arrowhead or *Sagittaria* but in this arum the veins branch off a midvein, while in arrowhead the veins all come from the point where stem meets leaf. Leaves are up to a foot long and about six inches in width. They grow from long succulent stalks up to two feet long. The flowers are small and pale yellow, spaced along a spike (or spadix) that is enclosed by a clasping hood (or spathe) usually yellow-green in color. Plants flower from May to July. The fruit is a cluster of brown berries, the one to three seeds enclosed in a gelatinous material. It is native from the Northeast down to Florida then west to Louisiana.

Arrow arum usually grows with its roots in water and is found in swampy areas not only in bright sun but in glooming shadows. Tony Avent, of Plant Delights Nursery, reports that his nursery has very good luck growing this plant in moist garden soil as well as shallow standing water. He suggests trying this native for its great tropical-looking foliage. When planting in the garden

Peltandra virginica

pond, push the root into the soft mud bottom, being sure the leaves are above the water. It also does quite well in a pot that stands in a saucer of water. Propagation is by seed kept in water or by division of the roots in early spring or fall.

USDA Zones 5 to 9

Pontederia cordata

Pontederia cordata, the pickerel weed, is a member of a small group of aquatic plants usually found in warmer regions of the world. Other common names include dog tongues and wampees. I don't know what the reference to dog tongues is, but the connection with wampees could be the similarity between the seeded pulp of the Chinese wampee tree (*Clausena lansium*), new to Florida at the end of the 1800s, and the seeded pulp of the pickerel weed. The genus celebrates the Italian botanist Giulio Pontedera (1688-1757).

Plants grow between two and three feet tall. The shiny green leaves are large and heart-shaped, averaging five inches wide and up to a foot long. They top fleshy stems. In the heat of summer showy six- to eight-inch spikes of violet-blue flowers adorn three-foot stalks. Individual flowers are an inch across and resemble the blooms of blue lobelia. White flowers occasionally appear. Pickerel weed blooms from June to November.

This is a common plant of wetlands and, like the cattails, inhabits those regions of transition between aquatic environments and dry land. They are found throughout the east ranging down to Texas and Florida and further, not only to the West Indies but down to Argentina. The fruit can be eaten like nuts while young, and fresh leaves are either cooked as a green or eaten in salads. Birds, animals, and insects also enjoy the plants.

Pickerel weed does best at the water's edge where it will be subject to periodic flooding. Some years ago we built a pond and among the plants set at the edge was pickerel weed, which did beautifully in mud that was mostly clay, under a few inches of water, and in hot sun. This plant also does well when grown in containers. Propagate by seeds or by the division of the roots in spring or fall.

USDA Zones 5 to 11

Sagittaria latifolia, the arrowhead, is one of some thirty species of aquatic perennials in the genus *Sagittaria*, usually submerged, and widely distributed in both temperate and tropical regions. The genus is taken from the Latin *sagitta*, "arrow," referring to the shape of the

Sagittaria latifolia

first on the showy staminate (male) blossoms, then transfer pollen to the pistillate (female) flowers. Flattened fruits have sharp beaks and are found on globular clusters.

Down in the bottom of the pond, the plants form long creeping stems or rhizomes, and at the ends developing starchy tubers. These tubers were a favorite food of Amerindians, who gave it such names as wapato and katnis. Early settlers also used them for food, calling them duck-potatoes. Lewis and Clark reported their diet, while traveling in Oregon, was elk meat and wapato bulbs.

Arrowheads can be used for most small water gardens, bog and pond gardens, and even along the edges of streams. In areas where arrowhead might become invasive, control it by planting in one- to three-gallon containers and garden soil. In areas safe for planting, put arrowheads directly in the soil, remembering that they will spread. They grow in moist bog areas to about six inches of water depth. Propagate by seed and by division of the roots.

USDA Zones 5 to 10

leaves in the most common species. The species name means "broad-leaved." There are a number of species in the Southeast usually differing in minor ways in the size and shape of the small fruits. Here we deal with the most common species and the one usually sold by nurseries. It is found naturally throughout the east, down to Florida and Mexico.

Sagittaria latifolia can have variation in leaf structure but most plants exhibit the distinct arrowhead silhouette, with the backward-pointing lobes like the base of an arrowhead. Plants are usually up to three feet tall with all the leaves coming up from the crown, but can be much taller in deep water; submerged leaves are lance-shaped or even linear and bladeless. Flowers have three green sepals and three white petals, usually with many stamens and pistils, the upper flowers having both and the lower flowers having pistils only. Insect visitors tread

Sanguisorba canadensis, the American burnet or Canadian burnet, is a great native wildflower that's limited in its endurance of high temperatures. It's included here for the gardeners in the Southeast who can either provide the necessary environment or have a sense of adventure. I am reminded of the North Carolina rock gardener Eve Whittemore, who once grew the fabled Himalayan blue poppy (*Meconopsis* species), a plant of the cooler parts of those mountains, outside of Brevard. She made a small greenhouse then each day put ice cubes beneath three small fans that circulated the cool air over the plants, and eventually they bloomed. The genus name is from the Latin *sanguine*, or "blood," and *sorba*, for "absorption," as the European species was thought to have the power to absorb blood. The species signifies the first description being made in Canada.

This is a large, tall plant of wet meadows, swamps, and bogs; when in bloom it is usually up to six feet in height, spreading about two feet, with attractive pinnately compound foliage. The small white flowers appear in dense spikes as long as six inches at the top of sturdy stems. They bloom from late summer into early fall. The plants are missing from most of the Deep South (except for one county in Georgia), but are found in Tennessee, North and South Carolina, Virginia, West Virginia, and Kentucky.

Sanguisorba canadensis

The American native is not to be confused with European burnet (*S. officinalis*, often added to salads and used to flavor wine). Our plant had medicinal uses, but is not in general use today. Burnet generally grows along the banks of streams and in wet places. The farther south you live the more necessary the wet becomes. Afternoon shade is also needed. Mulch well to conserve moisture and keep the root-run cool. There is one cultivar, a variegated form known as 'Variegata'. Propagation is by seed or division in spring or fall.

USDA Zones 4 to 8

Sarracenia species, the pitcher plants, are rather strange but attractive native insectivores (often called carnivorous plants), native to the Southeast; if given the right environment, they do very well in backyard water and bog gardens. The genus is named in honor of Dr. Michael Sarrazin (1659-1734) of Quebec who was the first to send species from North America to Europe in the 17th century.

The various species may differ but the principle remains the same: The leaves are hollow, leak-proof pitchers, with the area where leaf edges join sealed with a broad wing. The tube formed becomes much inflated and is topped by a hood to keep out excessive rain. The leaves are usually a dark maroon with purple lines or veining, about a foot high, and grow from the plant's crown. The pitchers are lined with glassy hairs that point toward the bottom. When insects are attracted by nectar-producing scent glands located at the rim of the pitcher, they wander over the edge, then find they can crawl down but can't go back up. Soon the slide to the bottom begins, where they drown in the watery fluid at the base and are slowly digested by enzymes.

Because many pitcher plants live in swamps where nitrogen is rare, the occasional meat provided by hapless insects helps to amend their diet. But if denied insects, they still manage to survive, bloom, and set seed. The flowers are almost as strange as the pitchers, being deep reddish purple, sometimes greenish or pink, about two inches across, nodding from a stem (or scape) up to two feet high. There are five sepals, with three or four bracts at the base and five overlapping petals surrounding a yellowish, umbrella-shaped style, ending in five hooked stigmas.

Much discussion continues on the number of pitcher plant species or varieties. I'm listing four; there are more.

Sarracenia purpurea ssp. *purpurea*, the best-known pitcher plant, is the most common of the insectivores. Because it likes cooler weather it is not that common in the Southeast, usually only found north of Georgia. Unlike its southern relatives, this plant needs at least six weeks of 40-degree temperatures to survive. It also does very well in terrariums.

Sarracenia purpurea ssp. *venosa* is the Southern subspecies, occurring throughout the Gulf Coastal Plain, and north to New Jersey. Because it has no winter dormancy temperature requirements, it's one of the easiest pitcher plants to grow. It differs in having pitchers that are shorter, broader, and often hairy on the outside.

Sarracenia psittacina, the parrot pitcher plant, has smaller pitchers that lay flat, with the hood above and the openings pointing to the side. The leaves resemble bird beaks and the flowers are dark crimson. They are limited in range to Florida, Louisiana, and southern Georgia.

Sarracenia flava, the trumpet pitcher plant, get its common name from the erect, flaring leaves with the hood leaning over the opening. The species name refers to the bright yellow color of the flowers; the trumpets may also be yellow. The flowers have a musky odor. They naturally inhabit wet pinelands from northern Florida to Alabama and up to Virginia.

These plants require moist to boggy, acidic soil and very little, if any, fertilizer. Provide full to slightly filtered sun. One of the most unusual plantings can be found in the garden of Steve Baldwin (co-owner of Farm House Gardens Nursery) of Charlotte, North Carolina, who grew a bathtub full of these bug-loving beauties, their tubular leaves glistening in the sunlight ready to call favored flies to stop and sample their deadly wares. Propagation is by seed or division.

USDA Zones 3 to 10

Sarracenia species

Saururus cernuus, the lizard's tail, swamplily, or water dragon, is another two-species-in-

Saururus cernuus

the-genus plant, one from America and one from Asia. *Sauros* is the Greek word for "lizard" and *oura* means "tail." The floral spikes droop at their tips and that's the meaning of *cernuus*.

Thin, dark-green, heart-shaped leaves have strong petioles and arise from jointed stout stems that can reach a height of five feet. The nodding flowers are white, very small, and crowded on slender spikes about six inches long. Stamens number from six to eight and the filaments are white; there are no showy petals or sepals. After maturity, the flowers become a string of nutlets that truly resemble a lizard's tail.

In the heat of summer, the dense, graceful terminal spikes of very fragrant flowers appear. If you observe the blooms produced by a colony of these plants, they appear to be tails of a group of white mice held high in the air. And because I have a moonlight garden (on moonless nights the light is from a nearby street lamp), when lit by lunar beams, the effect is sheer beauty. Add

the fragrance of vanilla tinged by the scents of other night-bloomers and you have true exotics in the garden—and they're native plants, for heaven's sake. For all that tropical beauty, lizard's tail ranges from Canada south to Florida, then westward to Texas.

The Cherokees used the roots as an astringent, a sedative, and an anti-rheumatic. Be warned, these charmers can spread about, but that tendency can also be used to hold a soil bank in check. They grow naturally in the muck along the edges of ponds, swamps, and streams, preferring mostly shade. As long as they don't dry out, they will take some southern sun. In my garden I sunk large Rubbermaid® pails at soil level, put lizard's tail in gallon pots and plunked them in the pails. I always keep some water at the bottom. If you have the room, use two- to five-gallon containers. Propagation is by seed or by dividing rhizomes and tubers.

USDA Zones 5 to 11

Saururus cernuus

159

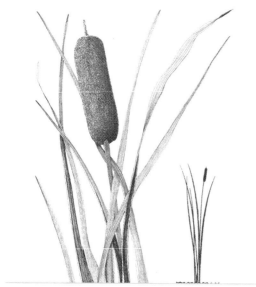

Typha angustifolia

Typha angustifolia, the common or narrow-leaved cattail, belongs to a genus with around ten species found in the temperate and tropical regions of both hemispheres. There is some confusion because in England and Europe, cattails are known as bulrushes, a name that in America is usually reserved for horsetails and sedges. The scientific name of *Typha* stands for *tuphe*, an ancient Greek name of the plant. The species name means "narrow-leaved."

These are tall water-dwelling plants with stout stems and grass-like foliage, widely distributed over the eastern and southern states and also found throughout Eurasia. Like many aquatic plants they are bridge-builders, starting in wet places, then eventually driving the water away, and turning mud into drier soil.

Leaves are erect and blade-like, up to three-fourths of an inch wide and between three and six feet in length. The flowers are sausage-like heads of tightly packed female flowers, topped with a thin, erect tail of staminate (male) flowers. And, except for the cultivars, cattails are very, very invasive, so care must be taken when using them, especially in a natural setting.

Amerindians made flour from the pollen and valuable thatching from the stems and leaves. The fluff is a good substitute for kapok (a silky fiber used for padding and insulation), and the thickened rootstocks make a great survival food. Fireworks manufacturers once used the flammable pollen.

Typha latifolia is the largest of the cattails, with leaves from six to ten feet tall. Cattails have a specific place to grow, thriving in mud or in shallow water. The rootstocks should be held by a stout container, or protected from spreading with a barrier sunk to at least two feet. Plant the roots to a depth of about six inches. Heavy clay or pond mud is essential for growth. They also need full sun. Propagate by division.

USDA Zones 5 to 10

Typha latifolia

I've gathered a goodly number of garden friends over the years, people who are not only there when help is needed, but particularly when seemingly insurmountable problems arise in the backyard. From many of the states in the Southeast, they've responded with individual interviews and letters about their experiences, including how they garden, the problems they face and, frankly, just how much they enjoy what they do. And, my apologies, because I live in North Carolina, I've picked two gardeners who cover different areas of that state.

I asked my gardening contacts to address the use of native plants in their gardens, including a few specific examples. While few gardeners among the general population, or even among the experts since they are typically intrigued by a variety of plant types, stick strictly to natives to populate their landscapes, but you would probably be surprised to know that most gardens include some native plants or their cultivars, whether the gardener knows it or not. Another subject I particularly wanted my gardening friends to discuss was hardiness, for in large part it is hardiness that determines whether or not a plant is, in fact, perennial in a region.

The brilliant red blossoms of our native cardinal flower are a special delight to hummingbirds.

Herewith, their feedback, on natives, hardiness, the process of growing things, and a bit of gardening philosophy.

Huntsville, Alabama

Carol Bishop Miller lives in Huntsville, Alabama. The city was named for a pioneer, John Hunt, who lived in a cabin next to a spring back in 1805, beginning a town that became a state in 1819. Carol is a garden writer, photographer, and occasional designer. She has a special interest in native plants and is a volunteer on the nature trail at the Huntsville Botanical Garden and is active in the Huntsville Wildflower Society. She is author of numerous articles and one book, *In a Southern Garden* (Macmillan, 1994).

"My garden is about one-third of an acre," Carol says. "It sits on the north-facing slope (closer to the bottom than to the top) of Monte Sano, the most prominent of several modest mountains overlooking our fair city. It's a fairly steep, lumpy yard, with limestone and tree roots protruding

Ratibida pinnata

though angel's trumpets (*Datura* spp.) will survive—even in a pot. "To me, a hardy plant is one that reliably reappears on a given site every year without replanting, whether by seed or roots that survive," Carol says.

She keeps her garden just tidy enough over winter to prevent the neighbors from reporting it to the city as a public nuisance. Anything that looks halfway decent she lets stand, both to feed the birds and because she would rather look at something, even if it's dead, than nothing. She usually sets out pansies and a few new bulbs in October. Tender tropicals go into the house or garage just before frost. Caladiums spend the winter in a box in the spare bedroom.

"I take cuttings of ornamentals like sweet potatoes, wandering Jews, and dicliperas (*Dicliptera suberecta*)," she says, "just keeping them in water on a window sill, changing the water once a week and adding a little liquid fertilizer. The angel's trumpets I cut down and mulch heavily right before the first frost. Plants in the cold, dark garage get a very tiny sip of water once a week. Occasionally during a warm spell, I'll set a couple of them on the patio to exercise their chloroplasts. Those in the hot, dry house, like angel-wing begonias, get two pretty good waterings per week." Carol mulches her flower beds with chopped leaves in late fall, then waits until February for a serious cleanup, just before things start really growing again.

She grows a number of Southeastern natives and particularly likes to grow the plants native to Monte Sano, because some of them are likely to be lost to development, and to the Asian bush honeysuckles that are swallowing the mountain. *Salvia azurea* var. *grandiflora* (*S. pitcheri*) sports graceful, sky-blue spires in late summer into fall and it's drought-resistant, too. Prairie coneflower (*Ratibida pinnata*) gives the garden six weeks of sunny yellow daisies with

through the soil. The house (a 1960s aluminum and brick split-level) faces north onto a lightly traveled residential street. The backyard pushes against the outside of a curve on a rather heavily traveled road that winds up the mountain. On Saturday nights, drunken speeders sometimes fail to properly negotiate the curve, so I've incorporated mangled headlights, busted side-view mirrors, bits of chrome, and sections of guardrail into the landscape on the upper level of the garden.

"A previous owner terraced the backyard with low stone walls and swooping bands of ground cover that follow the natural flow of the land—an effect I like so much that I've repeated it out front, where I've alternated lawn with rock-lined beds of shrubs and herbaceous plants. And, I'm pleased that the backyard is shady, and the front yard is mostly sunny, so I can at least attempt to grow almost anything." In the Southeast, "hardy" is a relative term. Carol rates her garden as USDA Zone 7b, but notes that she sometimes loses a salvia or two (rated as Zone 7) over the winter, elegantly down-swept ray flowers in late spring to early summer. She grows the giant coneflower (*Rudbeckia maxima*), not only for the towering yellow daisies, but also for the wonderful hosta-like gray-green leaves. Finally, she treasures butterfly weed (*Asclepias tuberosa*), that beautiful, tough, impervious, intensely colorful butterfly magnet. "I also filch seeds wherever I go!" she says.

Atlanta, Georgia

Sara Henderson has been a friend for many years. She gardens within the city limits of Atlanta, is a past Southeastern Flower Show winner, and is an advisor to many garden organizations. She has an incredible library, is a great cook, and a delightful speaker. She is also one of those rare individuals who is able to work on garden restorations—and get them right!

"My garden is in dry shade and presents a unique set of limitations," Sara says. "The

Hydrangea quercifolia

property runs along a ridge-line and is blessed with many mature oaks, but the combination of hot summers, drought, city water restrictions, and tree requirements make water a major concern. The other limiting factor is light. The canopy is oak of various types; the under-story is made up of dogwoods, redbud, and Japanese maples. The oaks, which I dearly love, block most of the sunlight. They're tall, allowing for morning sun and high light during the day, but little direct sunlight. I do what I can to limb up and thin canopies, especially the dogwoods, but my plant pallet is still limited to shade-loving plants. I'm often tempted by the beautiful colors possible in a sunnier space, but the mosaic of color and form possible from shade-lovers is truly delightful."

Sara's garden encompasses about 15,000 square feet. It's accessed by stone steps leading up a slight hill, then opens up to a large, mossy central area surrounded by a free-form border. Here she is more of a collector than designer so there are literally hundreds of plants (few are the same), filling the border. "By repeating key plants and using various cultivars, I've tried to develop a cohesive whole," she says. "Beneath the trees I've used many selections of *Hydrangea quercifolia*, laurels (*Kalmia* spp.), flowering quince (*Chaenomeles* spp.), camellias (*Camellia* spp.), witch hazels (*Hamamelis* spp.), and mahonias (*Mahonia* spp.), among others, to form a background for the smaller plants. The evergreen plants, along with aspidistras, hellebores, and autumn fern (*Dryopteris erythrosora*), give the garden winter form. What remains is filled with many shade-loving perennials and bulbs, designed with foliage combinations for added beauty. Ferns and hostas abound, as do *Astilbe*, *Tricyrtis*, *Pulmonaria*, *Epimedium*, *Asarum*, and *Polygonatum*. Another group of favorites are my spring ephemerals, including *Trillium* and

Arisaema. They, along with the *Phlox divaricata*, bring the garden alive in early spring and then are replaced by others as the season progresses.

"Several of the native plants are favorites of mine," she says. "I adore the oakleaf hydrangeas and am especially fond of the double-flowered form 'Snowflake', that was found as a chance seedling in the woods of Alabama. I also have many other selections and a number of the straight species, which I find has seeded around a bit. Many of my ferns, including Christmas (*Polystichum acrostichoides*), lady (*Athyrium filix-femina*), sensitive (*Onoclea sensibilis*), and northern maidenhair (*Adiantum pedatum*) are native and perform beautifully. A cross between our native lady fern and the Asian Japanese painted fern, called 'Ghost', has

Phlox divaricata

been outstanding. It has the vigor and upstanding form of lady with the silvery color of the Japanese painted fern. The many trilliums (mostly *Trillium cuneatum*) were obtained through rescues sponsored by the Georgia Native Plant Association and are a joy each spring. I love the many gingers and *Asarum shuttleworthii* 'Callaway' forms an especially nice carpet around the steps to the garden. It was very slow in the beginning but performed much better after I was advised to give it a bit of fertilizer.

"My specific site, while officially in USDA Zone 7b, is often a bit warmer than expected and is approaching a Zone 8. Being on the top of a ridge above the cold pockets, and in the city with residual heat, allows me to try things that might otherwise not be hardy. In reality, however, I am more limited by the summers than the winters. Since most of the more tropical plants tend to be sun-lovers, they would not thrive in my shady garden regardless of the winter lows. There are many woodland plants listed as Zone 7 that will not thrive here because of our summer heat. The daytime temperatures are within an acceptable range, but our nights do not cool down enough for them to rest and rejuvenate. Plants such as *Alchemilla* and *Hakonechloa*, while hardy in other Zone 7 areas, are not likely to do well here. While hardy simply means being able to survive, plants are not hardy in my opinion unless they can settle in and prosper. Native plants are also adapted to specific situations and will not flourish without these conditions."

As winter approaches Sara begins the process of preparing for spring. As the leaves fall, they are removed from the beds and the deciduous plants are cut down as they go dormant. All of this material is set aside. This is when she does most of her planting and dividing, as these new plants will have all winter to settle in and grow strong before spring. By early January most of the leaves will be down and the final winter cleanup can be done. All remaining leaves and dried material are removed from the beds, added to that reserved from earlier cleanup, run through a shredder and carefully put back onto the beds. The only material that is not shredded is anything that was diseased or might be harboring pests. Usually the trees provide enough leaves to put about an inch of mulch around the plants and this is a good amount.

Sara's goal is to protect the soil from leaching during the winter rains and to provide an ongoing supply of organic matter. The soil rarely freezes in this area so heaving is not an issue. The main drawback to mulching is that the mulch limits the number of seedlings. Weed seedlings are unwelcome, but she must leave certain areas un-mulched or will miss other desired seedlings. In February, she adds another inch or so of composted manure and by March new growth will have begun. Winter in Atlanta is often very brief but it's a good time to make sure that the garden, especially the soil, is ready to support the following year's growth.

Asimina triloba

Shreveport, Louisiana

Dr. Joe White, who with Dan Gill co-authored the *Louisiana Gardener's Guide: Revised Edition* (Cool Springs Press, 2002), has been both a student and teacher of Louisiana plant life for more than thirty years. He was Area Horticulture Agent at the LSU Ag-Center, and continues to appear on *Successful Gardener*, the Master Gardener television program that he helped to found. He worked closely with all of the above plus the Shreveport Rose Society, the Shreve-port Orchid Society, many local garden clubs, and a local association of nurserymen. He belongs to the American Horticultural Society, Shreveport Green, the Northwest Louisiana Master Gardeners, and serves on the boards of The Louisiana State Exhibit Museum Grounds and The American Rose Center, the headquarters for The American Rose Society.

Dr. White doesn't specialize in any particular plants but does enjoy a wide variety of plant materials including fruits, vegetables, shrubs, trees, vines, flowers, ornamental grasses, and more. He also grows many natives including American beautyberry, paw-paws, Indian currants, jujubes, Texas mountain laurels, muscadine grapes, Southern magnolias, and Texas star hibiscus. And he does have a vegetable garden that measures about thirty by forty feet. Additionally, he has numerous tree fruits, smaller fruits, and grape arbors. And he has a small planting (six feet-by-six-feet) of native Louisiana iris. "I have tall pine trees to the west and north of my property which shade all of my gardens in the late afternoon during the growing season," he says. "Since my various plants get sun from early morning until mid-afternoon, most of them do quite well. I like the balance between sun and shade that I have, but my plants would probably benefit from a couple of additional hours of full sun.

"My climate zone is 8a and I tend to agree with that designation, so 'hardy' to me means plants that can survive temperatures in the teens, and even lower, for three to five days during the winter season. At this latitude, however, we're in a transition zone between subtropical and temperate and we grow a lot of plants that with proper protection—the south side of buildings, heavy mulches, windbreaks,

Magnolia grandiflora

and more—can indeed survive fairly harsh conditions. "Actually, I make little to no preparations for the winter season. The twenty acres of trees adjacent to my property on the north and northwest sides of it provide a most effective windbreak that lifts the frigid air over my grounds."

Jackson, Mississippi

Felder Rushing is past president of his native plant society and is on the board of the American Horticultural Society and the Garden Writers Association. He attends many plant society meetings—often five or six different occasions each month—but belongs to none. He has a marvelous sense of humor and, I suspect, could survive a Category 4 hurricane with grace.

"My garden is endowed with a well laid-out overall design by highly acclaimed landscape architect Rick Griffin, also of Jackson, Mississippi," he says. "It has generous circular patios and decks—connected with meandering flagstone, paved, or mulched paths—and carefully-sited sections of fence-like visual 'baffles' with the tops cut into curves like scalloped rainbows. All decks and baffles are stained teal to help them blend with foliage and flowers. A dominant water feature in the front garden (just noisy enough to mute the city sounds) was designed by landscape architect Robert Poore, also of Jackson, and I have a well-used open 'fire pit' beside the water garden that becomes a fantastic combination of fire and water! The small gardens are completely private, even from the street and neighbors, with every entry marked with an arbor and a bottle tree.

"There are over 400 species of plants in my garden, all grown with no artificial life support—

no irrigation (except for the potted plants), no pesticides, and only an annual application of compost and cottonseed meal (high nitrogen, plenty of protein to feed my earthworms). The plants create a distinct cottage garden effect with lots of tree variety, evergreen and deciduous flowering shrubs, vines, ground covers, perennials, bulbs, potted plants, hanging baskets, and annuals. The plants—both native and nonnative—are an exciting blend of tried-and-true pass-along plants and cutting edge new cultivars that I drag home from seminars and travels around the country."

Felder accessorizes with native stone (one boulder is half the size of a Volkswagen Beetle) and collected folk art pieces (mostly metal sculptures), plus ten assorted bottle trees and a dozen or so fat, inverted, painted tire planters, placed for their zaftig shapes, which contrast with ferns and other medium or fine-texture plants. "In both the front and the back garden I have planted iron 'I-beam' posts," he says, "each twelve feet tall. Placed in a semicircle just outside my main front and back decks, their rusty color and solid form contrast well and provide a foil to the native jungle."

Felder started with full sun, but has carefully placed small trees for seasonal shade—in the winter his lean-to greenhouse and bulb beds are in the sun, but are shaded in the summer. He keeps an open area for meadow wildflowers and a small circular herb and vegetable garden in which he roots cuttings and trials new bulbs. Most of the garden, however, is kept shaded for summer comfort. I asked what his USDA climate zone designation is. "I straddle USDA 8b and 7a," he says, "but microclimates and a selection of universally hardy plants makes this completely moot. I have little use for artificial hardiness designations, because of both the dramatic swings in winter tempera-

tures and the very hot, humid summer nights—which throw off all bets other than experience and observation.

"My definition of hardy means a plant is tough enough to grow for a minimum of five years—through thick and thin—along a roadside fence row or in a cemetery—without the benefit of 'horticulture' or human intervention: no irrigation, no fertilization, no pesticides, no pruning, and no dividing." Getting ready for winter is not a Rushing activity. He's chosen plants for all seasons, placing them where their basic sun and moisture needs can be met naturally, then he just lets them go. "I wanted,

Salvia coccinea

and nearly get, as much color and texture in midwinter, late summer, and fall, as I have in the spring," he says. "And I attract winter migratory birds for their color and movement."

A few of his favorite native plants are winged sumac, euonymus ("hearts a'bustin"), yucca (*Yucca filamentosa*), goldenrod and aster combinations, equisetum ("In the water garden where it can't escape as easily," he says), red buckeye, magnolia 'Little Gem' (best magnolia for small gardens), smooth (spineless) prickly pear, bluestar, deciduous holly, bald cypress, palmetto, and all the coneflowers and river oats (*Chasmanthium latifolium*)—"Good grief, what an invasive thing!" As to seeds, Felder enjoys the annual wildflowers, coreopsis, black-eyed Susan, salvia (*Salvia coccinea*), and mulleins. He rarely needs more than five or six of any new annual plant, so he gives all his seeds to gardening friends in return for a few seedlings ready to make a home in his garden. "I root stuff like a fool!" he says.

Euonymus americanus

Asheville, North Carolina

Peter and Jasmin Gentling came to Asheville in 1971, moving from a third-floor San Francisco apartment where their gardening experiences ranged from scattered primroses to potted dahlias. Upon arriving in Asheville, they found a lovely old home on the side of Sunset Mountain. It seemed that nobody wanted the land around their property and they were able to buy about twenty acres piecemeal over the next few years. Both the Gentlings are gardeners for all seasons, doing all the work required by the plantings. Peter is a retired surgeon, a member of many horticultural societies, and an expert in Japanese style gardening. Jasmin is a retired nurse, an incredible cook, and is in charge of growing the vegetables.

The garden proper is known as Blue Briar and, of course, is nowhere near the size of the total property because most of it is in woods. They actively garden about three acres, mostly shaded or partly sunny. The soul of their garden is in the big trees: tulip poplars, oaks of several species, hemlocks, native magnolias, ash, walnut, and white pines. In addition, the previous owner, Dr. E.L. Demmon, was a U.S. Forestry advisor to the Chinese government, and responsible for bringing the dawn redwood (*Metasequoia glyptostroboides*) from China in the late 1940s. Blue Briar got two of them; these trees are now well over 100 feet tall. Various other folks in Asheville received dawn redwoods, but most of the trees went to New York and Boston for distribution around the world. The late JC Raulston was a close friend who told Dr. Gentling that the *Metasequoia* was a dominant tree in North America about thirty million years ago.

"In some ways we wish we had more sunny areas," Peter says. "To make them, we would have had to cut some large trees. Jasmin and I considered that, but decided that the trees really have powerful rights that take precedence over our selfish desires for more sun, so the trees remain. Actually, that's turned out well because our shady garden is cozy to work and sit in. The trees have become our wonderful friends. We have cut some access roads using heavy equipment, albeit very carefully. We put in a well and irrigation system that we've depended on during a prolonged severe drought. Even though our neighbors have had severe insect infestations with southern pine beetles, scale, and the like, we have had little loss from drought-stricken trees. The shady perennials we planted have fared well, too.

"Blue Briar is situated at about 2,500 feet in elevation. This puts the property about 300 feet above the city. The exposure is slightly west of south, so we get lots of winter sun. The good part of this is that there is never a winter month when you cannot find a few days of shirtsleeve weather and even take naps on the lawn in the sunshine. The bad part is that the garden wakes up in late February," Peter says. "The Japanese maples get rising sap, and then the temperature drops to 8 degrees, the bark freezes and splits, and we get fungus in the trunks. Consistent winter cold would be a better thing, but we don't get that.

"We are in Zone 6b, but in January 1985, we had a day of minus 18 degrees. All the azaleas died to the ground, the bamboo, and all the Zone 7 woodies went, although most of them sprouted up and re-established themselves. Because of rock walls and the large trees, however, there are lots of microclimates. When the north wind is howling over our heads, we don't feel it because we're about halfway up the mountain, and it blocks much of the wind. When it snows, the eddy currents usually bring us more snow, blown in off the top of the mountain. We can grow some things that are considered hardy in Zone 8, like calla lilies and cannas. Most dahlias overwinter just fine, particularly when they're situated close to the walls.

"In the past, we used heavy mulches to get us through the winter. That led to significant losses to voles. All the expensive hostas went. We couldn't grow lilies, and one winter we lost every tulip of 500 we planted except one! Why the voles left—that one I'm not sure about, but Jasmin thinks it was a nose-thumber. Now we place mulches, but only after the garden is cleaned up in late winter. All leaves are now raked away. This gives the voles no place to hide from Isabelle, my kitty, or from the raptors. We've found five kinds of owls here and three hawk species. They and the crows keep us entertained. It would be nice if crows ate voles, too. Nowadays, I buy a mulch made of half

Liriodendron tulipifera

Nature's Helper and half well-rotted manure or mushroom compost. This past winter we put twelve tons of this on in late January, before the winter aconite made its appearance. Since the garden is on a steep slope, I have to hump every bit of mulch up and down in a wheelbarrow. As Jasmin and I get older, this is going to be a problem. We don't use this mixture on the wildflower garden however, only on the exotica.

Even peonies love this stuff. We just spread it and let the earthworms work it in."

The Gentlings have been to Japan twice. They found Japanese gardeners do not use mulches because they think mulch is ugly, so the couple uses mulch with care in their garden. "When I left it on the leaves, or when we put on a cover mulch in the fall, we lost many perennials," Peter says. "Even trilliums and woody plants were gnawed and lost. So our trip taught us that timing of mulches might be a good compromise, and it does appear that we lose fewer things if the ground remains open most of the winter.

Carex plantaginea

"Because there is so much shade here, we have come to concentrate on the wildflower areas and on perennials that like the shade, such as Solomon's-seals, epimediums, arisaemas, asarums, thalictrums, sedges, and others. In the early days I was a plant collector, and really I am still hooked, although nowadays I generally look for a particular plant to fill a specific niche rather than buy with a shotgun approach. It's clearly difficult to be a good collector and a good designer. These comprise a distinct conflict of interests. I do have a greenhouse. I correspond with several of the seed exchanging plant societies, as well as with friends, both local and from other countries. I am always trying new things. It is surprising what will do well in a cool greenhouse. Lots of plants that hate heat, such as the blue corydalis, will do well in cool shade next to a wall. Our soil is acid except near some of the mortared walls.

"For, me the wildflower garden is of great interest. Both Jasmin and I love to hike, so we're always observing what's growing in our mountains. Since there are now good sources for nursery-grown natives it isn't necessary to collect from the wild. I'm always on the lookout for unusual variants though. I did find a variegated Solomon's-seal which I collected, but it had so little chlorophyll, that it expired. Some of the trilliums have interesting variations. I will collect a plant that's unusual and then grow it from seed when it is established enough to set seed. Getting wild seed is tough because dispersal can be so finicky and quick. There is a *Trillium vaseyi* here that Mrs. Demmon had collected many years ago. We think it may be a tetraploid form because the flower is about four inches across. It has set large quantities of viable seed and will bloom in about five years from planting.

"As an old member of the International Plant Propagators Society, I will try my hand at growing just about any plant. I'd love to try Gray's lily, although I am having trouble getting a permit to collect seed. There is a new carex we've found with wide blue leaves. It is not *Carex flaccosperma* or *C. pensylvanica*. In fact, no one is really sure just what it is. We are watching to see if it will make a good garden subject. Ferns are useful here. I buy them or occasionally collect the spores to germinate in the gravel of the greenhouse. We have a bog garden that's full of native grasses, sedges, primulas, iris, skunk cabbage, lobelias, and a host of other things. New plants appear there yearly, particularly mosses and ferns. It's a sunny place. We diverted a spring to make this garden and to supply the neighboring pond."

The Gentling garden is as pretty in winter as at other seasons, just more austere. The promise of spring is never far away. Asheville has four distinct protracted seasons, each about three months long. To residents, summer, believe it or not, is the least favorite because it's hot, muggy, and hazy, and the light is flat most of the day. But at least summer is reasonably dependable: Residents can go around with minimal clothing and no shoes. "It would be nice if winter ended and spring started," Peter says, "but that is almost never to be. The extremities of the seasons intertwine, often with disastrous results. But that is part of the pathos and charm, the paradox that keeps us both worried and hopeful. Perhaps my favorite plant of all is April grass. It has all the essence and promise of the metaphor, the richness, fragrance, and delicacy—that tells me what life is about. I never lie down in it without thinking of Brahms' *German Requiem*. Both are so beautiful they make me cry."

Charlotte, North Carolina

Ann Armstrong spent many delightful hours in the wildflower-filled ravines that surrounded her childhood home in upstate New York. In 1967, upon moving to Charlotte, North Carolina, she bought *Wild Flowers of North Carolina* by C. Ritchie Bell and William S. Justice to take on hiking and camping ventures,

as well as to help her identify plants she might want to add to the gardens. Her city garden is simply beautiful, and she's an accomplished writer. In addition to a gracious city garden, Ann and her husband Beverly (an acknowledged master of the Japanese art of bonsai) have a great Siamese cat named Paku.

Tiarella cordifolia

"We've developed our present gardens over the past twenty-two years," she says. "It is a small, one-third-acre, fenced corner lot in Zone 7b to 8a. The total property is under cultivation with the exception of a small patch of St. Augustine grass. The gardens are both sunny and shady but no one garden is in full sun, not even the kitchen garden. As time went by, the front gardens became more shaded from the hollies, *Cryptomeria*, and river birch. The walled garden in the back has always been relatively shady, as are the fenced gardens along the side of the house.

"For five years I wrote a weekly gardening column for a local newspaper and I used approximately 2,000 species in these gardens as a laboratory to see how various plants, shrubs, and herbs performed in this climate. It's the high humidity and hot summer nights that we endure in this area that cause the demise of a number of plants. Since we have little snow cover in the winter, we must protect the crowns of plants from standing water or they will decay.

"My basic love of wildflowers has carried over from childhood, when I made terrariums out of small ferns, mosses, and bird's foot violets from our woods." In the spring, the gardens have drifts of *Aquilegia canadensis*, the native red and yellow columbine. Over the years it's seeded about and hybridized so that some of the flowers are actually soft pink and light yellow. If the leafminer damage becomes too unsightly after it finishes flowering, Ann simply cuts the plant to the ground and in a few weeks up springs fresh foliage. Close to the drift of columbine is *Thermopsis villosa*, its yellow blooms blending with those of the columbine.

The seeds of blue-eyed grass (*Sisyrinchium angustifolium*) have cast themselves throughout the gardens. If they become too rambunctious, it is a simple matter of pulling them out. "However, their tiny bright-blue stars add gaiety to the borders," Ann says. "If their foliage looks tattered and worn after blooming, I pull them out, confident that the remaining seeds will provide fresh plants the following spring." Other favorites include Queen Anne's lace (*Daucus carota*) and butterfly weed (*Asclepias tuberosa*), adding a punch of long-lasting orange flowers to the summer garden. "However, it's

late emerging from its winter dormancy," Ann says, "and a thump with the hand cultivator can do irreparable damage to the underground plant. Another wildflower that needs foot and tool protection is *Baptisia australis*. It took me a few years to realize my foot had harmed the flower bud."

Ann wouldn't be without two native vines: *Gelsemium sempervirens*, often called Confederate jasmine, graces trellis and arbors with its sweetly scented early spring blooms. Another spring-bloomer is *Lonicera sempervirens*, whose bright red tubular flowers light up the gray leaves of the wax myrtle through which it grows. This vine, along with the aforementioned

Gelsemium sempervirens

columbine, serves as a nectar supplier for early arriving hummingbirds.

There are numerous native plants for the shade garden. Rue anemone (*Anemonella thalictroides*) is one of Ann's favorites that spreads about, competing with tree roots and bearing dainty, blue-green foliage and white flowers in early spring before going dormant for the summer. "I grow both the false Solomon's-seal (*Smilacina racemosa*) and Solomon's-seal (*Polygonatum biflorum*)," she says. "The leaves of the former are similar to the *Polygonatum biflorum* in appearance, and the flowers are borne in white trusses at the ends of the stalks whereas the Solomon's-seals are born in little bells along the axils. Both add elegant, graceful structure to the shade garden, especially if you grow the variegated form of the Solomon's-seal (which is a cultivar of an Asian species). In fall, the leaves of both species turn a luscious butterscotch color. I also found that *Polygonatum biflorum* is capable of becoming a garden thug as it spreads about with rhizomatous roots. But it certainly is a beautiful thug. The false Solomon's-seal seems to hold its ground against the neighboring tree, large rocks, and ferns; but I wish it would increase. Perhaps it will if I give it more light and less competition.

"I've found that the wild gingers have done very well for me in dry shade. I grow *Asarum canadense*, a deciduous species with wandering ways. It is kept within bounds by being planted under a large evergreen azalea and next to a fence. My favorite gingers are those that are evergreen with delightful patterning to the leaves: *A. virginianum* with heart-shaped, glossy leaves, and *A. arifolium*, the arrow-leaf ginger, whose attributes are triangular to arrow-shaped, mottled leaves. Bellworts (*Uvularia sessilifolia*) are ephemerals that have hung in with me for years but never increase. Called the straw lily bellflower, they're only eighteen inches tall with small leaves and little yellow bells that hang down from the upper branches in early spring. It would be more impressive if I had more of them.

"I have foamflower (*Tiarella cordifolia*) strewn throughout the shade gardens. I can't get enough of it. It makes a perfect ground

Asarum canadense

cover with evergreen, heart-shaped, variegated leaves and delicate, pink-tinged flower buds that break forth into racemes of starry cream flowers. It is simply magical when the lot is in bloom. They require shade and moist, organic soil, which I am delighted to give them. Finally, there are two wildflowers I depend on for my fall garden. The first is the hardy ageratum (*Eupatorium coelestinum*). The flowers of this perennial look similar to the annual short blue ageratum we buy for bedding plants. Hardy ageratum blooms arrive on the scene about the time the sky clears of its humid haze and reflects the color of the flowers. This perennial is stoloniferous and would love to take over the entire border. However, I pull out the spent plants, which leaves just enough roots to refurnish this part of the garden the following year. And the other perennial I count on in late autumn is swamp sunflower (*Helianthus angustifolius*). Mine begins flowering around the end of September with bright, yellow daisy-like flowers."

As winter approaches Ann tries to clear the garden of spent perennials and other detritus. Although the garden is small, and there are always people wandering by or through, and it's good to have things looking halfway tidy. She keeps a lookout for the cool weather weeds and removes them while they are young. She sows a few hardy annuals like larkspur, poppies, and love-in-a-mist (*Nigella* spp.) the first of November. She grows many plants from seed, the source being specialty catalogs, and plant society seed exchanges such as the Royal Horticultural Society, American Horticultural Society, and The North American Rock Garden Society.

"I like to believe that all my plants are hardy with the exception of the annuals, some of which re-seed and act like perennials," she says. "I guess the plants are hardy that survive the onslaught of rabbits, errant feet, and the pugnaciousness of neighboring plants that want to shoulder the little ones out of the way. Life in this garden follows the law of the jungle, but loving care and sometimes tough love are given in equal measures."

Pickens, South Carolina

Tom Goforth is a fern expert par excellence. He maintains the Crow Dog Native Fern Garden, a seven-acre garden and research station located in the inner Piedmont of northwestern South Carolina at 1,200 feet above sea level. At the southernmost limit of Zone 7, the garden is about a mile from Table Rock Mountain and the 2,500-foot precipitous rise of the Blue Ridge Front, regionally known as the Blue Wall. Native fern ecology research, fern propagation, experimental fern landscaping, and native fern education are the primary activities at the Crow Dog Native Fern Garden. The garden includes a research and teaching facility, greenhouses, experimental plots, and a developing diverse fern garden. The goals of the garden are to expand and disseminate native fern and fern ecology knowledge, identify and document fern habitats, encourage the preservation of fern communities, and maintain a comprehensive collection of native Eastern U.S. species, excluding species of the subtropics.

"The nursery has close ties with the Carolina Vegetation Survey, based in the Triangle area of North Carolina," Tom says. "[The Survey] is affiliated with universities and colleges throughout the Carolinas, and with regional botanical gardens, native plant nurseries, landscape designers, and gardening groups. We're funded privately through sales of native ferns propagated on site, and workshops, lectures, and demonstrations for diverse groups. Ecologically, the Inner Piedmont of western

Polystichum acrostichoides

South Carolina is a narrow north-south transition zone for many fern species and a steep gradient of floristic variation. The region offers unique geographic, geologic, climatic, and floristic perspectives, as well as a close proximity to plant community sites and climatic zones that are similar to those of upper Midwestern and Northeastern states and lower Southern states.

"Our topography varies from steep rocky slopes to rich coves and floodplains to topsoil-depleted former farmland. Gentle to moderate slopes in the Carolina Piedmont were terraced in the 19th to mid-20th centuries for farming. Non-restorative agricultural practices and erosion stripped hundreds of thousands of acres of A-horizon soils and floristic diversity. But relatively intact natural gardens occur within the Southern Appalachian Province and in rugged coves and rocky ridges of the Inner Piedmont in close proximity to the Blue Wall."

Crow Dog Native Fern Garden land is forested with mixed hardwoods and pines that are more than fifty years old, last farmed in the late 1940s. All the land lacks significant topsoil. The average growing season canopy is sixty-five percent, with scattered deep shade below laurel thickets and sunny areas below tall and dispersed poplars, maples, and oaks. There are several springs and seeps in low areas. In a central cove on the property, a small spring-fed pond paved with bedrock granite gneiss provides a dependable irrigation source. The garden is within earshot of waterfalls of the Blue Ridge Front and close to rich acidic, transitional, and circum-neutral plant communities to the north and south.

A high majority of fern species of the Eastern United States occurs within a 100-mile radius of Tom's nursery. Research data is used to create a broad spectrum of habitats for fern species and communities in the garden through improving and modifying parts of the garden, designing new niches, and maintaining naturally established sites. "In our garden native fern plants are propagated from spores in the garden's lab and greenhouses using protocols that encourage cross-fertilization within species only," Tom says. "Spores were originally obtained from fertile fronds collected in the wild. Except for new species research, spores for

Dennstaedtia punctilobula

each species are collected yearly from a variety of plants in the garden. The details of the spore propagation protocol for each species have been established through literature study and propagation research and development in the garden's lan.

"Spores are collected from early spring to late fall when fertile fronds of each species are mature. The spores are sown in a sterilized mixture of fine sphagnum moss and vermiculite in closed, 100-percent-humidity containers. Gametophytes and proto-sporophytes are reared through the summer, fall, and winter in climate-controlled conditions using artificial lighting. In the spring, young sporophytes are placed in greenhouses under an open forest canopy that provides a variety of direct sunlight durations needed for individual species and groups of species. Juvenile and mature ferns are sold, planted in experimental plots or the fern garden, or maintained in containers in the greenhouses and outdoor flats." All ferns at the Crow Dog Native Fern Garden are native to the Eastern United States and are overwintered outside. Native fern species, excluding those from subtropical locations in the Deep South, require a cool to cold dormancy period and have a poor survival rate when a dormancy period is denied. The fern species planted in the garden are placed in locations with similar ecological conditions and companion.

Groups and individuals from universities, garden clubs, nurseries, and landscaping firms visit the Crow Dog Native Fern Garden for workshops, demonstrations, and garden tours. The garden also sponsors and leads field trips to regional fern community sites, presents lectures and workshops at conferences, and assists university students and faculty who have interests in native fern ecology and the correlation of geology with plant communities.

Nashville, Tennessee

Jenny Andrews is not only a favored editor, but also a gardener of long history in Tennessee. She has lived and gardened in Nashville for over seventeen years, both as a horticulturist specializing in wildflowers at the local Cheekwood Botanical Garden, and as a home-owner. Her home garden is a blend of native and non-native plants, including annuals, perennials, vines, shrubs, and trees. "I am fasci-

nated by plants in general," Jenny says, "and am interested in everything from the unusual, rare, and even the strange, to new forms of old favorites. Of course I love native species, and after working in a botanical garden for so long, seeing them in the wild is like seeing a celebrity. That feeling never changes, year in

Geranium maculatum

and year out. No matter how many times I've seen bloodroot, trillium, wild geranium, or Jacob's ladder, it doesn't get old—every spring it's like seeing an old and dear friend again.

"The fact that so many natives are great garden plants makes them even more special. They can absolutely hold their own, side by side with plants from anywhere in the world. One of my favorite plants, which looks good throughout the growing season, is *Amsonia illustris*—ice-blue flowers in spring, dark green shiny foliage in summer, yellow fall color, and very low maintenance, never needing watering during a drought or even staking. I don't mind a little special care for something really unusual, but I really appreciate a plant that takes care of itself. Another favorite is a huge *Callicarpa americana* planted in the front yard near a downspout. Every fall when it sets berries, all my neighbors want to know what it is. It practically stops traffic."

As far as hardiness, Jenny has long known, as have so many of her fellow gardeners, that she can "get away with" many plants typically considered tender for her region, which is Zone 6b. "The feeling among horticulturists is that most plants aren't really thoroughly tested to find out what their hardiness zones truly are. And cold hardiness is only part of the picture. I've lost as many plants from the heat and humidity of Nashville as I have from the cold, especially since the nights don't cool off. And the inconsistency of winter temperatures can be really rough on plants. We'll be inching our way toward spring, with temperatures slowly rising, and then, wham, there will be a sudden drop, knocking some plants back to square one as far as spring growth. And our winters can be damp, which is a killer for anything that doesn't like to be cold and wet."

Jenny hastens to add, "But that's another good thing about native plants—they are far less likely to be damaged by weird Tennessee weather, if you choose natives suitable for the region. There are some fascinating plants native to the Nashville area, and they are becoming more available in the nursery trade, especially from native plant specialty nurseries."

There are some shady areas in Jenny's garden, but it is primarily sunny. "When a tornado came through the back yard a few years ago it took out two big hackberry trees, turning my new shady garden into a full sun garden. So I adapted, and now I can't imagine not having a sunny landscape area." A long border on either side of a fence includes numerous sun-loving plants, such as coneflowers, grasses, asters, goldenrods, hardy mums, daylilies, penstemon, shrub roses, pink chaste tree, salvias, and summer phlox. These are seasonally interspersed with coleus, pansies, Persian shield, zinnias, angelonia, diascia, and other annuals. "I enjoy the changing scenery of perennials and shrubs coming in and out of flower, paired with longer-blooming annuals. And mixing in interesting textures and colored foliage, and certainly plants for birds, butterflies, and other creatures."

While her main interests have been perennials and annuals, in recent years Jenny has also become more interested in trees, shrubs, and vines. "One of the first things I did after the big storm was plant a tulip poplar, knowing it would offer a bit of shade, but also grow tall and straight, avoiding the electric,

Callicarpa americana

phone, and cable lines stretching across that part of the yard. While I am drawn most often to herbaceous plants, you need woody plants for structure, and their textures and fall colors can be valuable assets." She has also added to the original landscape (which included a large, old, perfectly shaped dogwood and two large crape myrtles) a dogwood, Japanese maple, redbud, crape myrtle, purple smoke tree, and native smoke tree. "Smoke trees are some of my favorite plants. The native species, *Cotinus obovatus*, is a particular gem."

Like many gardeners, especially those with formal training in botany or horticulture, Jenny uses her garden as both an enjoyable place to be and as a laboratory of sorts. Each year she finds plants to experiment with, and often plants something new in several places to see where it will perform best. "You really just never know what's going to thrive and where it will be happy. I've put things in places that I just knew were perfect, and had them die or look too pitiful to keep. But then something will go beyond all expectations that I had thought would fail. The long border outside the fence, along the road, gets morning sun, afternoon shade, and has great drainage. Plus the proximity of the road (and the fence) adds warmth. So I've been able to grow such things as little skullcaps, native to dryer regions, and that's been a nice surprise."

During the process of putting this book together Jenny has actually embarked on a new venture and will be living in Florida, but she is taking some of her most prized plants with her. She says, "One of the most exciting things about living in a new place is finding out what plants you can grow that you couldn't before, but there are so many I hope I can continue to include in my garden."

Free Union, Virginia

C. Colston Burrell is a garden designer, photographer, naturalist, and award-winning author. A certified chlorophyll addict, Cole is an avid and lifelong plantsman, gardener, and bird watcher. He gardens on ten wild acres alive with birds and butterflies in the Blue Ridge Mountains near Charlottesville, Virginia, where he grows natives and the best plants of the global garden. He is the principal of Native Landscape Design and Restoration, which specializes in blending nature and culture through artistic design, and has written several popular books, including *Rodale's All New Encyclopedia of Perennials*, *Perennials for Today's Gardens*, and *A Gardener's Encyclopedia of Wildflowers*, which won the 1997 American Horticultural Society book award. He is also a contributing editor to *Horticulture* magazine, and writes regularly for many other publications.

"Bird Hill is a pleasure ground, a pastiche of woodland, meadow, and garden inspired by the beauty of the regional landscape," Colston says. "I designed my collector's wonderland to be viewed from the house, and to be viewed with the house as the garden's centerpiece. I emphasized plantings rich in texture, color, and scent to envelop comfortable circular spaces conceived for reverie. Circular elements repeat throughout, inspired by Midwestern landscape architect Jens Jensen, who used them as I do to add order to the randomness of nature. Though natives make up the heart of the palette, plants from around the world blend together within the natural framework. Shaded beds surround the house, filled to overflowing with sedges, ferns, bulbs, wildflowers, shrubs, and flowering trees. In sunny areas, temperate and tropical plants meld for a season-long feast of foliage and flowers that overwhelm the senses. Potted plants, small water features, and antique stone pieces abound.

"I believe that gardening is a partnership with nature. I have a light hand, but I also have a standard of excellence for the aesthetics of the garden. I do water during drought, as the garden is often open to tours and people do not want to see wilted or shriveled plants. I do garden organically. I feel a responsibility to make sure that my garden has a positive impact on the environment. I encourage and welcome birds, butterflies, reptiles, and amphibians. Dealing with destructive mammals is an issue. I have fenced out deer, but rabbits, voles, moles, and raccoons wreak havoc with the garden. Mostly I complain, but I do some baiting for voles, carefully sealed underground so that birds have no access. I use repellents on some plants to keep the rabbit damage down."

Colston's garden sits at the center of a parcel consisting of seven acres of woodland and three acres of meadow. The heart of the garden is about three acres, and is constantly expanding. Approximately four acres are within a deer fence, and ultimately, the entire property will be fenced. Once fenced, the woodlands will be restored with regionally native species, many of which the deer devour. A lovely stream flows through the property, and runs all season with regular summer rains. The stream is at the base of the ravine, outside the more cultivated limits of the garden, but once the deer are fenced out, this beautiful area will become a carpet of native spring wildflowers. The area currently supports some deer-resistant species, and he's added seeds of many plants to augment the existing natives.

Hogs grazed the area until well into the 1950s, so only the toughest plants survived. *Tipularia, Goodyera, Cimicifuga racemosa, Geranium maculatum, Dennstaedtia punctilobula, Polystichum acrostichoides*, and *Monotropa* are a few of the persistent natives. *Polygonatum, Smilacina*, and

Arisaema triphyllum

Uvularia hold on in spite of constant browsing. Plants now established from seeding include *Sanguinaria canadensis, Arisaema triphyllum, Caulophyllum thalictroides*, and a few *Trillium grandiflorum*, but the deer persecute these. The meadows are also in need of restoration, as they have been overrun by invasive exotics.

"I've a perfect mix of sun and shade," Colston says, "though at times I do long for more sun within the deer fence. Outside the deer fence, awaiting restoration, is a meadow struggling with invasion by Korean lespedeza. Many native wildflowers and grasses thrive in spite of the invasion. The shady areas of the garden are filled to overflowing with plants perfectly suited to the environment. I am trilled to have so much shade as woodland plants are my first love. I do have a love of tropicals as well, many of which are grown in containers."

Colston gardens at a 900-foot elevation on a mountain that is 2,300 feet high, with excellent air drainage, and loads of micro-climate effects. The garden is sloped to the east and south, so it warms up early. Plants begin growth precociously, and are occasionally damaged by early frosts. But, frost is late to settle on the garden in autumn; it often stays frost-free until November, which is unusual for USDA Zone 7a. In the six years he's been gardening here, the lower temperature limits of the zone (0⁻F) have been reached only once. The usual minimum winter temperature is about 7, with occasional dips to 4. The past two years, he has had up to a week where the daytime temperature did not rise above 32°F, which is much more significant than a 6 a.m. dip to 4 or 7.

"I like to leave herbaceous plants standing in winter, for interest and for food and cover for birds," he says. "This produces copious seedlings of some species, such as *Eupatorium* and *Helianthus*, but the trade-off is worth it. I remove diseased or succulent growth that could be prone to disease, but most cleanup, top-dressing, and chopping of leaves for mulch is done after the first of the year. The garden is outfitted with a drip system to send the water directly to the plants' roots with minimal waste.

"I'm a certified chlorophyll addict, and grow plants from around the world in my garden, but my original interest in gardening, and lifelong experience, has been with natives. I am still an outspoken advocate for our native flora as well as our native ecosystems. The overriding criterion for non-natives is they are non-invasive. I am constantly evaluating new introductions for their invasive potential. Genera of particular interest include *Trillium, Anemone, Helleborus, Galanthus, Narcissus* species and old hybrids, *Corydalis, Cimicifuga, Aralia, Iris, Tricyrtis, Disporum, Polygonatum,* plus ferns and sedges. I am particularly interested in precocious plants

and winter gardening. Having spent eleven years in Minnesota, my return to my home state of Virginia has brought the possibility of having something in bloom at least nine months of the year, so I am always looking for the latest and the earliest."

Renick, West Virginia

Barry Glick is a nurseryman and owner of Sunshine Farm & Gardens. He has a great sense of humor and a complicated history, and he not only sells plants but also collects them with a passion. His nursery Website (www.sunfarm.com) is the closest thing to a horticultural encyclo-pedia available on the Internet. "I guess I'd have to say that I envision Sunshine Farm & Gardens to be a bridge between the most knowledgeable people on a particular genus of plants and the home gardener," Glick says. "I take full responsibility for all of the chaos and havoc surrounding the incredible palette of rare and unusual, but mostly idiot-proof plants.

Cymophyllus fraseri

180

"In the past thirty-two years, we've managed to amass a diverse collection of well over 10,000 hardy-to-Zone-5 perennials, bulbs, trees, and shrubs from every corner of the Earth on our sixty-acre mountain top at 3,000 feet in beautiful Greenbrier County, West Virginia. When asked about the size of his garden, Glick says, "It's about equal to 500 football fields, or in reality, some sixty acres of land, perched on a mountainside. Fifteen acres are now under intense cultivation, with the rest waiting in the wings. Right now I have the finest collection of *Taraxicum officinale* [dandelion] on the East Coast. My six-acre Hellebore Hillside has over 68,000 mature plants."

I asked Barry about light levels in his gardens. "We control the light balance with a seventeen-foot power pruner and limb up the trees where necessary, and I never really yearn for anything except longer days, more manpower, and more money. As to USDA Zones, there is such a fine line on their maps, that around the house we grow some Zone 7 plants like *Aucuba japonica*. Most years we get a good snow cover and nobody ever informed the plants when our area was changed from Zone 5 to Zone 6, so their feet are buried as deep as possible.

"We try to do all of our planting as early in the growing season as possible. We try to avoid fall planting, because we feel there's not sufficient time for most plants to make enough root growth to anchor the roots. [This way] heaving due to freezes and thaws is avoided." "Well, just what is your definition of hardy?" I asked. "A matter of life or death. We never pamper anything: We plant it, feed it, mulch it, and if it grows that's great—if not, we plant something else in its place. There's a long list featuring plants in our trial beds waiting for a place in the garden." "What do you do for preparation if winter comes?" I asked. "I pray in advance for an early spring while we are edging the beds, deadheading, and mulching."

When I asked Barry about particular plants he specializes in, he included some exotics like the hellebores, the hardy cyclamens, and primulas. Then he tugs at my heart when, with no hints offered, he adds Fraser's sedge (*Cymophyllus fraseri*) to the list. "Others among my favorite native plants are *Hymenocallis caroliniana*, all the hepaticas (*Hepatica* spp.), *Diphylleia cymosa*, and the beautiful and little known Carolina bugbane (*Trautvetteria caroliniensis*)," he adds. He belongs to many gardening organizations and grows thousands of seed packs a year provided by seed exchanges, botanic gardens worldwide, and societies like the Alpine Garden Society and the Hardy Plant Society.

Apopka, Florida

According to Tom MacCubbin, "How lucky could one be but to live in Florida where we garden year-round? Sure, the summers are brutal, being hot and humid, but the rest of the nine months are like a northern springtime." He wouldn't want to garden anywhere else. "Luckily this gardener and horticulturist landed in Central Florida just over thirty years ago, where you can often grow the best of the northern temperate climate plants plus many tropicals. The spot is near Apopka, which we were told means 'land of potato eaters.' This may relate to the usually fertile soils that will grow just about anything, surrounding many lakes. Today this area is the heart of Central Florida foliage-plant production. In fact, Apopka is now known as the 'indoor foliage capital' of the world.

"This gardening oasis lies nearly in the middle of USDA Hardiness Zone 9, which covers the center of the state, including areas from Jacksonville to Ocala and south to Lake Okeechobee. Some areas experience winter temperatures well below freezing, while other areas hardly ever see a frost. The summers are all hot. Central Florida gets just enough cold to be able to grow many of the plants that need a chill in order to leap into spring growth and flower. We get enough of a frost to nip the tops out of many perennials, induce a slight period of dormancy, and help control run-away growth. There is the feeling you are in a more northern climate with the benefit of mostly warm and very pleasant gardening weather".

Tom suggests, "With these growing conditions you cannot have just one garden. You need a full sun site for plants that want high light levels, shady spots for plants that prefer filtered sun, and then you need dry and moist areas too. If you had to pick just one site, let it be a sunny spot where you can grow a majority of the Florida plants and maybe construct a little overhead cover just for those that like the shade."

Visitors to the MacCubbin landscape are bound to find gardens everywhere. "There are gardens for that burst of color, featuring bright yellow black-eyed Susans and coreopsis that poke out from nearby shrubbery as you meander along walkways. And then there is the stop at the gathering place for butterflies as they wing in to sip nectar atop butterfly weeds. It's just the right spot for a bench where you can sit, rest, and observe. Then there is the spot with the northern look that includes some native iris and Stokes' aster. But you're in the subtropics now, so the next stop has a tropical look, with spider lily, coontie, blazing star, wild petunia, and scarlet hibiscus.

"And yes there is the hodgepodge garden too. It's the spot where you don't know where to put everything else. Every gardener has one

don't they? This garden has the big native Walter's viburnums and saw palmettos in the background, plus a tall southern magnolia for shade. You can grow just about anything here. The taller crinums are clustered as a focal point with smaller blue-eyed grass, rain lilies, and gaillardia in the forefront. There is room for a seasonal planting of phlox and some late-spring-blooming shasta daisies.

"The gardens are always changing," explains Tom. "Many Florida perennials like coneflowers and goldenrod are short lived and may need replanting from season to season or certainly from year to year. Some, like the dotted horsemint, grow gangly by midsummer and need a good pruning, and tropical sage has seeds that sprout everywhere, needing frequent transplanting to new locations.

"In a land with an almost ideal climate it may seem like perennials could be planted and expected to grow, but it's not usually the case. For one thing, the soil isn't always the best. Gardeners relocating to the Sunshine State are often in for a real shock—the soil is sand. Some

Monarda punctata

call it beach sand, though the official state soil as designated by the Florida legislature is a Mayakka fine sand. It resembles the sand in an hourglass, and retains little water and very few nutrients." But, Tom adds, "In defense of sands, they do anchor plants in the ground very well and make for easy digging. In our gardens there are no rocks except for some relocated at a substantial cost from some select areas of the state or hauled in from north of the border. With some care, such as water and fertilizer, Florida sands grow some might pretty perennials.

"If you can, it's always best to beef up the sands with lots of organic matter," advises Tom. "You will find most local gardeners visiting the municipal compost piles to obtain bags, trash cans, or pickup truck loads of this good brown earth to add to their gardens. Many also add peat moss and liberal quantities of manure to the sands. Some improve the soils by incorporating bags of potting soil. One thing you learn in Florida is, don't ask for a load of topsoil without checking out the source first. You just might get another load of sand. There is no good definition of topsoil in the state. It's just what is available and, shall we say, on top of the soil. Also, topsoil may bring weeds and other pests you may not already have.

"Fall through spring is our really great gardening time. While many northern gardeners are putting their beds to rest, Florida gardeners are busy digging and planting. It's the most enjoyable time to plant as the temperatures begin to moderate into the 70s and 80s during the day and 50s at night. Pulling out the weeds, tilling the soil, adjusting the acidity, and working in organic matter is just a matter of routine. Then you can have lots of fun planting." When asked, if you have plenty of room for a great selection of native perennials what would you plant, Tom replied, "That is a

Asclepias tuberosa

tough question. But thirty years of gardening locally has produced some favorites." Below are a few of the plants Tom says you should consider and why:

- *Black-Eyed Susan:* Very colorful with yellow petals and a dark center—this short-lived perennial is sure to attract attention. It's in bloom from May to November and attracts butterflies.
- *Blue Porterweed:* Use as a backdrop for flower gardens and along walkways. Grows to four feet tall. Bright blue, small flowers appear above the foliage almost year-round.
- *Butterfly Weed:* A very easy-to-grow perennial, to three feet tall, with yellow to orange blossoms. A "must" for butterfly gardens. Plants are drought tolerant and in bloom most of the year.
- *Climbing Aster:* A little-used flower that makes an excellent backdrop when trained to a trellis or fence. The blossoms are pink to lavender with yellow centers, opening almost year-round, attracting butterflies. Needs a late winter trimming to keep it in bounds.

- *Coreopsis:* Plant our state wildflower in clusters to enjoy cheery yellow blossoms with a dark center almost year-round. It's easy to grow, reseeds, and is a favorite of butterflies.
- *Dotted Horsemint:* Easy to grow in sandy or improved soils, producing stalks of lavender bracts with yellowish flowers on plants to three feet tall. Flowers from May to November and attracts hummingbirds and butterflies. Needs periodic pruning to remain attractive.
- *Gaillardia:* A safe bet for even drier sites, opening orange to red blossoms with yellow tipped petals and growing to two feet tall. The hybrids of native selections are very colorful and a favorite of butterflies.
- *Stokes' Aster:* A low-growing, clump-forming perennial, opening white to blue blossoms late spring through summer on plants growing to one foot tall. Plant to form a nice border or ground cover.
- *Tropical Sage:* In bloom year-round this is a real favorite, with bright red blossoms flourishing in dry and poor soils, growing to three feet tall. It can be aggressive and needs periodic trimming or even removal to keep in bounds.

Gaillardia pulchella

"Perhaps you can get your starts for the perennial garden from friends or even as container-grown plants at the garden center. But it is lots fun growing your own plants from seed saved from a local planting or purchased as packets." According to Tom, "Starting new plants from seed is enjoyable, but in Florida it often means more than just tossing them on the ground. Even with the easy ones like tropical sage and butterfly weed, it's best to start them in pots or cell packs. Just fill the containers with potting soil and then sow the seeds. Keep them moist and in a warm location. Most germinate in just a few days. Give them the light level they need for good growth and then keep them moist and feed every week or two with a 20-20-20 or similar fertilizer solution. Most are ready for the garden in two to three months. Luckily for Florida gardeners, transplants can be started year-round. You normally don't have to worry about cold temperatures affecting them, but you do need to keep storms from washing the young seedlings away.

"If you need more help with your perennial gardens, Florida is full of people with good information. One great source is the Florida Federation of Garden Clubs, which has many local chapters. All would love to have a new member. It is also a major sponsor of native wildflower plantings within the state. I am a member of the local men's circle started by the ladies to get the men more involved in gardening, and some say out of the house. Central Florida also has a very active native plant society that meets monthly. There are also weekly gardening features in the Sunday section of the *Orlando Sentinel* newspaper. And don't forget to stop by a local University of Florida IFAS Extension office for wildflower and native plant information—that is where you will find me at work."

Bailey Hortorium. *Hortus Third: A Concise Dictionary of Plants Cultivated in the United States and Canada*. New York: The Macmillan Publishing Company, 1976.

Bell, Michael. *The Gardener's Guide to Growing Temperate Bamboos*. Portland, Oregon: Timber Press, 2000.

Birr, Richard E. *Growing & Propagating Showy Native Woody Plants*. Chapel Hill, North Carolina: The University of North Carolina Press, 1992.

Bisset, Peter. *The Book of Water Gardening*. New York: A.T. De La Mare Printing and Publishing Co., Ltd., 1905.

Brookes, John. *Room Outside: A Plan for the Garden*. New York: The Viking Press, 1969.

Earle, Alice Morse. *Old-Time Gardens*. New York: The Macmillan Company, 1901.

Fitter, Richard and Alastair Fitter. *Collins Guide to the Grasses, Sedges, Rushes, and Ferns of Britain and Northern Europe*. London: William Collins Sons & Co Ltd., 1984.

Foote, Leonard E. and Jones, Jr., Samuel B. *Native Shrubs and Woody Vines of the Southeast*. Portland, Oregon: Timber Press, 1989.

Gleason, Henry A., Ph.D. *The New Britton and Brown Illustrated Flora of the Northeastern United States and Adjacent Canada*. New York: Hafner Publishing Company, Inc., 1963.

Halfacre, R. Gordon and Shawcroft, Anne Rogers. *Landscape Plants of the Southeast*. Raleigh, North Carolina: Sparks Press, Inc., 1989.

Jarman, Derek. *Derek Jarman's Garden*. Woodstock, New York: The Overlook Press, 1995.

Loewer, H. Peter. *Growing and Decorating with Grasses*. New York: Walker and Company, 1977.

_____. *The Indoor Window Garden*. Chicago: Contemporary Books, 1990.

_____. *Solving Weed Problems*. Guilford, Connecticut: The Lyons Press, 2001.

Loewer, Peter and Mellinchamp, Lawrence. *The Winter Garden: Planning and Planting for the Southeast*. Mechanicsburg, Pennsylvania, 1997.

Ohwi, Jisaburo. *Flora of Japan*. Washington, D.C.: Smithsonian Institution, 1965.

Oudolf, Piet. *Designing with Plants*. Portland, Oregon: Timber Press, 2000.

Stearn, William T. *Botanical Latin*. Third Edition. North Pomfret, Vermont: David & Charles, 1983.

Thomas, Graham Stuart. *Perennial Garden Plants*. Third Edition. Portland, Oregon: Sagapress, Inc./Timber Press, Inc., 1990.

Walker, Jacqueline. *The Subtropical Garden*. Portland, Oregon: Timber Press, 1992.

by Botanical Name

Acorus calamus, 146
Actinomeris alternifolia, 116
Adiantum pedatum, 95, 124, 125, 164
Adiantum capillus-veneris, 124
Adlumia fungosa, 17
Aesculus pavia, 106
Agave manfreda, 77
Ageratina altissima, 52
Alchemilla, 164
Allium cernuum, 17
Allium tricoccum, 18
Amarcrinum belladonna, 42
ùAmarcrinum memoria-corsii, 42
Ambrosia spp., 59
Ammophila breviligulata, 134
Amsonia ciliata, 19
Amsonia ciliata var. filifolia, 19
Amsonia hubrichtii, 18
Amsonia illustris, 176
Amsonia tabernaemontana, 18
Andropogon gerardii, 134
Anemone, 180
Anemonella thalictroides, 19, 172
Annogramma leptophylla, 123
Aquilegia, 20
Aquilegia caerulea, 21
Aquilegia canadensis, 20, 106, 172
Aralia, 180
Archilochus colubris, 106
Arisaema, 21, 164
Arisaema dracontium, 22
Arisaema species, 22
Arisaema triphyllum, 21, 179
Artemisia ludoviciana, 22
Aruncus dioicus, 23, 28
Aruncus, 23
Aruncus spp., 31
Asarum, 24, 163
Asarum arifolium, 173
Asarum canadense, 24, 173
Asarum europaeum, 24
Asarum shuttleworthii, 24, 164
Asarum virginianum, 173
Asclepias, 26
Asclepias exaltata, 25
Asclepias incarnata, 25
Asclepias syriaca, 26
Asclepias tuberosa, 25, 26, 163, 172, 183
Asimina triloba, 165
Asplenium platyneuron, 125
Asplenium resiliens, 126
Asplenium trichomanes, 126

Aster azureus, 27
Aster carolinianus, 27
Aster divaricatus, 27, 57
Aster lateriflorus, 27
Aster novae-angliae, 27, 28
Aster oolentagiensis, 27
Aster species, 26
Astilbe, 28, 163
Astilbe biternata, 28
Athyrium filix-femina, 95, 126, 164
Athyrium filix-femina var. asplenioides, 127
Aucuba japonica, 181
Baptisia, 111
Baptisia alba, 29
Baptisia australis, 28, 172
Baptisia sphaerocarpa, 29
Boltonia asteroides, 30
Caladium species, 8
Callicarpa americana, 177
Caltha, 146
Caltha palustris, 146, 147
Camassia, 31
Camassia leichtlinii, 31
Camassia scilloides, 30, 31
Camellia spp., 163
Campsis radicans, 107
Cardamine, 31
Cardamine concatenata, 31, 32
Carex, 135
Carex flaccosperma, 135, 170
Carex grayi, 135
Carex muskingumensis, 136
Carex pensylvanica, 170
Carex plantaginea, 136, 170
Carex platyphylla, 137
Carex species, 135
Cassia marilandica, 32
Caulophyllum thalictroides, 179
Cercidiphyllum japonicum, 24
Chaenomeles spp., 163
Chamaelirium luteum, 33
Chasmanthium latifolium, 137, 168
Chelone, 35
Chelone cuthbertii, 36
Chelone glabra, 35, 80
Chelone lyonii, 36
Chelone oblique, 36
Chimaphila maculata, 33
Chimaphila umbellata, 34
Chrysogonum virginianum, 34
Chrysopsis mariana, 36
Cimicifuga, 180

Cimicifuga americana, 38
Cimicifuga racemosa, 37, 179
Cimicifuga species, 37
Cinnamomum cassia, 32
Clausena lansium, 155
Claytonia caroliniana, 38
Claytonia virginica, 38
Commelina virginica, 39
Conoclinium coelestinum, 51
Coreopsis, 40
Coreopsis auriculata, 40
Coreopsis grandiflora, 40, 41
Coreopsis rosea, 40
Coreopsis species, 40
Coreopsis tinctoria, 40
Coreopsis verticillata, 40
Corydalis, 180
Corydalis species, 73
Cotinus obovatus, 178
×Crinodonna 'Summer Maid', 42
Crinum, 41, 42
Crinum americanum, 41
Crinum moorei, 42
Cryptomeria, 172
Cymophyllus fraseri, 138, 180, 181
Cypripedium acaule, 43
Cypripedium calceolus var. pubescens, 42
Datura spp., 162
Daucus carota, 172
Decumaria barbara, 13
Delphinium carolinianum, 44
Delphinium exaltatum, 44
Delphinium tricorne, 43
Dennstaedtia, 127
Dennstaedtia punctilobula, 127, 175, 179
Dentaria, 31
Dianthus, 91
Dicentra, 44
Dicentra canadensis, 45
Dicentra cucullaria, 45
Dicentra eximia, 44
Dicentra species, 45
Dichanthelium clandestinum, 142
Dicksonia, 124
Dicliptera suberecta, 162
Dieffenbachia, 153
Dieffenbachia seguine, 8
Dieffenbachia species, 8
Dioscorea villosa, 45
Diphylleia cymosa, 46, 113, 181
Diphylleia sinensis, 46
Disporum, 180

Dodecatheon meadia, 46, 47
Dracocephalum virginianum, 92
Dryopteris erythrosora, 163
Dryopteris marginalis, 128
Echinacea pallida, 47, 48
Echinacea purpurea, 47, 48
Enemion biternatum, 73
Epimedium, 163
Equisetum hyemale, 147
Eryngium yuccifolium, 48, 49, 77
Erythronium albidum, 50
Erythronium americanum, 50
Erythronium species, 49
Euonymus americanus, 168
Eupatorium, 180
Eupatorium capillifolium, 50, 51
Eupatorium coelestinum, 51, 173
Eupatorium fistulosum, 52
Eupatorium maculatum, 52
Eupatorium perfoliatum, 52
Eupatorium purpureum, 52
Eupatorium rugosum, 52
Eupatorium species, 50
Filipendula rubra, 53
Gaillardia aristata, 54
Gaillardia ù grandiflora, 54
Gaillardia pulchella, 54, 184
Galanthus, 9, 180
Galax, 55
Gillenia, 58
Galax aphylla, 55
Galax rotundifolia, 54
Gasteria species, 8
Gaultheria procumbens, 34
Gaura lindheimeri, 55
Gelsemium sempervirens, 172
Gentiana andrewsii, 56
Geranium maculatum, 57, 176, 179
Gillenia stipulata, 58
Gillenia trifoliata, 58
Goodyera, 179
Hakonechloa, 164
Hamamelis spp., 163
Helenium autumnale, 59
Helenium flexuosum, 59
Helenium nudiflorum, 59
Helenium species, 8
Helianthus, 180
Helianthus angustifolius, 60, 61, 173
Helianthus annuus, 60
Helianthus decapetalus, 61
Helianthus giganteus, 61
Helianthus × multiflorus, 61
Helianthus grosseserratus, 61

Helianthus salicifolius, 62
Helianthus species, 60
Heliopsis helianthoides var. scabra, 63
Heliopsis helianthoides, 62
Helleborus, 180
Hemerocallis fulva, 84
Hepatica acutiloba, 63
Hepatica americana, 63
Hepatica americana var. acuta, 63
Hepatica americana var. obtusa, 63
Hepatica nobilis, 63
Hepatica spp., 181
Hesperaloe, 64, 65
Hesperaloe nocturna, 65
Hesperaloe parviflora, 64, 65
Heuchera, 112
Heuchera americana, 65
Heuchera cannabis, 66
Heuchera pubescens, 65, 66
Heuchera sanquinea, 65
Heuchera species, 65
Heuchera villosa, 66
Heucherella, 112
Hexastylis, 24
Hibiscus coccineus, 66, 67
Hydrangea quercifolia, 163
Hymenocallis, 67
Hymenocallis calycinum, 68
Hymenocallis caroliniana, 67, 68, 181
Hymenocallis coronaria, 68
Hymenocallis denticulatum, 68
Hymenocallis liriosome, 68
Hymenocallis × moseranum, 68
Hymenocallis occidentalis, 67
Hymenocallis palmeri, 68
Hymenocallis patulum, 68
Hymenocallis species, 67
Hypericum densiflorum, 69
Hypericum kalmianum, 69
Hypericum species, 68
Hypoxis hirsuta, 69, 70
Hystrix patula, 138, 139
Impatiens capensis, 107
Indigofera, 29
Ipomoea pandurata, 70, 71
Iris, 180
Iris brevicaulis, 72
Iris cristata, 2, 71
Iris fulva, 72
Iris giganticaerulea, 72
Iris hexagona, 72
Iris nelsonii, 72
Iris pseudacorus, 71
Iris species, 71, 73

Iris verna, 72
Isopyrum biternatum, 73
Jeffersonia diphylla, 73, 74
Jeffersonia dubia, 73
Juncus effusus, 149
Kalanchoe pinnata, 8
Kalmia spp., 163
Kassia, 32
Liatris, 74
Liatris microcephala, 75
Liatris pycnostachya, 75
Liatris scariosa, 74
Liatris species, 75
Liatris spicata, 74
Lilium canadense, 75, 76, 106
Lilium superbum, 76
Liriodendron tulipifera, 169
Lobelia, 149
Lobelia cardinalis, 106, 148
Lobelia siphilitica, 149
Lonicera sempervirens, 107, 172
Lupinus perennis, 76
Lupinus polyphyllus, 77
Lupinus texensis, 77
Magnolia grandiflora, 150, 166
Magnolia tripetala, 16
Mahonia spp., 163
Manfreda variegata, 78
Manfreda virginica, 77
Manihot esculenta, 120
Marshallia grandiflora, 78
Matteuccia struthiopteris, 128, 129
Meconopsis species, 156
Mertensia virginica, 79
Metasequoia, 168
Metasequoia glyptostroboides, 15, 168
Mimulus ringens, 80
Miscanthus sinensis 'Gracillimus', 32
Mitchella repens, 80, 81
Mitchella, 80
Mitella diphylla, 81
Monarda didyma, 82, 106
Monarda fistulosa, 83
Monarda punctata, 82, 83, 182
Monotropa, 179
Muhlenbergia capillaris, 139, 140
Muhlenbergia dumosa, 140
Muhlenbergia emersleyi, 140
Muhlenbergia filipes, 139
Muhlenbergia lindheimeri, 141
Muhlenbergia pubescens, 141
Muhlenbergia rigens, 141
Muhlenbergia species, 139
Narcissus species, 180

Nelumbo, 150
Nelumbo lutea, 149, 150
Nelumbo pentapetala, 149
Nigella spp., 174
Nuphar luteum, 151
Nymphaea elegans, 153
Nymphaea mexicana, 153
Nymphaea odorata, 152
Nymphaea tuberosa, 152
Nyssa sylvatica, 87
Oenothera, 83
Oenothera biennis, 83
Oenothera fruticosa, 83, 84
Oenothera macrocarpa, 10
Oenothera missouriensis, 10
Oenothera speciosa, 14
Onoclea sensibilis, 129, 164
Opuntia compressa, 84, 85
Opuntia humifusa, 84
Orontium aquaticum, 153
Osmunda cinnamomea, 129, 130
Osmunda regalis, 130, 131
Pachysandra procumbens, 85
Pachysandra terminalis, 86
Panicum amarum 'Dewey Blue', 142
Panicum clandestinum, 142
Panicum miliaceum, 141
Panicum species, 141
Panicum virgatum, 142, 143
Parthenocissus quinquefolia, 86
Passiflora, 87
Passiflora incarnata, 87
Passiflora lutea, 88
Passiflora species, 87
Pedicularis canadensis, 88
Pedicularis lanceolata, 89
Pelargonium, 57
Peltandra virginica, 154
Penstemon digitalis, 89
Penstemon frutescens, 89
Penstemon hirsutus, 90
Penstemon species, 89
Phalaris arundinacea var. picta, 112
Phlox, 90
Phlox amoena, 91
Phlox amplifolia, 91
Phlox carolina, 91
Phlox divaricata, 91, 164
Phlox floridana, 91
Phlox paniculata, 90
Phlox pilosa, 7, 91
Phlox stolonifera, 92
Phlox subulata, 91, 92
Phragmites australis, 143, 144

Physostegia virginiana, 92, 93
Phytolacca americana, 25
Pinus strobus, 16
Plantago major, 136
Podophyllum diphyllum, 73
Podophyllum hexandrum, 93
Podophyllum peltatum, 46, 73, 93
Polemonium reptans, 94
Polygonatum, 163, 179, 180
Polgonatum canaliculatum, 95
Polygonatum biflorum, 95, 173
Polygonatum commutatum, 95
Polygonatum giganteum, 95
Polygonatum odoratum, 95
Polygonatum pubescens, 95
Polypodium, 131
Polypodium polypodioides, 131
Polypodium virginianum, 131
Polypodium vulgare, 131
Polystichum acrostichoides, 95, 132, 164, 174, 179
Pontederia cordata, 155
Porteranthus, 58
Porteranthus stipulata, 58
Puccinia podophylli, 94
Pulmonaria, 163
Quercus virginiana, 131
Ratibida pinnata, 162
Rhododendron catawbiense, 15, 107
Rhus spp., 87
Rhus typhina, 96
Rubus odoratus, 97
Rudbeckia, 98
Rudbeckia fulgida, 10, 98
Rudbeckia fulgida var. sullivantii, 98
Rudbeckia hirta, 98
Rudbeckia laciniata, 98
Rudbeckia maxima, 163
Rudbeckia species, 97
Rudbeckia triloba, 98
Ruellia caroliniensis, 99
Ruellia ciliosa, 99
Ruellia humilis, 99
Sagittaria, 154, 155
Sagittaria latifolia, 155, 156
Salvia azurea, 100
Salvia azurea var. grandiflora, 162
Salvia coccinea, 167, 168
Salvia lyrata, 100
Salvia officinalis, 100, 157
Salvia pitcheri, 100, 162
Sanguinaria canadensis, 74, 179
Sanguisorba canadensis, 156, 157
Sansevieria trifasciata, 8, 77

Sarracenia flava, 158
Sarracenia psittacina, 158
Sarracenia purpurea ssp. purpurea, 158
Sarracenia purpurea ssp. venosa, 158
Sarracenia species, 157, 158
Saururus cernuus, 158, 159
Scilla, 31
Scutellaria incana, 101
Sedum nevii, 102
Sedum purdyi, 102
Sedum smallii, 102
Sedum spathulifolium, 102
Sedum ternatum, 101
Senecio aureus, 102
Shortia galicifolia, 55
Silene, 103
Silene virginica, 103
Sisyrinchium angustifolium, 103, 172
Smilacina, 179
Smilacina racemosa, 104, 173
Solidago altissima, 105
Solidago canadensis, 105
Solidago juncea, 12
Solidago odora, 105
Solidago rigida, 105
Solidago rugosa, 105
Solidago sempervirens, 106
Solidago species, 9, 104, 105
Spigelia marilandica, 106
Spiraea, 53
Spiranthes cernua forma odorata, 107
Spiranthes cernua, 107
Stokesia laevis, 108
Stylophorum diphyllum, 108, 109
Syndesmon thalictroides, 19
Taraxicum officionale, 181
Tephrosia virginiana, 109
Thalictrum anemonoides, 19
Thermopsis, 111
Thermopsis caroliniana, 110
Thermopsis villosa, 110, 172
Tiarella, 112
Tiarella cordifolia, 111, 171, 173
Tiarella wherryi, 111
Tillandsia usneoides, 131
Tipularia, 179
Tradescantia, 9
Tradescantia × andersoniana, 112
Tradescantia ohiensis, 113
Tradescantia virginiana, 112
Trautvetteria caroliniensis, 181
Tricyrtis, 163, 180
Trillium, 163, 180
Trillium cuneatum, 114, 138, 164

Trillium grandiflorum, 113, 179
Trillium kamtschaticum, 113
Trillium luteum, 114
Trillium stamineum, 114
Trillium sulcatum, 114
Trillium underwoodii, 114
Trillium undulatum, 114
Trillium vaseyi, 170
Typha angustifolia, 160
Typha latifolia, 160
Uniola, 144
Uniola latifolia, 137
Uniola paniculata, 144
Uvularia, 179
Uvularia grandiflora, 114

Uvularia perfoliata, 115
Uvularia sessile, 115
Uvularia sessilifolia, 173
Veratrum viride, 46
Verbena bonariensis, 115
Verbena canadensis, 115
Verbena 'Homestead Purple', 116
Verbisina alternifolia, 116
Vernonia altissima, 117
Vernonia gigantea, 117
Vernonia noveboracensis, 117
Vernonia species, 116
Veronica, 117
Veronicastrum virginicum, 117
Viola odorata, 118

Viola pedata, 118
Wisteria, 119
Wisteria frutescens, 118, 119
Xanthorhiza simplicissima, 149
Xerophyllum asphodeloides, 119, 120
Xerophyllum tenax, 119
Xyris, 120
Xyris arenicola, 120
Xyris fimbriata, 120
Yucca, 120
Yucca aloifolia, 121, 122
Yucca filamentosa, 120, 121, 167
Yucca gloriosa 'Variegata', 122
Zigadenus leimanthoides, 122

by Common Name

Aaronsbeard, 68
Aaron's rod, 110
Adam's needle, 120
adder's-tongue, 49
agave, 77
ageratum
    American, 52
    hardy, 51
alligator bonnet, 152
alligator-lily, 68
aloe
    American, 77
    false, 77
alum bloom, 57
alumroot, 57, 65
    downy, 66
    hairy, 66
amaryllis, 67, 69
American
    ipecac, 58
    Jacob's ladder, 94
anemone, 19
    false rue, 73
    rue, 19, 20
arum, 146
    arrow, 154
arrowhead, 154, 155
asparagus, 29
aster, 16, 50
    blooming, 26
    calico, 27
    climbing Carolina, 27
    cornflower, 108
    heath, 27
    Maryland golden, 36
    New England, 28

starved, 27
    Stokes', 108
    wood, 27, 57
baptisia, 29
Barbara's buttons, 78
barberry, 73
beardtongue, 89
    foxglove, 89
    hairy, 90
bee-balm, 82, 106
beetleweed, 55
bellwort, 114
bergamot, wild, 83
betony, wood, 88
black-eyed Susan, 97
blanket flower, 54
blazing star, 33, 74
bleeding heart, 45
    fringed, 44
    wild, 44
bloodroot, 74
bluebells, 80
    Virginia, 79
bluebonnet, Texas, 77
bluestar, 19
    creeping, 19
    dog, 18
    eastern, 18
    willow, 18
bluestem, big, 134
boltonia, 30
boneset, 50
    white, 52
bowman's root, 58
bride's feathers, 23
brown-eyed Susan, 98

buckeye, red, 106
bugbane, 37
bulldog, 146
bunny-ears, 84
burnet
    American, 156
    Canadian, 156
    European, 157
butterfly weed, 25, 26
cactus, 84
    beavertail, 84
caladium, 23
campion, crimson, 103
cardinal flower, 106, 148
catgut, 109
cattail
    common, 160
    narrow-leaved, 160
celandine, greater, 109
chamomile, false, 30
chigger-flower, 26
chinquapin, water, 149
colic root, 45
columbine, 19, 21
    American, 20
    Colorado, 21
    red, 106
coneflower, 48, 97
    branching, 98
    cut-leaf, 98
    orange, 98
    purple, 47
coral-bells, 65
coreopsis, thread-leaved, 40
cough-weed, 102
cow-lily, 151

cowslip
    American, 46, 146
    Virginia, 79
cranesbill, American, 57
crazy-berry, 146
crowfoot, 57
culver's root, 117
daisy, 26, 146
    bluegrass, 40
    gloriosa, 98
daylily, 16
    wild, 84
death camas, 30, 122
    coastal, 122
delphinium, 11
devil's-bit, 33
devil's-shoe-strings, 109
dog-fennel, 50
dog tongue, 155
dogwood, 15
dove's foot, 57
dumb cane, 153
Dutchman's-breeches,
    eastern, 45
fairy-candle, 37
fairy-spuds, 38
fairy-wand, 33
false-dragonhead, 92
fern, 138
    American wall, 131
    bead, 129
    Christmas, 31, 95, 132
    cinnamon, 129
    hay-scented, 127
    lady, 95, 126
    maidenhair, 95, 124

Northern maidenhair, 124
ostrich, 128
resurrection, 131
rock, 131
royal, 130
sensitive, 129
shuttlecock, 128
Southen lady, 127
Southern maidenhair, 124
fescue, dwarf, 35
fire pink, 103
flag
giant blue, 72
myrtle, 146
sweet, 146
yellow, 71
flowering onion, nodding, 17
foam-flower, 111
fragrant-balm, 82
fumitory, climbing, 17
galax, 54
Garfield tea, 22
gaura, white, 55
gayfeather, 74
Kansas, 75
gentian, bottle, 56
geranium
spotted, 57
wild, 57
ginger, 25
Canadian wild, 24
European, 24
mottled, 24
goat's-rue, 109
goatsbeard, 23, 24, 28, 31
false, 28
golden
club, 153
star, 34
goldenrod, 16, 26, 29, 50, 105
anise-scented, 105
common, 105
field, 105
seaside, 106
stiff, 105
sweet, 105
goldflower, 68
grass
American beach, 134
bear, 119
bitter panic, 142
blue-eyed, 103
bottlebrush, 138

bull, 140
common reed, 143
deer, 139, 141
deer-tongue, 142
dudder, 124
hairy yellow star, 69
panic, 141
ribbon, 112
spike, 144
switch, 143
turkey-foot, 134
yellow-eyed, 120
yellow star, 69
green-and-gold, 34
green dragon, 22
ground squirrel-pea, 73
grundy-swallow, 102
Helen's flower, 59
hellebore, great, 46
helmet-pod, 73
helonia, 33
hemp, Indian, 66
hepatica, 63
round-lobed, 63
sharp-lobed, 63
hibiscus
scarlet rose, 66
Texas, 66
hog-apple, 93
honeysuckle
trumpet, 107
wild, 55
horsemint, 82, 83
horsetail, common, 147
hosta, dwarf, 35
hyacinth, wild, 30, 31
hydrangea, 16
climbing, 13
Indian
blanket, 54
fig, 84
hippo, 58
physic, 58
pink, 106
rattle, 28, 29
Indian-chief, 46
indigo
wild blue, 28
wild, 29
yellow, 29
indigo-weed, 29
iris
dwarf crested, 71
lamance, 72

Louisiana, 71, 72
ironweed, 116
New York, 117
tall, 117
Jack-in-the-pulpit, 21, 153
jeffersonia, 73
jewelweed, spotted, 107
Joe-Pye weed, 50, 52
Johnny-jump, 46
katsura tree, 24
lady's-slipper, 42
yellow, 43
lamb's lettuce, yellow, 84
larkspur
dwarf, 43
wild, 43
lemon, wild, 93
liatris, dwarf, 75
lilac, 112
lily, 114
American swamp, 41
Canada, 75, 106
fawn, 49
milk-and-wine, 41
spider, 67
swamp, 67, 158
Texas spider, 68
Turks-cap, 76
water, 152, 153
yellow pond, 151
liver-leaf, kidney, 63
liverwort, 63
lizard's tail, 158
lobelia
blue, 155
great blue, 149
lotus
American, 149
East Indian, 150
yellow, 149
lousewort, Canadian, 88
lungwort, smooth, 79
lupine, wild, 76
magnolia, umbrella, 16
mallow, marsh, 66
mandrake, 93
man-of-the-earth, 70
marigold, marsh, 146
May-apple, 46, 73, 93
Maypop, 87
meadow-gowan, 146
meadowsweet, prairie, 53
mecha-meck, 70
merrybells, great, 114

milkweed
common, 26
swamp, 25
woodland, 25
millet, proso, 141
mint, 92
mistflower, 51
miterwort, 81
monkey-bell, 146
monkey flower, Allegheny, 80
moss-pink, 92
moss, Spanish, 131
mother-in-law's tongue, 77
mountain asphodel, 119
mugwort
darkleaf, 22
white, 22
muhly, 139
hairy awn, 139
Lindheimer's, 141
Mexican, 141
nelumbium, 149
never-wet, 153
nodding ladies tresses, 107
oak, 15
live, 131
oats
river, 137
sea, 144
upland sea, 137
wild, 115, 137
obedient plant, 92, 93
Oconee-bells, 55
old maid's
bonnet, 76
nightcap, 57
orchid, 107
orpine
elf, 202
three-leaved, 101
Oswego-tea, 82
partridge berry, 80
passion flower, 87, 88
peony, 19
pepper-root, 31
petunia
glade wild, 99
wild, 99
philodendron, 146
phlox
blue, 91
creeping, 92
garden, 90
hairy, 91

large-leaved, 91
thick-leaf, 91
pickerel weed, 155
pinebarren, 122
pinkroot, 106
pinks, 91
pipsissewa
common, 34
spotted, 33
pitcher plant, 157
parrot, 158
trumpet, 158
pleurisy root, 26
pokeweed, American, 25
pond nuts, 149
poppy
celandine, 108
European, 109
Himalayan blue, 156
potato vine, wild, 70
prairie-pointers, 46
prickly-pear, 84
pride of Ohio, 46
primrose, evening, 46, 83
queen-of-the-prairie, 53
rabbit's-pea, 109
ragweed, 59
ragwort, golden, 102
ramp, 17, 18
rampion, German, 84
ramson, 18
randy bottle, 151
raspberry
purple-flowering, 97
Virginia, 97
rattlesnake master, 48, 77
red catchfly, 103
redwood, dawn, 15
rheumatism-root, 73
rhododendron, 15
Rosebay, 107
Roanoke-bells, 79
rudbeckia, purple, 47
rue, meadow, 19
ruellia
hairy, 99
smooth, 99
rush, common, 149
sage
azure blue, 100
blue, 100
Louisiana, 22
lyre-leaf, 100
man, 22

pitcher, 100
white, 22
wild, 22
sagewort
Chihuahua, 22
Mexican, 22
saxifrage, 28, 81
sedge, 133, 135, 149
blue wood, 135
Fraser's, 138
Gray's, 135
palm-leaved, 136
plantain-leaved, 136
seersucker, 136
silver, 137
senna
Maryland, 32
wild, 32
seven-sisters, 41
shame-face, 57
shepherd's-cress, 101
shooting star, 46
skullcap
downy, 101
hairy, 101
skunkweed, 55
snake-button, 48
snakeroot, 52
button, 48, 74
white, 52
sneezeweed, 59
purple-headed, 59
soapwort, variegated, 122
Solomon's-plume, 104
Solomon's-seal
false, 104
great, 95
hairy, 96
smooth, 95
variegated, 95
sour gum, 87
sourwood, 15
Spanish
bayonet, 121
moss, 131
spatterdock, 151
speedwell, 117
spiderwort, 112
spike, interrupted, 100
spirea, wild, 23
spleenwort, 124
black-stem, 126
ebony, 125
maidenhair, 126

spring beauty, 38
spurge, Allegheny, 85
squawberry, 80
squaw-weed, swamp, 102
squill, 31
squirrel-corn, 45
squirrel cup, 63
St. John's-wort, 68
bushy, 69
Kalm's, 69
stagger-weed, 43
star flower, golden, 35
starwort, drooping, 33
stonecrop, mountain, 101
stork's-bill, 57
strawbell, 114
string-lily, 41
striped prince's-pine, 33
sumac, staghorn, 87, 96
sundrops, 83
sunflower, 60
false, 62
giant, 61
narrow-leaved, 60
orange, 62
ox-eye, 62
swamp, 59, 60
tall, 61
thin-leaved, 61
willow-leaved, 62
sun glory, 62
sun-lotus, 153
swallow-wort, 26
sweet
Betsy, 114
William, wild, 91
tephrosia, Virginia, 109
through-wort, 52
tickseed, 40
toothwort, 31
trillium, 11, 138
great showy, 113
painted, 114
Southern red, 114
twisted, 114
yellow, 114
trinity-lily, 113
trumpet creeper, 107
turkey-beard, 119
turkey-corn, 44
turkey-foot grass, 134
Turks-cap lily, 76
turtlehead, 80
Cuthbert's, 36

pink, 36
red, 36
white, 35
twinberry, 80
twinleaf, 73
umbrella leaf, 46
unicorn's horn, 33
valerian
American, 43
Greek, 94
variegated huaco, 78
Venus's-hair, 124
verbena, rose, 115
veronica, 117
vervain, 115
violet
bird's-foot, 118
dogtooth, 49
Virginia
creeper, 86
dayflower, 39
wampee, 155
tree, Chinese, 155
wandflower, 55
water dragon, 158
water lily
banana, 153
blue, 153
fragrant, 152
yellow, 153
whippoorwill flower, 138
wild pea, 76
wind root, 26
wingstem, 116
wintergreen, 34
spotted, 33
wisteria, American, 118
woodfern
evergreen, 128
leather, 128
marginal, 128
woodpoppy, 108
wormgrass, 106
wormwood, silver, 22
yam, wild, 45
yellow root, 73, 149
yucca, 64
common, 120
red, 64
yucca-leaf, 48

Peter Loewer is an accomplished writer, photographer, and botanical illustrator who has authored over thirty books on gardening, native plants, and the natural sciences, including *The Evening Garden*, *The New Small Garden*, *Secrets of the Great Gardeners*, *Winter Gardening in the Southeast*, *Fragrant Gardens*, and *The Moonflower*, one of three children's books co-authored by his wife, Jean Jenkins. His popular *The Wild Gardener* was named by the American Horticultural Society as one of the seventy-five best gardening books of the twentieth century. Peter has also served as editor, art director, and a regular contributor for a variety of

publications, and has authored numerous articles for such magazines as *Green Scene*, *American Horticulturalist*, *Organic Gardening*, and *Carolina Gardener*.

For over ten years he has hosted "The Wild Gardener" of WCQS, Asheville, North Carolina's public broadcasting station, and has been the lead commentator for the monthly garden show "Conversations." He is the owner of Graphos Studio of illustration and design and several of Peter's botanical drawings are in the permanent collection of the Hunt Institute for Botanical Documentation at Carnegie-Mellon University. Peter and his wife live and garden in Asheville, North Carolina.